How They Shine

Melungeon Characters
in the Fiction of Appalachia

Appalachia

Map by permission of *Penn History Review.*

An imaginary oval on this map that includes Eastern Kentucky, Southwest Virginia, and Northeast Tennessee, will comprise the geographical area where almost all the fiction discussed in this book is set. The several counties where Melungeons are prevalent are deep in the Appalachian mountains and close to the Cumberland Gap, that point where Kentucky, Virginia, and Tennessee touch each other. The two exceptions are Dykeman's *The Tall Woman*, which occurs in North Carolina, and Hamilton's *M. C. Higgins, the Great*, that is set just north of the river in southern Ohio. Some of the places are real, others fictionalized—yet they all are situated in this small region that has very particular characteristics.

How They Shine

Melungeon Characters in the Fiction of Appalachia

by Katherine Vande Brake

MERCER UNIVERSITY PRESS   2001

ISBN 0-86554-721-1 (casebound)   MUP/H541
ISBN 0-86554-983-4 (perfectbound)   MUP/P324

How They Shine
Melungeon Characters in the Fiction of Appalachia
Copyright ©2001
Mercer University Press, Macon, Georgia USA
All rights reserved
Printed in the United States of America
Paperback reprint, February 2006

The paper used in this publication meets the minimum requirements
of American National Standard for Information Sciences—
Permanence of Paper for Printed Library Materials, ANSI Z39.48-1984.

Library of Congress Cataloging-in-Publication Data

Vande Brake, Katherine.
    How they shine : Melungeon characters
    in the fiction of Appalachia / by Katherine Vande Brake.
        pp. cm. — (The Melungeons ; 3)
    Includes bibliographical references (p. 285) and index.
    ISBN 0-86554-721-1 (casebound; alk. paper)
    ISBN 0-86554-983-4 (perfectbound; alk. paper)
        1. American fiction—Appalachian Region—History and criticism.
2. Racially mixed people in literature. 3. Appalachian Region—
In literature. 4. Mountain life in literature. 5. Melungeons in literature.
I. Title. II. Melungeons (Series) ; 3.

PS286.A6 V36 2001
813.009'3520304—dc21   2001034524
                                                  CIP

Contents

Series Editor's Preface

In February 2000 Mercer University Press sent me Katherine Vande Brake's proposal for a book that would analyze the use of Melungeon characters in works of Appalachian fiction. When I reviewed the manuscript, I was immediately impressed by the general concept for the book, Vande Brake's sensitivity, and her gift of language. Now that the work is completed I am eager to recommend it to both scholars and lay readers as the first book of its kind. Vande Brake's background in literary studies and her long residence in Appalachia give her insight that both Melungeon insiders and literary critics from other parts of the country might lack.

This book shows how writers take the fact of Melungeons' presence in Appalachian communities and the mystery that surrounds us as a people and then weave those elements into powerful stories that help readers experience our reality. Vande Brake points out that writers of fiction are drawn to Melungeon characters because of the unpredictability, the passion, the legends, and the lore that labeling a character "Melungeon" can add to a narrative.

I have faced the writer of this book across my desk and I know her sincere desire is to convince her readers that a Melungeon character in a narrative is an honorable and a wonderful thing. She has analyzed authors from Mildred Haun and Jesse Stuart, who wrote in the 1940s, to such contemporary writers as Sharyn McCrumb, Lee Smith, Adriana Trigiani, and Phyllis Reynolds Naylor.

Vande Brake's point is that the writers she discusses chose Melungeons (and not some other group) as characters because they wanted to capture something important that is both unique and universal. *Almost belonging* is different from *belonging*. Many people have experienced being marginalized at some point in their lives. Some of us Melungeons have known the outcast experience all day every day. The fiction tells this tale. Yet, these carefully chosen narratives with Melungeon characters also celebrate worlds where Melungeons truly belong—Sanctuary Mountain, Sarvice Valley, Canara. The isolation of some of the depicted communities is jewel-like and clear, exotic and nostalgic.

Vande Brake does not enter into the academic debate about the origins of Melungeons even though she has done extensive reading of the books and articles that comprise the literature of that debate. Instead she accepts Melungeons as a recognizable group of people in the culture of the Southeastern United States and looks both quizzically and sympathetically at how Melungeon characters figure in novels, stories, and even one outdoor drama script written in the twentieth century. But she also does something else of great importance. In the process of her literary exploration, she isolates and clarifies for the reader the most important social and psychological aspects of the Melungeon search for self. As a Melungeon descendant, I finished Vande Brake's book not simply with a sense of "a good read," but with an unexpected deeper sense of self. This is a testament not only to the author's grasp of the literature, but to her gut-level understanding of—and empathy with—the Melungeon experience. For this, we all—Melungeon and otherwise—owe her a debt of gratitude.

Thank you, Katherine Vande Brake.

July 2001   *N. Brent Kennedy*

Author's Preface

Booktalking is one of my favorite pastimes. This project began as booktalking one autumn afternoon as I sat in the King College office of one of my colleagues, Professor Kimberley Kidd. Kim was the presiding expert for me and a senior English major named Heidi Henderson, who had approached me about doing an honors project on Appalachian women writers. Kim had done some serious work in Appalachian literature at East Tennessee State and had written her master's thesis on Celtic mythology in the work of Sharyn McCrumb. As we sat looking out toward the ridge of Holston Mountain on that gray November afternoon, we made two lists, one of authors, the other of themes to watch for in the fiction. Melungeons were an item on the second list.

A second initiative was also underway at that time. I had applied to begin a doctoral program in Rhetoric and Technical Communication at Michigan Technological University (MTU) in Houghton, Michigan. During the spring semester as Heidi and I were making our way through the novels and short stories we had chosen, I received a letter from the admissions committee at MTU. They needed a piece of academic writing to complete my admissions dossier. Since my matriculation date was not until the fall semester of 2000, they did not need the writing sample until January 15, 2000. I decided to do a paper titled "Melungeon Characters in the Fiction of Appalachian Women Writers." I thought limiting my topic to Melungeon characters and women writers would provide a narrow focus.

I began my research in the summer of 1999. As I investigated Brent Kennedy's book, other books, periodical articles, web sites, and several theses and dissertations, I was truly fascinated by the Melungeon people and their plight. In the fiction the Melungeon characters are marginalized in cruel and vicious ways. As I read the social science "literature," I began to understand why. I subscribed to the Melungeon e-mail list and started to get to know people through their postings. Then I went to the Fall Festival in Sneedville on the first weekend in October. The rest—as they say—is history.

I sat down at Thanksgiving to write what I kept calling "my paper." I turned out 23,000 words in four days. I realized that it was more than a paper. It was the beginning of a book. By then, I had read most of the work by men and *Sang Spell* by Phyllis Reynolds Naylor. All I lacked was to read *Kinflicks* by Lisa Alther. I could definitely see a book taking shape. *M. C. Higgins, the Great*, by Virginia Hamilton, was a late addition, my treatment prompted by the fact that it was featured in a presentation by Susan Mead at the Spring 2000 Appalachian Studies Conference. *Big Stone Gap*, by Adriana Trigiani, published in April 2000, was another serendipity.

From the outset I thought the distinction between "outsiders" and "insiders" is crucially important. All the fiction I have considered is written by non-Melungeons except for *Kinflicks*: Alther has now publicly affirmed her kinship to Brent Kennedy. Her upcoming book that will focus on Melungeon characters and history will be a groundbreaker—the first work of fiction consciously composed by one inside the legend. When she wrote *Kinflicks*, she was not aware of any Melungeon connections in her ancestry. This outside/inside distinction is also what makes Brent Kennedy's book so pivotally important. He writes from *inside*. A novelist consciously writing from inside will have a perspective on the Melungeon experience as different from the existing works as Kennedy's work is from that of his detractors, such as Virginia Easley DeMarce and David Henige.

I started with curiosity—I wanted to know more about the who, what, and why. I am finishing with a passionate burden to explain, to share, to convince. I want people outside to read, to learn, to understand. But even more than that I want the people on the inside, those with Melungeon heritage, to realize that it is their unusual circumstances of life and fascinatingly mysterious ancestry that lead authors to employ the *Melungeon* metaphor. Treatment of Melungeon life and depiction of Melungeon characters can show what happens to human beings who are pushed to the edge of a society—something important for all people everywhere to know.

Acknowledgments

When I think about the writing of this book, I have to acknowledge that its genesis was surely divinely orchestrated. God must have fashioned the circumstances that here in the middle of my life made such a scholarly endeavor possible. Through the 1980s and the early 1990s as my three sons completed high school and college, I was a utility person in the King College community. I filled several roles simultaneously—director of the English for Speakers of Other Languages Program (ESOL), director of New Student Orientation, and coordinator of Summer Conferences and Events. Any one of these jobs could have been full time; I begged Dean Greg Jordan (now college president) to find me *one* job to do that wouldn't pull me in so many directions. He moved me to a vacancy in the English Department saying I was to be the technology person and to focus on teaching writing and working with students who were preparing for secondary teaching (since I had taught in both public and private secondary schools). That job change was the beginning.

A second contributing factor was a trip to my high school class reunion in 1996. I was surprised to discover that my classmates were intrigued by what they termed my success. "You're a college professor! That's cool!" I had been so busy for fifteen years trying to keep my family together and make ends meet that I never gave success a thought. After the reunion I began corresponding with a classmate by e-mail. Over and over, he called me a scholar. Our discussions ranged over the fields of his interests in the social sciences and mine in the humanities—the volumes of e-mail that we wrote began to change my own perception of who I am. A scholar? Well, perhaps.

A third factor was my being appointed to serve as the King College liaison person for the Appalachian College Association-sponsored Writing across the Curriculum with Technology project (ACA/WAC). This responsibility brought me into contact with professors throughout Appalachia who are interested in writing. As a part of the educational thrust of the Culpeper Foundation grant that funded the project, I went to conferences, met with the other ACA/WAC representatives, and attended a spectacular two-week workshop called Computers in Writing-Intensive Classrooms at Michigan Tech. After that workshop, my skills using computer technology improved dramatically, my interests were broadened, and I began to think seriously about enrolling in MTU's

Rhetoric and Technical Communication Program as a doctoral student. In addition, four colleagues and I, from a cluster of institutions in Northeast Tennessee and Western North Carolina, identified a need for a training manual for undergraduate peer writing tutors, wrote this manual, and posted it, that is, "published" it, online.[1] All these things that I experienced as a result of being designated ACA/WAC representative for King College were important in the making of the scholar, someone capable of conceiving and writing a monograph.

The graduate school application did become a reality. I was surprised when the committee asked for a writing sample, but grateful I had the germ of an idea—I would write about Melungeon characters in the fiction of Appalachian women writers. I had thought I could do the project during the month of May 1999. However, a death in my immediate family filled May completely with many family responsibilities, including the sorting and packing that takes place when someone who has lived long in one house dies. I was not able to even begin to think about gathering materials for my paper until mid-June. And I didn't start working until mid-July. (Sometimes it is a good thing not to be able to see very far into the future.)

Finally, after twenty years of teaching at King College, I was given the opportunity to take a sabbatical semester in the spring of 2000. This time not only gave me a semester without classes to pursue my research and work on the manuscript, it also offered a respite. I was able to spend time and energy in research and writing during the fall of 1999 because I knew I was not facing the prospect of a busy spring. I could extend myself further than usual because I knew I did not need a reserve of strength for teaching in January.

All five of these things were critical components of the process that resulted in this book. I really believe God decided it was time for me to move in a new direction and put his plan into effect. In my own shortsighted ignorance, I would not have chosen to be a technology expert on the King College faculty or to add the responsibilities of the ACA/WAC initiative to an already full teaching load. If I had known about the required sample of academic writing, I might not have bothered with the MTU application. As things played out, these factors were out of my hands. *Soli Deo gloria!*

Of course, in addition to supernatural nudges, I have had help from colleagues and friends. There are wonderfully helpful people at King

---

[1] The internet address is <http://www.montreat.edu/tutor>.

College. I am deeply indebted to Professor Kimberley H. Kidd, who was always ready to examine texts with me, to talk without ceasing about the Melungeons, and finally to edit the manuscript. Without Daniel J. Bowell, then director of the E. W. King Library, and Terrie K. Sypolt, then research librarian, I never could have gathered the materials I needed to accomplish my reading and research. Then, too, there is Gregory D. Jordan, longtime friend, who really thinks I can do whatever I put my mind to.

My gratitude also goes to Allen Radtke, who believed in me as a writer and encouraged me to live inside the process, in order to—as he put it—give myself over to the pace of the work. Then there is my neighbor John Viskant, who has read the entire manuscript, practically at one sitting, and then had a thousand questions about the books, the authors, and the Melungeon people. Sandra Grubbs, closer than a sister, has prayed for me to have wisdom, integrity, and courage at all stages of the process. Finally, two of my sons, Peter and Timothy, read sections as I worked, quizzed me on my conclusions, and even keyed in some of the text. My third son, Matthew, answered my computer questions at all hours of the day or night as the document took shape.

To all, thank you.

1

Epiphany in Sneedville: The Project Becomes a Crusade

My trip to the 1999 Fall Festival in Sneedville, Tennessee, at the foot of Newman's Ridge proved to be a life-changing experience. Until that day in early October Melungeons were for me an academic topic, one that was interesting and important about people who are marginalized and mysterious. After that day Melungeons were undeniably flesh and blood, personal and palpable—people with singularly memorable pale blue and pale green eyes gazing out of unmistakably Mediterranean faces. Months of research crystallized, and I was aware of emerging resolve. Discussing Melungeon characters in Appalachian fiction suddenly took on a new dimension. I wanted to share with people having Melungeon heritage my belief that writers of fiction use Melungeon characters and Melungeon lore and customs not to humiliate or ridicule but instead to illustrate and incarnate the most important truths about being human, understanding relationships, and making one's way in this sometime inhospitable world.

No one has said what being a Melungeon means any better than Ted Anthony, a writer for the Associated Press:

> One word. One lousy word. An obscure word. A powerful word, uttered over the centuries in confusion, derision and, most recently, pride.
>
> *Melungeon.*
>
> One word. And behind it, a tapestry of truth and possibility, of people wanting to be what they're not and not wanting to be what they are. Of understanding your life by owning a chunk of your past. Basic things. Complicated things.
>
> For 300 years, racial, social, and cultural stigmas made second-class citizens of anyone in [Appalachia] who was branded with that one word. Scattered in pockets through the mountains, they sat at the bottom of the white-trash pile—discriminated against, denounced, denied voting rights, branded "colored" by the government in the days when that was a fighting word.[1]

---

[1]Ted Anthony, "Forging a Common Present from Mysteries of Long-Hidden Past Lineage: A Quest for Ancestral Secrets in the Appalachians Leads a

In 1994 Mercer University Press published *The Melungeons: The Resurrection of a Proud People*, written by a man of Melungeon heritage named
Brent Kennedy.[2] Like the biblical two-edged sword that rightly divides
the word of truth, this book divides people who have an interest, either
personal or scholarly, in Melungeons. It also divides Melungeon studies
into definite categories of *before* and *after*. Since 1994 and *The Melungeons*,
the landscape has changed. Identifying with the group has taken on new
importance; searching for family history has become an open enterprise
for many; talking about living inside this Appalachian legend has become
public discourse both in print and on the internet. In spite of opposition
from persons both inside and outside Melungeon circles, Kennedy himself articulates his position and his presuppositions clearly in the preface
to his book:

> I do not want this book to be interpreted as the final word on the
> Melungeons. It is not. . . .
>   I strongly emphasize that I am not a historian, an anthropolo-
> gist, or a professional writer. . . .
>   There is no pride of authorship here, nor an agenda to prove
> any particular point of view or heritage. . . . I have been and
> remain open to any and all possibilities.[3]

Some academics believed Kennedy, embraced him as a fellow seeker,
and agreed to join the Melungeon Research Committee, a group of professional scholars and laypeople who are continuing to examine the
Melungeon mystery. Others were vituperative. Virginia DeMarce, past
president of the National Genealogical Society has little, if anything, good
to say about Kennedy's book.

> Mercer University Press has placed its imprimatur on a book that
> attempts to cross the disciplines of anthropology, genealogy, and
> history—with genetics as a periodic refrain. However, the author
> does not apply the standard methodology of any of these
> disciplines. Racial prejudice and persecution, as the title implies,
> are the themes that meld all this together. . . . no evidence—not

---

Researcher to the Melungeon People—and to Controversy," *Los Angeles Times*, 28
June 1998, Bulldog Edition, A:1.
    [2]N. Brent Kennedy with Robyn Vaughn Kennedy, *The Melungeons: The Resur-
rection of a Proud People, An Untold Story of Ethnic Cleansing in America* (Macon GA:
Mercer University Press, 1994; 2nd rev. and corr. ed., 1997).
    [3]Kennedy, *The Melungeons*, vii-viii.

even census records, . . . not a single instance in which his named ancestors, from 1790 through 1900, appear in public documents as anything but white. . . . Other links, relationships, and conclusions do not withstand fact checking.[4]

DeMarce continues throughout her review to indict Kennedy for supposed irresponsibility as both a scholar and a family historian, citing her own documented research on the members of Kennedy's family that are chronicled in his book.

David Henige, a historian at the University of Wisconsin, particularly interested in historical method, source criticism, and oral history, author of a 1984 article labeling Melungeons as "tri-racial isolates," is also critical of *The Melungeons*.[5] Calling Kennedy's book an "egocentric work," Henige asserts that, in spite of a disclaimer, Kennedy is in fact writing history, "in the usual prescribed fashion by culling through historical sources to reconstruct some portion of the past in the line with a particular theory."[6] Henige calls Kennedy's interest in linguistic similarities between Turkish and familiar American English words long thought to be Cherokee anachronistic "linguistic pratfalls."[7] Henige gives precious little grace:

> Kennedy clearly views his work as an ongoing enterprise, so perhaps it would be expedient for him to publish as soon as he can the documentation for the 100 or so assertions that now lie exposed and undefended in *The Melungeons*. Until he does so, whatever credibility his argument might have is fatally compromised.[8]

Others, like Chester DePratter, one of the archaeologists excavating the ruins of the sixteenth-century Spanish city of Santa Elena at Parris Island, South Carolina, became part of Kennedy's team of investigators. DePratter says, "Brent is running the whole gamut—from oral history to 'real' history and into the realm of science. I do find myself having to caution him from time to time, but if he had been totally out there on the

---

[4]Virginia Easley DeMarce, "Review Essay: *The Melungeons*," *National Genealogical Society Quarterly* 84 (1996): 134, 137, 140.

[5]David Henige, "Origin Traditions of American Racial Isolates: A Case of Something Borrowed," *Appalachian Journal* 11 (1984): 210-13.

[6]David Henige, "Brent Kennedy's *Melungeons*," *Appalachian Journal* 25 (1998): 271.

[7]Henige, "Brent Kennedy's *Melungeons*," 276.

[8]Henige, "Brent Kennedy's *Melungeons*," 278.

fringe, I never would have gotten involved."[9] Another supporter is Scott Collins, a court official in Sneedville, Tennessee, who has spent twenty-five years researching his own Melungeon ancestry.[10]

A third person who has entered the scholarly debate over Kennedy's book is Darlene Wilson, a doctoral student in history at the University of Kentucky. Wilson grew up in Wise, Virginia, and went to eighth grade with Brent Kennedy; she calls the book "a cross between one family's saga and a sociopolitical manifesto."[11] Wilson goes on to say:

> I immediately recognized in Kennedy's theories a probing attempt to recount the real experiences of so many of our neighbors and, yes, of probably my own ancestors. I . . . came to the conclusion that Kennedy had, albeit incompletely and with errors of fact and omission (of which I have been reminding him good-naturedly ever since), opened an important topic for consideration. . . . simply stated, Kennedy opened the closet door on Appalachia's ugly history of racism, caste- and class-differentiation, and showed that it isn't ancient history but something quite current.[12]

Wilson's voice is an important one in the debate over this book because she points out that it has a significance that is more than scholarly:

> This book has (as of November 17, 1997) sold 10,600 copies[13] roughly three-to-four times the average initial sales of an academic work by any university press. . . . Kennedy's book is indeed considered a single family's history by the readers I have heard from; only a fraction of that audience are academics. Thus we need to consider *The Melungeons'* impact among a predominantly Appalachian-connected lay readership.[14]

These grassroots readers are the second group that this book polarizes. These are the people who write to Brent Kennedy sending "emo-

---

[9]Anthony, "Forging a Common Present."

[10]A picture of Scott Collins and some results of his research are available at the website of the Hancock County Tennessee Historical and Genealogical Society, as accessed 10 October 1999: <http://www.korrnet.org/overhome/page3.html>.

[11]Darlene Wilson, "A Response to Henige," *Appalachian Journal* 25 (1998): 287.

[12]Wilson, "Response to Henige," 287-88.

[13]According to sources at Mercer University Press, as of April 2001, more than 20,500 copies had been sold.

[14]Wilson, "A Response to Henige," 287.

tional letters, thank-you letters, hate letters, [even] death threats."[15] These are the people who accessed "A Melungeon Homepage" via <http:// www.melungeon.org> and e-mail Wilson, the "Web Spinning Granny," the page's creator. These are the people who subscribe to the Melungeon genealogy e-mail list (<melungeon-l@rootsweb.com>). Some of them are honest seekers of family history "who have become frustrated with the glaring inconsistencies of documentary 'proofs' such as those relied upon by Henige and DeMarce."[16] Others are like some of Brent Kennedy's family members who destroyed photos rather than let him have access to them and who told him to "burn in hell."[17]

There is a third group, outsiders whose knowledge about Melungeons is a reader's familiarity, people like me and (presumably) Ted Anthony. We read a novel or a feature story. We are curious. Initially we may wonder why a Melungeon might have such a chip on his/her shoulder, why a character behaves in a self-destructive way, or what all the fuss is about. Then, in the order of things, there is a change, perhaps a real or a symbolic trip to the Sneedville Fall Festival. The words and the paragraphs take on new meanings. We read, "Kennedy has a distinct advantage over Henige in that his Melungeon experiences were at least *lived* ones, his knowledge of Melungeons acquired firsthand."[18] And we understand that there is a real gap between living the legend and reading about it. We talk to someone on the inside. Perhaps, like Anthony, we even talk to Brent Kennedy. We notice things we didn't get just from reading about these people and their situation. Anthony has had an epiphany similar to mine, evidenced in the following:

> And then there's this. Unseemly, politically incorrect even, but here it is: Though they fit our nation's modern definition of white, many with Melungeon ancestry just plain look different from the majority of white folks around here [Wise County, Virginia]. Long, regal noses, dusky faces, jet-black hair, shining blue eyes. One glimpse can evoke foreign lands, strange tongues.[19]

After my own trip to Sneedville, I read these words. Real experience and my appreciation for the way someone else, another outsider, has written about that experience come together. "Aha!" I think. "I know

[15]Anthony, "Forging a Common Present."
[16]Wilson, "A Response to Henige," 289.
[17]Anthony, "Forging a Common Present."
[18]Wilson, "A Response to Henige," 293.
[19]Anthony, "Forging a Common Present."

about the Spanish faces.[20] I've looked into the pale blue eyes. I understand." Once this epiphany occurred, my research and reporting of that inquiry took on the trappings of a personal crusade. Myth and truth, facts and prejudices, white and "colored," marginalization and misbehavior, moonshining and counterfeiting, Collins and Mullins, Gibson and Goins. I determined to find the truth inside the fiction and tell the story behind the stories that have risen from the lore and experience of the Appalachian region and are forming future attitudes of countless readers toward the people who now openly call themselves Melungeons.

The most apparent reason that these people have suffered persecution by the white majority is their phenotype. Darker than the Anglo-Saxon Scotch-Irish who were in charge politically, Melungeons were designated "free persons of color." This designation could mean "a child born to free-Negro parents, a true mulatto born to a free-Negro mother, a true mulatto born to a white servant or any free-white woman, a manumitted Negro slave, a person with Indian ancestry, a person with Middle-Eastern or Mediterranean ancestry whose complexion was darker than Anglo-Saxon white, or the offspring of any combination of the above."[21] Being "free colored" in postcolonial society was better than being a slave, but not much better. Many in Melungeon families served in the Revolutionary War, especially at the Battle of King's Mountain. As veterans, many went west and bought land with bounty money, traded for it, squatted on it, or acquired it by land grant.

Chris Everett succinctly explains what happened in the first half of the nineteenth century to persons of color. In 1830 the U.S. Congress passed the Indian Removal Act.[22] Following the Nat Turner slave rebellion in Virginia, that state passed a law in 1831 threatening to enslave free mulattos if they did not leave the state.[23] In 1834 Tennessee disfranchised all persons of color denying them suffrage and other rights of citizenship they had enjoyed for more than thirty years; North Carolina passed a similar law in 1835.[24] In 1857 the Dred Scott decision further

---

[20]"Spanish faces" is the term used by Eloy Gallegos in *The Melungeons: The Pioneers of the Interior Southeastern United States, 1526–1997,* vol. 2 of *The Spanish Pioneers in United States History* (Knoxville: Villagra Press, 1997).

[21]Pat Elder, *Melungeons: Examining an Appalachian Legend* (Blountville TN: Continuity Press 1999) 94.

[22]C. S. Everett, "Melungeon History and Myth," *Appalachian Journal* 26 (1999): 369.

[23]Everett, "Melungeon History and Myth," 370.

[24]Everett, "Melungeon History and Myth," 370.

endangered free colored: "black" meant noncitizen, "and, by implication, anyone so classified ('free person of color,' 'Mulatto,' or 'Indian') could potentially be enslaved."[25] The situation was desperate. It is easy to see why a person would want to be "white." If claiming Portuguese ancestry was the way to be "white," it is understandable that people said they were "Portyghee."

These 1830s laws denied persons of color the right to vote, access to education, and the right to testify against a white person in court.[26] Even though Pat Elder, author of *Melungeons: Examining an Appalachian Legend* (1999), claims that most Melungeons who were listed as "free-colored" in the 1830 census were listed as white in 1840—this would imply that the laws worked in favor of those with Melungeon heritage—there are stories of persecution passed down in Melungeon families that are impossible to ignore.[27] Melungeons *looked* different, and they were persecuted because of it.

In the twentieth century the infamous Walter Plecker, Virginia's first "Registrar of Vital Statistics," tackled the "race problem" by insisting on only two categories: white and colored. Plecker worked through physicians and midwives by having them single out all who fell into the "colored" category and then prescribing that an attachment be affixed to birth certificates stating that the particular family was not white and that the individual and all of his/her descendants never could be so designated.[28] Plecker's purpose was to prevent miscegenation. In addition, on the Melungeon e-mail list I have read accounts of young women who were sterilized against their will, of stores in Wise and Coeburn, Virginia, that refused to sell merchandise to Melungeons, of county records in Sneedville, Tennessee, burning three different times. In Wayne Winkler's taped public radio documentary and speech about Melungeons in the popular press there are references to the fact that families who managed to get the "white" designation on census, birth, and marriage records abandoned any allegiance to their Melungeon heritage, claiming instead that they were English or Scotch-Irish, anything but Melungeon. The prejudice was real. The prejudice was based on skin color.

[25]Everett, "Melungeon History and Myth," 370.

[26]"Sons and Daughters of the Legend," audiotape of a National Public Radio (NPR) documentary compiled by Wayne Winkler, WETS-FM, Johnson City TN.

[27]Elder, *Melungeons*, 182.

[28]"A Melungeon Homepage: The Plecker Folder," accessed 10 October 1999 at <http://www.melungeons.org/archive.htm#TOP>. (The Melungeon homepage is currently offline.)

People with Melungeon ancestry often share other physical characteristics—the Anatolian bump or ridge on the back of the skull, Asian
"shovel teeth," the Asian eyefold, or six fingers on each hand.[29] Many are
dark-skinned; others are light. Stories about Melungeons often stress the
fact that children in the same family had wide variations in color—implying the children had different fathers, a promiscuous mother, obvious ties
to Africa, or all three. Such variation, however, may well be due to
atavism or *reversion-to-type.*[30] Brent Kennedy's odyssey to unravel the truth
about his heritage was prompted by a serious illness—sarcoidosis—that
is common in Mediterranean and Middle Eastern people. That illness and
the realization of what it implied enabled Kennedy to take an unbiased
look at certain physical characteristics of members of his family, which
in turn convinced him that the family's presumed Scotch-Irish lineage
was bogus.

What about Origins?

So, if Melungeons look different, a logical next question is, "Where did
they come from originally?" The answer is, "No one knows for sure."
There are concentrated pockets of Melungeon people in Northeast Tennessee, Southwest Virginia, and Eastern Kentucky. Genealogical research
among them is fascinating, but difficult. Many family stories have been
lost. A voice on the audiotape of Wayne Winkler's NPR documentary
says that the "white designation" was a gift from ancestors who thought
they were doing a good thing.[31] Laypersons and researchers who are outside the group continue to insist that every assertion about family history
be documented by the usual means—census records, tax rolls, church
records, birth certificates, marriage certificates. This is difficult, however,
as many persons on the inside trying to find out about their ancestors
quickly corroborate. The persecution caused some people to destroy family documents or to fabricate "acceptable" family histories. According to
the Melungeon homepage, "In Wise County, Virginia, an estimated 60%
of all original marriage certificates are now 'missing,' either destroyed by
friendly clerks or stolen by family members."[32] Census takers, though
they sometimes could be bribed, were persons to be avoided at all costs.

---

[29]Nancy Morrison, "What Are the Physical Characteristics of Melungeons?"
accessed 10 October 1999 at <http://homepages.rootsweb.com/~mtnties/
physical.html>.

[30]Elder, *Melungeons*, 109.

[31]"Sons and Daughters of the Legend" audiotape.

[32]"A Melungeon Homepage: The Plecker Folder."

Connie Clark, a teacher in Wise, Virginia, remembers how her grand-mother, as recently as the 1950s, feared and avoided the census taker.

Were the Melungeons Portuguese? Through the years, Melungeons themselves have claimed to be "Portyghee."[33] Many researchers, including Brent Kennedy, have taken this claim at face value and looked for links to Portugal in the years between Columbus and Jamestown, documenta-tion asserting, for example, that Portuguese sailors were shipwrecked on the coast of North America, moved inland, and married Native American women. However, a recent article by doctoral student Chris Everett advances another theory. He claims that, from the early 1800s until about 1930, "Portuguese" was a euphemism for African-American heritage.[34] According to Everett, the term was a defensive mechanism "to hide or disguise racial identity in an oppressive social climate where skin color essentially determined one's legal status."[35]

Were the Melungeons originally Turks or Moors? Kennedy recounts how sea battles in the Caribbean between Sir Francis Drake and his adversaries resulted in Drake's taking as many as 600 "Turks" and/or North Africans on board his ships with the intention of getting ransom money for them from the Sultan of Turkey.[36] However, records suggest that only one hundred were actually ransomed. Kennedy presumes the rest were put ashore when Drake stopped at the Roanoke colony and was prevailed upon to transport the discouraged English colonists back to Britain. Then, too, there is the fact that the Turkish terms *melun* and *can* and the Arabic words *malun jinn* (both combinations pronounced *muh-lun'-jun*) mean "cursed soul" or "one whose life has been damned."[37] This evidence plus the discovery of as many as 600 Turkish words that can be linked to American English words often attributed to Native American languages as well as some similarity in physical characteristics between Melungeons and eastern Mediterranean people lead Kennedy to posit links.[38]

Were the original Melungeons Spanish? A recent book by Eloy Gallegos details the Spanish presence in what is now the Southeastern

---

[33]Jean Bible, *Melungeons Yesterday and Today* (Rogersville TN: East Tennessee Printing Co., 1975) 95-98.

[34]Everett, "Melungeon History and Myth," 369.

[35]Everett, "Melungeon History and Myth," 369.

[36]Brent Kennedy, speech at East Tennessee State University (ETSU), 29 September 1997.

[37]Kennedy, speech at ETSU; and see Kennedy, *The Melungeons*, xviii.

[38]Kennedy, speech at ETSU; and see Kennedy, *The Melungeons*, esp. 130-36.

United States.[39] He mentions the expedition of Hernando de Soto who
came up from present-day Pensacola, Florida, as far as where the Etowah
and Ostanaula Rivers join to form the Coosa at present-day Rome,
Georgia. He tells in detail about the journeys and settlement attempts by
Lucas Vasquez de Ayllon in 1526 and Captain Juan Pardo in 1566–1567.
Ayllon himself died, but some of the people with him left his settlement
on foot and were never heard from again. Gallegos points out that Pardo
and one of his men kept detailed journals as they traveled and carried
out King Philip II's mandate to claim and hold the land for Spain by
erecting forts in the interior, to Christianize the native peoples they found
there, and to mark out a land route from Santa Elena on the Atlantic
coast to the confluence of the rivers at Chiaha (Rome, Georgia) so there
would be a way to go from the Atlantic coast to the Gulf of Mexico
without sailing around the Florida peninsula.[40] The journals report that
the native peoples were friendly to the Spanish adventurers. Santa Elena
was abandoned in 1587, its inhabitants ordered to St. Augustine where
a defensive position against the marauding English seamen would be
easier to maintain. However, Pardo's men at the forts, soldiers and clerics
alike, were left to their own devices; "none drifted back to Santa Elena as
they dared not. . . . Pardo made no promise nor had any intention of
returning to the interior. His orders to the soldier/settlers were to hold
the land, a promise to which they swore under oath. They dared not
return to the coast."[41] Both Gallegos and Kennedy agree that these men,
soldiers and clergy, were probably forbears of the people who today call
themselves Melungeons. The Spanish faces and the many Spanish place-
names throughout the southeastern states are evidence.

Other theories that have been proposed for many years are detailed
in Jean Bible's 1975 book and in other places.[42] Melungeons could be
descendants of Sir Walter Raleigh's "Lost Colony." The fact that the
earliest Melungeons spoke Elizabethan English and had some common
English family names supports this theory.[43] Another suggested possibility is that a Welshman named Madoc came to Mobile Bay in 1170 and
sailed up the Tennessee River. There are rumors of blue-eyed, fair-
skinned "Welsh Indians" who built stone forts and spoke a Welsh

[39]Gallegos, *The Melungeons* (see n. 20, above).
[40]Gallegos, *The Melungeons,* 48.
[41]Gallegos, *The Melungeons,* 146.
[42]See n. 33, above. Elder and Kennedy also rehearse the theories of origin.
[43]Bible, *Melungeons Yesterday and Today,* 88.

dialect.[44] Some scholars have thought that the Melungeons' forbears were Mediterranean seamen from Phoenicia or Carthage who came across the Atlantic Ocean more than 2,000 years ago.[45] This hypothesis is supported by the discovery of several stones having what appear to be inscriptions in Semitic languages.[46] Melungeons have long claimed Jewish heritage. The stones mentioned above, the discovery of some Hebrew coins in Kentucky that date to Bar Kokhba's Rebellion against Rome in 132–134 AD, and a Yuchi Indian feast similar to the Hebrew Feast of Tabernacles support this idea.[47]

Last, but not least, is the theory that academics and researchers like DeMarce, Henige, Everett, and Elder hold, which maintains that Melungeons are "tri-racial isolates." This term means that Europeans, Indians, and African-American blacks blended through intermarriage during and possibly even before the eighteenth century. When the Scotch-Irish settlers pushed into the "new" lands that were opened up to settlement after the Revolution, they found nonaborigine or nonnative people already in residence—Melungeons. As Kennedy often points out when he speaks, the winners write the history. The winners in America were clearly the English—fair-skinned and for the most part intolerant of people darker than themselves. American schoolchildren, like me, grow up believing the first Europeans in North America were the Jamestown settlers in Virginia and the Pilgrims in Massachusetts. We are taught to write off the Spaniards as exploiters of the natural resources of the Western Hemisphere—remember what they did to the Incas!—and seekers after fantasies like the infamous "fountain of youth." We get no hint that there were many on the seas and some who walked the land of North America who were neither American Indian nor English. It is startling to learn otherwise.

Does this speculation and even now the emerging documentation about Melungeon origins make a difference? Many voices say "Yes." Even in the very late twentieth century, people in Appalachia with Melungeon heritage are engaged in a struggle to establish community and credibility. The fact remains that still today they look different from others in the society around them, and that fact has caused them to be treated differently than their fairer-skinned English, German, and Scotch-Irish neighbors. It has been and continues to be the outsiders versus the

---

[44]Bible, *Melungeons Yesterday and Today*, 81-85.
[45]Bible, *Melungeons Yesterday and Today*, 61-72.
[46]Bible, *Melungeons Yesterday and Today*, 68.
[47]Bible, *Melungeons Yesterday and Today*, 74-77.

insiders. To those inside it feels important to learn as much as possible. First Union in 1997 was a summer meeting of Melungeons to exchange genealogical information and celebrate their heritage. Three hundred people were expected; 1,000 people showed up. Second Union, which brought 2,000 people together, took place in 1998.[48] Third Union was in May 2000. Subscribers to the Melungeon e-mail list continue to talk about being Melungeon as though it is something they—at the very least— understand. Outsiders continue to demand documentation. Debate among them rages in the academic journals.

However, there is an aspect not yet mentioned that reveals another dimension. A person's experience has a reality that, for that person at least, cannot be denied. I went to Sneedville. As a result of that journey, I changed. My experience has informed my research in a new way. Being Melungeon is a particular existence for a group of people in the mountains of Northeast Tennessee, Southwest Virginia, and Eastern Kentucky. People who grow up in the region recognize the term "Melungeon" and assign meaning to it. Even though scholars insist Melungeons have no distinct folklore of their own,[49] certain themes, legends, myths, stories, customs, assumptions, and ideas surface again and again in both nonfiction and fiction about Melungeons.[50] The Melungeon e-list often has discussions that go on for several days about customs, stories, legends, assumptions, and ideas. References to many of these same customs,

---

[48]Information about many aspects of Second Union and Third Union can be found at <http://www.melungeons.org>. (This internet Melungeon homepage is currently not online.)

[49]Saundra Keyes Ivey, "Oral, Printed, and Popular Culture Traditions Related to the Melungeons of Hancock County, Tennessee" (Ph.D. diss., Indiana University, 1976) 430-31.

[50]All these terms seem "loaded" and difficult to discuss unless their definitions are agreed upon. I am using them in the following ways. *Folklore* has to do with the traditional beliefs, practices, legends, sayings, songs, and tales of a group of people that are passed down orally. *Theme* means a concept or truth that is evident in writing. A *legend* is a story that has a basis in fact; for example, the Mahala Mullins story starts with an actual person who lived in a definite place and is known to have done certain things. Over time the legend may be embroidered, and details are added that may or may not be true. *Myth* is a story about, among other things, origins; often a writer in the popular press will use this word to mean "a lie," but a myth can be a very positive story that helps people understand beginnings. A myth can be "true" in the sense that it is factual; it may be unverifiable. A *story* is a narrative. *Customs* are practices that exist within a group of people in a particular place at a particular time.

stories, legends, assumptions, and ideas recur again and again in the many articles and now books about Melungeons. And, of course, the fiction about these people often turns on one piece of "lore." So, I must disagree with those who say there is no such thing as Melungeon folklore. Insiders tell stories and celebrate certain people and events. Outsiders have notions that, right or wrong, cause them to think and behave in definite ways. These ideas/themes/narratives/preconceptions/myths are one of the things that make fiction with Melungeon characters distinctive in the larger body of Appalachian literature.

In her 1982 doctoral dissertation, Melanie Sovine asserts that there is a wide gap between the written depiction of Melungeons and the people themselves.[51] Sovine says, "the literature offers a mythical image that is rarely congruent with the empirical reality corresponding to the people who are labeled 'Melungeon.' "[52] Yet the stories persist. Sovine thinks popular writers tend to reference other popular writers, which perpetuates what she calls "the myths."[53] However, the stories are very present inside the tradition—on the Melungeon homepage, on the Melungeon e-mail list—as well as in print over the years. Is it a question of which came first? If the Melungeon Research Committee and the gatherings in Wise (First, Second, and Third Unions) have done anything, they have gotten all the players talking. Associated Press writer Ted Anthony calls the phenomenon "community" and exhorts his readers:

> [C]onclude what you will about their origins, today some of them are shouting together. And the shouts are being heard. The Melungeons, whatever, whoever they may be, are here. They are loudly, passionately, indisputably, irreversibly here.[54]

One story, a legend, that comes up again and again is the tale of Mahala Collins Mullins.[55] "Big Haley" Mullins was a moonshiner who

---

[51]Sovine uses the term *literature* as a social scientist. She means articles printed in both the popular press and in scholarly journals. She *does not mean* fiction, poetry, or drama (*literature* in the way a person in literary studies would use the word).

[52]Melanie Sovine, "The Mysterious Melungeons: A Critique of the Mythological Image" (Ph.D. diss., University of Kentucky, 1982) 2.

[53]Sovine, "The Mysterious Melungeons," 55.

[54]Anthony, "Forging a Common Present."

[55]Read one version of the story in James Aswell's *God Bless the Devil! Liars' Bench Tales*, compiled for the Tennessee Writer's Project (1940; repr.: Knoxville: University of Tennessee Press, 1985). (There also is an extended discussion of

weighed at least 350 pounds (she was a victim of elephantiasis). This maker of exceptionally high quality "corn likker" was a virtual prisoner inside her log cabin on Newman's Ridge because she was too fat to get through the cabin door. Deputies who tried to arrest her for her illegal activities are reported to have returned to Sneedville and said, "She's ketchable, but not fetchable."[56] She was so big that when she died her coffin was built around her bed and she could only be removed for burial by taking her out through an opening in the cabin wall.

Another story that is told often is that Melungeons were skilled metalworkers who made counterfeit dollars. "Brandy Jack" Mullins and "Counterfeitin' Sol" Mullins did go to jail for counterfeiting. And there have been persistent references to the Swift silver mines in stories and articles for many years.[57]

Other themes and ideas occur again and again. Melungeons have certain surnames: Collins, Mullins, Goins, Bolin, Denham, and Minor. Melungeons have certain given names: Eulalia, Canara, Deniza, Mahala, Sylvester, Sylvania, and Sarelda. Melungeons will do about anything; they can't be trusted to behave predictably. Melungeon baby boys will have dark skin. Melungeons suppress the truth about their origins. Melungeons live in extreme poverty on the highest ground in any given area. Melungeons sneak around through the woods, light eyes peering questioningly out of dark faces. Melungeons are fiercely loyal to each other and impeccably honest. Melungeon girls are exceptionally pretty with dainty feet and small hands. Melungeon men are dark and handsome. Melungeons have a long history of little or no education. Melungeon heritage is mixed; there are many theories of origin. Melungeons love their mountain homes. Laws in Virginia, Tennessee, and North Carolina discriminated against Melungeons and other persons of color. Melungeons were "discovered" by John Sevier—this event was

---

Aswell's version of the story in this book.) See photographs of Big Haley's house on Newman's Ridge at <http://www.geocities.com/bourbonstreet/inn/1024/mahala.html> and at <http://freepages.genealogy.rootsweb.com/~appalachian/melungeons/melungeons.html>. The Vardy Community Historical Association has raised money to dismantle Mahala Mullins's cabin on the ridge and move it to Vardy near the Presbyterian Mission Church so it will be safe from vandals and provide a visible link to the past.

[56]Kennedy, *The Melungeons*, 17; and see an 1870 likeness of Big Haley on the same page.

[57]Elder, *Melungeons*, 120.

documented in a letter.[58] Melungeon cemetaries sometimes had small houses built over the graves. Melungeons decorate the graves of dead family members every year in May. The typical Melungeon phenotypes and the various theories of origins already discussed are also mentioned.

Some of the recurring themes and ideas attached to Melungeons are things that could be said about many people from the mountainous region where Melungeons live. Many mountaineers are affiliated with Pentecostal Holiness, Methodist, and Baptist churches. Holiness churches often practice snake-handling and the other "signs" that mark the indwelling of the Holy Spirit mentioned in Mark 16:18. Mountain people lost land that had been in their families for generations because they did not have proper current titles to that land. "Antiquers" from the outside came into the region early in the twentieth century and bought up family heirlooms. Cash was often in very short supply. Many aspects of life were governed by superstitions. Herbs were used for medicine. "Granny women" (midwives) delivered babies and doctored the sick. Most of the things mentioned in this second category could be true for any mountain community and its members.

Now to the Fiction

In my discipline, English, the word "literature" means not nonfiction articles (newspaper, magazine, journal, and now web-published), but novels, short stories, plays, and poems. To people outside my discipline, including countless students who have sat in my middle school, high school, and college classrooms, reading—and by extension writing— literature can a confusing endeavor because things in books are not what they appear to be at first glance. The good guys wear white hats, oak trees represent strength, roses, thorns and all, stand for love, and stories from as far back as the ancient Hebrews and the Greeks inform stories written as recently as yesterday. "How," demand my students upon encountering a given figure of speech, "are we ever supposed to know *that*?" "Hush!" I tell them. "Listen. . . . " And then I begin to read out loud. Sometimes some of them get it—one student finds a character in a story she can completely identify with, another hears a line in a poem that says better than he could ever hope to what a particular situation has

---

[58]According to Barbara Langdon's bibliography, Manuel Mira is the first writer to document this letter, which he says is in the Newberry Library in Chicago. Manuel Mira, *The Forgotten Portuguese: The Melungeons and Other Groups: The Portuguese Making of America* (Franklin NC: The Portuguese-American Historical Research Foundation, 1998).

been for him. When such a thing happens I have a convert—a person who will take my word for it from then on that important things are found in books. Eventually some readers stop demanding that what they read relate directly to their own experience. They will read to build their own caches of vicarious experiences. For them the "Aha!" can go both ways: they can validate their own lived experiences by finding examples in literature, and they can experience new things in books that they may never know in "real life." The new things, even though they may not be knock-on-wood reality, are true. In fact, the new things can be the most important kind of true things because these true things can build bridges to people and ideas that are outside any one human's limited perspective.

So, for me, literature is vitally, crucially, seminally important. Reading it, knowing it, and experiencing it are at the center of what it means to be human. Literature creates experience. I read a story or I hear a song lyric . . . I live in the world that the author creates. If the author is adept, if the story or song is good, I experience what the characters or the narrator experiences. I trust or distrust the voice of that speaker. I chuckle. I smile to myself. I get a queasy feeling. I feel tears welling in my eyes. I collar a friend so I can read her a passage. All these things are possible responses to literature. When I read a story or poem, when I hear a song, I participate imaginatively in someone's life, a life that was lived in a particular place at a particular time.

There is one more thing about literature that is very important. This *experience* that literature creates for readers is significant and very concentrated, even synthesized. The story has a definite beginning and a discernible end. My life, on the other hand, seems to be ongoing. It is difficult for me to *see* the real issues and questions in my own day-to-day existence. In a story, the action is concentrated and sharply clear because the author has imposed a structure on her material to convey certain ideas.[59] I can extract truth; sometimes it fairly hits me over the head. My personal experience is broadened and deepened as a result. I come to understand things I could never otherwise know.

Back in the 1980s I read an article about Melungeons. I remember it discussed the stone inscribed with Semitic writings and speculated about possible Melungeon origins. On one of the pages, there was a picture of a dark-haired young woman with memorably haunting eyes and dangly earrings. From that article and subsequent conversations with people who had lived in Appalachia much longer than I, I knew a little. Then last

---

[59]Laurence Perrine and Thomas R. Arp, *Sound and Sense: An Introduction to Poetry*, 8th ed. (Fort Worth: Harcourt Brace Jovanovich, 1992) 5.

year a student came to me and asked if I would supervise a directed study on Appalachian women writers. We started with a list of novels and another list of themes that often appear in Appalachian works. Melungeons was one of the items on the second list. It was in the voluminous reading for that course that my curiosity was piqued and the idea for this project was born. There are interesting and important things to discover in looking at the way writers have represented Melungeon characters in fiction.

2

Just over the County Line: Melungeon Characters in The Hawk's Done Gone, *by Mildred Haun*

Mildred Haun (1911–1966) was born in Hamblen County on 11 January 1911, but grew up in Cocke County, Tennessee, at the head of Haun Hollow, Hoot Owl District. She left East Tennessee in 1927 to live with a relative in Franklin, near Nashville, so she could go to high school. She hoped to go on to college to become a doctor so she could go back to Cocke County as an educated "granny woman" in order to doctor the sick, deliver babies, and care for the mothers.[1] She matriculated at Vanderbilt in 1931. However, in the course of her time there, she gave up her dream to be a doctor and discovered her writer's voice during her senior year in John Crowe Ransom's Advanced Composition class. In his introduction to *The Hawk's Done Gone*, Herschel Gower relates what transpired:

> Ransom saw enough originality in her work to encourage her to keep on writing until she had a full book of stories. "I promised him I'd stay in the class for the spring quarter if I wouldn't have to write poetry," she later recalled. And with this request Ransom gave her a dispensation. While the rest of the class wrote verse, the shy senior sat in the back of the room and kept on with her prose ballads of Cocke County.[2]

The stories she wrote that became *The Hawk's Done Gone* are truly remarkable. Haun's narrator, Mary Dorthula White, speaks from the pages with utter authenticity. The world is one of superstition, of

---

[1] Herschel Gower, introduction to Mildren Haun, *The Hawk's Done Gone and Other Stories*, ed. Gower (1940; repr.: Nashville: Vanderbilt University Press, 1968) xii.

[2] Gower, "Introduction," *The Hawk's Done Gone*, xiii-xiv. See also the excellent summary biography, "Mildren Haun," by Stephanie Baker, at <http://athena.english.vt.edu/~appalach/writersG/haun.html>.

poverty, of cruelty, of male domination of women, of the fragility of life
in a harsh environment, of revenge, of fatalism—a very real and palpable
world. Haun, using Mary Dorthula's voice, tells about the place where
she grew up and about the people who inhabit that place. The book is
often viewed as a collection of short stories, but I really think it is more
like a novel. The stories are told by a common narrator (except for the
last one told by a daughter after Mary Dorthula's death), and the order
in which they are read makes a difference in the level of understanding.

The organizing principle is a reproduction of the Births/Deaths/
Marriages page of the family Bible of Mary Dorthula White. This woman,
the narrator of all but the final story, is a midwife or "granny woman,"
in a mountain community in Cocke County, Tennessee. She is not
Melungeon, but she knows about the Melungeons who live in nearby
Hancock County and two of her daughters marry Melungeon men. This
woman emerges from her narrative as a "strong mountain woman" in the
tradition of characterization evident in several Appalachian writers. She
witnesses and is even party to incredible violence. There is little evidence
that anyone expects the society to be other than violent—no law officer
intervenes to protect anyone (except in the story about the family whose
land was taken to create the Great Smoky Mountain National Park where
a deputy protects not the humans but the United States Government).
Even though life is hard, Mary Dorthula does not complain or whine, nor
does she expect other than what she gets. The final story is narrated by
daughter Amy Kanipe, who concedes that her mother even protected and
shielded Ad, the scoundrel husband/father.

"The New Jerusalem"

There are three stories in *The Hawk's Done Gone* in which Melungeons
play big roles. "The New Jerusalem" focuses on Effena, Mary and Ad's
daughter. Effena marries a Melungeon, Murf Owens, after she has been
seduced by (raped by?) her half brother Linus. She tearfully tells Murf on
their wedding night, "I'm not pyore (pure)." Murf and Effena do
conceive a child. Murf understandably harbors anger against Linus. The
two men eventually have a fight in which Murf is killed. Linus comes
over to comfort Effena. (He gets in her bed with lustful intentions even
though she is pregnant—I guess he just assumes she will let him have sex
with her since he did that at least once before.)

Effena is like a wild thing. Murf haunts her in the bedroom where
she sleeps, coming once when Linus is there and once when her mother
has come over to stay with her/comfort her. Effena also has two dream-
visions that advance the plot of the story and implicate Linus in the

murder. The first one is about King Solomon's swimming hole. She talks about being there with Murf, having snakes and scorpions crawling all over her feet, and coming home on horseback. The second dream occurs one night when she has wandered out on the mountainside to get away from Linus. She dreams that she talks with Murf's mother who tells her that Murf was killed, that he wouldn't be getting to heaven for ninety-one days, and that Effena should go to the New Jerusalem (a church over in Hancock County where Melungeons worship).

Both these dreams have an effect on Linus. When Effena is narrating the one about King Solomon's swimming hole, the narrator notes, "He looked like somebody just come out of a trance. Set there and his eyes looked like two cups in a saucer. He didn't say a word. He got up and left the table."[3] When Effena tells him she saw Murf's mother "Linus wouldn't let her go any further. He looked at her real hard and said, 'Aw God damn it, shut your mouth and dry up this crazy stuff around here.' And he started to hit her."[4]

Right before she is due to give birth, Linus agrees to take her to the New Jerusalem. It is a long journey. Effena and her mother sit in the back of the wagon and talk all the way to the church. During the service, there is an altar call that produces amazing results. The preacher issues the invitation saying, " 'What is your sin?' . . . [Linus] turned and spoke uneasy-like to Effena. 'Murf is pushing me around,' he said. She looked at him. 'I done it,' he owned. 'He picked a fuss with me.' "[5]

This story shows the strong anti-Melungeon feelings that exist in the mountain community. Linus, who emerges in all the stories where he appears as evil and depraved, is Ad's son by his first wife, which makes him a half brother to Effena who is Mary and Ad's daughter. Mary Dorthula says at the opening of the story that

> Linus was against Effena marrying Murf Owens from the start. Said Murf would make Effena join the New Jerusalem church over in Hancock County where all the Melungeons went. . . . Murf was a Melungeon, but I didn't see why that should make any difference. Linus claimed there was a man come over in Hancock County from somewhere down the country and tried to let on like Melungeon folks had Negro blood in them. But of

---

[3]Mildred Haun, *The Hawk's Done Gone and Other Stories* (1940; Nashville: Vanderbilt University Press, 1968) 94.
[4]Haun, *The Hawk's Done Gone*, 87.
[5]Haun, *The Hawk's Done Gone*, 96.

course that man didn't know anything about it—no more than a frog does. Melungeon folks can tell about themselves—how they are an old race of folks, and how they were started somewhere on a ship. They had some kind of trouble on the ship and ended up here. The old folks know about it.[6]

There is a sense of foreboding in this story, but the narrator tries to quiet her own fears saying, "Everything was peaceful with her and Murf and she was going to have a baby—a boy baby, she said, one that looked just like Murf. Smooth black skin, and had his ways. I didn't ask her any questions. I thought it best not to."[7] The story as I have told it here seems simple, but it is actually very complex. The fact that Linus has killed Murf is not revealed for sure until the very last line. The dreams and the haunting give the story an eerie quality. Linus looms large and scary; Effena is a terrified victim until she gains supernatural strength from the knowledge of what Linus did. Her calm certainty is his undoing and gives her the upper hand over him, her rapist. It's as if she is almost a spirit herself and no longer of the flesh. Linus does what she tells him to and wants him to, completely spooked by her unearthly calm. "Linus said he wasn't sleepy and he was going to stay up for a while longer. But Effena went on and turned down the cover for him. He got in. Looked like there was something that pushed him about—something that made him do everything Effena told him to do."[8] Later that night Murf's ghost wakes them all and Linus storms into the lean-to room where Effena and Mary Dorthula are sleeping, "He looked like an egg-sucking dog. 'We'll get up soon in the morning and take you to that damblasted New Jerusalem if that's what you are taking such a spasm for,' he hollered and then flounced out of the room."[9]

In this story it is not immediately clear why Linus kills Murf. There are two possible reasons: Linus is jealous that another man will have the girl he fancies (even though this girl is his half sister); or Murf is Melungeon. No matter what the reason, we are glad as readers to see Linus humiliated in the New Jerusalem. The double meaning of the church's name is not wasted, for we hope that Linus will truly get his on Judgment Day. It is worth noting that neither Effena nor Mary Dorthula seems disconcerted by the notion that Effena's baby could be dark—

---

[6]Haun, *The Hawk's Done Gone*, 80-81.
[7]Haun, *The Hawk's Done Gone*, 81.
[8]Haun, *The Hawk's Done Gone*, 94.
[9]Haun, *The Hawk's Done Gone*, 95.

Melungeon-colored. Both of these women also are at peace with the supernatural events of the story such as the repeated visits by Murf's ghost and the two prophetic dreams.

"Melungeon-Colored"

In the story, "Melungeon-Colored," Mary Dorthula tells the story of her "grandyoungen" Cordia. Cordia was Effena's first child, a girl, not the boy she was hoping for. Effena, Mary Dorthula's oldest and sickliest child, died only two days after Cordia was born. On her deathbed Effena pledged her mother to silence about the fact that Cordia's pa, Murf, was a Melungeon. Effena also made her mother promise to forbid Cordia to marry.

> So when Effena saw she was going to die she asked me not to ever let Cordia know that her pa had been a Melungeon. Said some folks were getting so they held it against a body for being a Melungeon. I reckon it was because of what that ignorant man from down the country said about them having Negro blood in them. . . . But other folk claimed that Melungeons were a Lost Colony or a Lost Tribe or something. I don't know.[10]

The narrator continues, "I could see how Effena thought, I knowed if Cordia ever had any boy youngons they would be Melungeon-colored and her man might not understand."[11]

This deathbed promise sets up the tension in the story: Cordia is a pretty young girl who does run off to marry against the wishes of her grandparents. Then the grandmother, who is also the community's midwife or Granny woman, schemes to be sure that Cordia will miscarry if she becomes pregnant. As fate would have it, Cordia waits until she is three months along to confess that she is "in the family way." It's too late for the pennyroyal tea to cause an abortion. There is nothing to do but wait for the birth.

More tension is created in the narrative by the recitation of many superstitions. Bad omens abound: the cat washes her face in front of the door (a sign someone is coming); the narrator sees a snakeskin (bad luck); there is a terrible storm the night of the birth of Cordia's baby; the

---

[10]Haun, *The Hawk's Done Gone*, 98. (An electronic-text version of "Melungeon-Colored" conveniently may be accessed at <http://athena.english.vt.edu/~appalach/readings/melungeon.htm>.)

[11]Haun, *The Hawk's Done Gone*, 98.

narrator dreams of snakes the night before; and she hears death bells before midday the day before (which means someone will die before midnight). She adds to the ominous atmosphere by declaring

> I felt all shook up inside. . . . I felt certain something terrible was bound to happen that very night. I had been feeling it all day. . . . For the last nine days I had been feeling all turned upside down. The feeling I always had when something was going to happen. . . . I caught myself hoping the world would come to an end. . . . I was so tore up I didn't care what washed away. . . . I never had been into such a shape before."[12]

Mos, Cordia's husband, comes to get Granny for the birthing in the midst of the storm. When they arrive back at Mos and Cordia's cabin, the baby has already come and Cordia is having convulsions. "I threw back the quilt. 'Its skin!' I said. 'A Melungeon! I knowed it.' I don't know what made me say it."[13] When Mos sees the dark-skinned Melungeon child, he goes crazy and kills Cordia with a stick of stove wood. Mary Dorthula thinks "It would be for Cordia's good. It would save her name."[14] Mos builds a coffin out of boards from the house loft.

> When we got the coffin done we didn't even stuff it and put a lining in it. We piled some quilts down in it and laid Cordia on them. I did wash Cordia and wrap her up in a new quilt. But we had to break her knees to get her legs to go down into the coffin. And the baby, it kept on living. Mos, he just picked it up and put it on in. . . . I had to stay there in the room while Mos went to dig a grave. And the baby alive.
>
> It poured down rain while Mos was gone. . . . And that cat. That cat kept on clawing at the window. It meowed and screamed and went on. . . . When we set the coffin down, it jumped upon it. Mos couldn't knock it off. It fit him right back. It followed us every jump of the way. I could hear the baby smothering and that cat meowing.[15]

A reader might think the story would end at this point, but it doesn't. Haun goes on and has the narrator tell about the funeral seven months

---

[12]Haun, *The Hawk's Done Gone*, 101, 104, 104-105, 107.

[13]Haun, *The Hawk's Done Gone*, 108.

[14]Haun, *The Hawk's Done Gone*, 109.

[15]Haun, *The Hawk's Done Gone*, 109-10.

later by which time Mos already has himself another woman. This is Granny again:

> It seemed like every body was hollering about something. Then I seed. They were just singing loud. I went to singing too:
>> In vain to Heaven she lifts her eyes
>>> But guilt, a heavy chain,
>> Still drags her downward from the skies
>>> To darkness, fire and pain.
> Darkness, fire and pain. They were what I had been through. But God said he understood. . . .
> We stopped down there in the hollow and I picked my dress tail full of poke sallet for supper. . . . I felt peaceful as a kitten.[16]

Whamo! This is certainly an example of a story that elicits actual physical sensations in the reader. The violence is justified by silence on the part of the narrator. She assumes the fact that the victims are Melungeons is the only information the reader needs to understand the story. As the subtitle of Kennedy's book asserts, this is an example of "ethnic cleansing in America." The story is very tight and filled with foreboding. From the outset the signs make it clear that disaster will overtake the characters. The narrator is not much help. She accepts the horror as something that happens in her world and goes about the business of her life picking greens for supper on the way home from Cordia's funeral.

This story gives both an outside and an inside perspective. Haun is not Melungeon, but she knows how her community views them and is able to show that attitude with haunting clarity. When Mos sees the black baby, he loses control and submits to blind anger. His violent act is not explained away. We get no clue about Cordia's reaction to the "Melungeon-colored" child—unless she has taken too much gunpowder on purpose, knowingly causing the convulsions that precede her murder. Do such atrocities actually happen in America?

"Wild Sallet"

"Wild Sallet" is another story in which Linus is violent. A second similarity to "The New Jerusalem" is that one of his half sisters is involved. Meady, the youngest daughter of Ad and Mary, runs off and marries Burt Hurst, another Melungeon. Linus, "twenty-two years older

---

[16]Haun, *The Hawk's Done Gone*, 111.

than Meady—nigh old enough to be her pa" is against this marriage, too, and against Burt from the very beginning, as is his father Ad.[17]

> Ad hated Burt too. He hated him for that (the fact that he tried to "spark" Meady when she was only fourteen). And because he was a Melungeon. Ad hated nigh all Melungeons. He hated them because they claimed they were in this country before our kind of folks come. And Ad thought some of his own kin ought to have the credit of finding the whole new country.[18]

Everyone thinks the two young men have resolved their differences, but one day they have a fight. Linus is seriously hurt. Burt and Meady carry Linus to their house. Meady doctors Linus and "she took the spite out on Burt, of course. She was two months called to straw (pregnant) and easy to upset. She told Burt she couldn't tolerate him any longer— she hated him. She didn't want to have his youngons. All sorts of things she told him. . . . Burt got enough of it So he upped and left her. He went back home."[19]

Linus stays on with Meady. He expects her to wait on him and does not go get Granny when Meady's time comes. Meady lies on the kitchen floor to have her twin baby girls. Linus is enraged that she has two babies; he takes one, kills it, and burns the tiny body.

> He said one of Burt Hurst's youngons was enough for him to keep up. He allowed as how he would fix one of them— nobody would ever know. Nobody had reason to know that there were two of them. They were both girl babies. It didn't matter which one he fixed.
>
> Meady tried to snatch it out of his hands. She couldn't. She was too weak. She couldn't raise her body up. She was wore out from having to get up and wash both of them. And not knowing whether she fixed their bellies right or not. She just laid there and held the other one.
>
> She heard flesh spewing and crackling in the other room. Like ham meat frying, she said. Smelled like it too—sort of. She heard something pop like a rifle. The bones. The smell and sound

---

[17]Haun, *The Hawk's Done Gone*, 112.
[18]Haun, *The Hawk's Done Gone*, 113-14.
[19]Haun, *The Hawk's Done Gone*, 117.

of a cholery hog being burnt. And she had cut the wood that burnt it.[20]

"Linus took to acting funny after that—like his brain wasn't in his head—like it was off somewhere, up in the air. He drunk and drunk. And kept on drinking till he got too much of Ad's old buckeye liquor. . . . He took such a spasm that Meady got scared. Got scared and blowed the fox horn."[21] The community then comes to her rescue.

Meady names the baby that lives Rozella. One day Rozella gets a bad case of thrush. Tradition says that the only cure is to have a person who has never seen his own pa to blow in the baby's mouth.[22] Burt is such a person, but he will not oblige Meady's request even to save his own child. He does change his mind and comes to Meady's house, but too late. Rozella dies. Oddly enough this brings them back together. As the story ends the two of them are going to gather violets for the baby's coffin and wild sallet.

In "Wild Sallet" it is easy to hate Linus and to sympathize with Burt until he refuses to come to Rozella's rescue. Then, at that point we no longer need to sympathize with him because Meady inexplicably takes his part and forgives him totally. This story is full of violence and death, one death—supposing the superstition is true—that could have been prevented. Yet, the ending feels peaceful. Even though it is hard to believe that Meady can come through rape, abandonment by her husband, the murder of one child and the death of the second, she does. And, her forgiveness pervades the atmosphere. Like Mary Dorthula at the end of "Melungeon-Colored," Meady is picking greens for supper.

Without a doubt, Mildred Haun's book meets my criteria for what literature does. Through her narratives and with her characters I live for

---

[20]Haun, *The Hawk's Done Gone*, 118.

[21]Haun, *The Hawk's Done Gone*, 118.

[22]It is interesting to note that Geoffrey of Monmouth in *The History of the Kings of Britain* (trans. with an introduction by Lewis Thorpe [London: The Folio Society, 1966] 145-49) tells how Merlin, who doesn't have a father, will be able to save King Vortigern's tower by virtue of having his blood sprinkled on the foundations. Merlin's mother tells a story of his conception which implies that Merlin's father was a spirit, an incubus. Merlin proves he is supernatural by revealing two dragons sleeping inside two hollow stones at the bottom of a pool under the foundations of Vortigern's tower. Merlin's prophecies not only explain the meaning of the battle of these two dragons but preserve his own life. The similarity to Haun's story is striking.

a season in a mountain community. I trust Mary Dorthula White even after her daughter tells me her mother protected and shielded her scoundrel husband Ad. I hear the things she has to tell me like "Drusilla had just enough of Burt's Melungeon blood in her to make her pretty—big black eyes and long black hair. And a low voice, soft as he wind rattling through sycamore leaves."[23] I appreciate the beauties of the mountain environment, I understand the subservient role the women adopt as their lot in life. The violence of the men—Mos, Linus, Burt—I cannot accept even though I see it clearly. I experience the mountain culture and perceive the ways they—at least the ways the men in that community—treat Melungeons. The women have a different attitude: Mary Dorthula is never approving of Ad's and Linus's hatred, two of her daughters marry Melungeon men, and Effena's prayer is clear evidence of her beliefs:

> Oh God, you are a good God, and you love Melungeons and widows and orphans as well as anybody else. And God, Murf loved You. He said You did everything right.[24]

I read *The Hawk's Done Gone*, and while I'm reading, I live in the Hoot Owl District south of the Hancock County line.

---

[23]Haun, *The Hawk's Done Gone*, 124.
[24]Haun, *The Hawk's Done Gone*, 85.

3

Black-Haired and Violet-Eyed: Wilma Dykeman's Bludsoes *in* The Tall Woman

Wilma Dykeman (1920–), born and raised in Asheville, North Carolina, attended Northwestern University. She has written award-winning fiction and nonfiction. Dykeman married James Stokely with whom she coauthored several books. Known as a novelist who portrays both place (the Appalachian Mountains) and people with exquisite grace, Dykeman continues to write and speak with intelligence and dignity. Of her own work, she says:

> In an article, "The Philosophy of Travel," George Santayana spoke of "the rooted heart and the ranging intellect." From where I frequently write I can see in the distance the whole range of the Great Smoky Mountains through the changing seasons of the year. Through the 10,000 books in my personal library and through many trips across the U.S.A. and travels to familiar and remote parts of Mexico, Canada, most of the countries of Europe, and China, I reach out to know and understand other people, other landscapes. The rooted heart suggests an intense sense of place; the ranging intellect reveals concern for the human values and issues of our time. I believe that both of these are central to all that I have written. . . . Being considered a Southern, an Appalachian, a regional writer has diminished serious evaluation of my work in some circles. I believe that much of the world's best literature is regional, in the largest sense of that word. Discovering all that is unique to a place, or a person, and relating that to the universals of human experience may be old-fashioned, but I feel it is one of the challenges of writing.[1]

---

[1]"Wilma Dykeman," *Contemporary Authors*, New Revision Series, vol. 1, ed. James R. Ethridge (Detroit: Gale Research Co., 1981). See also the biographical essay by Leslie Beckner, "Wilma Dykeman," at <http://athena.english.vt.edu/~appalach/writersA/dykeman.html>.

I couldn't say it better. The hallmarks of Dykeman's fiction are her powerful sense of the mountains and her sympathetic and sensitive treatment of her characters. She deftly weaves facts about Appalachia together with strong images of Appalachia's inhabitants.

Like many other novels by Appalachian writers, Dykeman's *The Tall Woman* does have Melungeon characters even though the term "Melungeon" is never used. Dykeman's Melungeons are the Bludsoe family. The members of this family are not central characters and never really take form as distinct individuals, yet they are important in the novel, which is set in the time just after the War between the States, for these isolated strangers add a bit of the mysterious to life on Thickety Creek and are mentioned consistently throughout the story.

The first meeting with a Bludsoe in the narrative occurs when main character Lydia Moore McQueen has gone to fetch her cow Pearly after outliers have ransacked the Moore farm.[2] Pregnant Lydia is exhausted and still has miles to walk.

> [A] half-naked boy perhaps ten years old, coming around a curve ahead, jumped out of the road and hid behind a laurel bush until she was past. He was almost certainly one of the Bludsoe children: she had caught a glimpse of curly black hair. . . .
>
> The Bludsoes, they were as unfamiliar to the valley, as untamed, as the owls or the panthers she sometimes heard at night. Big Matt Bludsoe was the pappy of them all, although they said his mother, when she was still alive, had ruled even him. . . . For as long as she remembered or had heard, the Bludsoes, from their eyrie up on Stony Ridge and Creek, had supplied the valley and the county seat beyond with whiskey. . . .
>
> There were many stories of Stony Ridge and Bludsoe cruelty and rage, withdrawal from the rest of the world for fifteen, twenty years, since Big Matt and Callie his wife, had first gone in there with his mother, Vashti, who was tall and strong as any man. . . . Lydia had often wondered about these women—they

---

[2]During the War between the States bands of outlaws terrorized the women, children, and old men left on the farms when the men went off to fight. The outliers, or bushwackers, would attack a farm and take all the food, stock, and anything else of value to either use themselves or to sell to whichever army would pay the highest price. Sometimes they would rape or otherwise torture the women on a farm. The social order was fragile, particularly in the border states, and these outlaws took advantage of the situation.

had been from the Low County of South Carolina was all she ever heard—and she wished she could know the true story of their coming here and how they endured the wildness and the loneliness of the mountains and the hard men who ruled their lives.

Some folks in the valley said the Bludsoes on Stony Creek were rich with treasures few outsiders had seen, hauled in the wagons brought when they came taking up some vague land grant from the days of the old war, the Revolution. . . . Always for certain, however, was the evil aura around the Bludsoes, the shadow of blood.' They've got dark blood in them from somewhere. . . .

'They're mixed. They claim from Indian or Portugee,' . . . there was a wide distance of pride and arrogance and ignorance on both sides between the valley and Stony Ridge."[3]

From this it is easy to see that Dykeman makes a clear reference to Melungeon culture, history, and origins. There are Melungeon families that trace their heritage to the South Carolina low country, the site of one of Juan Pardo's original forts.

Many people in the mountain community come to comfort the Moore family after the ravaging by the bushwackers and to offer what help they can. One, Emma Caldwell, suggests that "there's just one set of folks around here could do a thing like that to neighbors, and that's the savages that live up on Stony Ridge. . . . [W]hen the bottom's touched, I'd be willing to bet there's Bludsoes there."[4] Another says "That heathenish offspring of Big Matt Bludsoe, this is some of their doing."[5]

Lydia's husband Mark, who has suffered his own hell in the prison at Andersonville (betrayed by someone from Thickety enraged that Mark would dare to fight for the Union) and who was an orphan and outsider in the community even before the war, has no fear of the Bludsoes. He buys a piece of land from them saying "They won't cheat us in a trade. No matter what else may be said about the Bludsoes, nobody ever gave them a name for anything but straight-out honesty."[6] Mark in fact sees the Bludsoes as friends and sometimes hunts with them in the mountains.

---

[3]Wilma Dykeman, *The Tall Woman* (Newport TN: Wakestone Books, 1962) 37-39.

[4]Dykeman, *The Tall Woman*, 45-46.

[5]Dykeman, *The Tall Woman*, 46.

[6]Dykeman, *The Tall Woman*, 74.

Mark is haunted by his war experiences and by the knowledge that one of their neighbors not only betrayed him and sent him to Andersonville but also set the outliers on Lydia's parents' farm. He and Lydia both attribute their son David's brain damage to the desperate circumstances Lydia endured during her pregnancy when she had to be the strong person who took care of her mother and siblings, cooking, cleaning, plowing, and planting. These dark rememberings in their lives haunt Mark. Dreaming and waking, he is filled with spite and vengeance. To calm him, Lydia mentions that some suspect the Bludsoes, but Mark will have none of it: "If I thought it was the Bludsoes," he says, "I'd go up there on Stony Ridge and rip that den apart, clean them every one out."[7]

There are indications that the Bludsoe family is trying to make peace. They bring a side of deer meat to the Moore farm when Sarah Moore dies, and Morgan Bludsoe butchers a hog for Lydia without taking any payment in kind when Mark is gone out West for a more than a year. However, in spite of their actual good intentions, whenever any mischief is perpetrated in the valley, the Bludsoes get the blame. When some of her meat is stolen, Lydia suspects the Bludsoes, but finds out later that they are innocent. Her ginseng bed is destroyed, and Lydia again suspects her mysterious neighbors. We never find out the culprits for that crime. The precious school building burns to the ground, and the Bludsoes are the first to be mentioned as perpetrators.

Mark and Lydia are traveling to the valley to find out what they can about the school fire when they meet a rowdy bunch of drunken men on horseback who are on their way up the mountain to torch the Bludsoes' cabins. Mark tries to reason with the vigilantes, but is forced to threaten them with his gun before they turn back down to the valley. Mark pledges that he will question his neighbors on the mountain. "The Bludsoes don't lie," Mark [says]. "You all know that. Fight and kill and make liquor, yes, but their word's their bond."[8]

Lydia has championed the school from the first and is determined to discover the truth about its destruction even if that means accompanying Mark to see Big Matt. "I want to see all those chests of riches Old Vashti and the others brought with them when they came to this country,"[9] Lydia says. Two days later they make the trek up to Stony Ridge meeting Black Matt, Big Matt's son, on the way.

---

[7]Dykeman, *The Tall Woman*, 125.
[8]Dykeman, *The Tall Woman*, 244.
[9]Dykeman, *The Tall Woman*, 245.

As they rode along, Lydia had the same feeling she had known the time Morgan Bludsoe came down to help her with her hog killing: that everything they had been doing was already known to the Bludsoes. She could hardly wait to see their homes. . . .

[S]he . . . thought that there must be something rare and exotic about the lives of these people who lived apart from the humdrum community she knew. Now she found that they were not the stuff of mysterious legends but miserable subjects for pity. They were outcasts, and nature had not redeemed them from the wildness and poverty to which men had sentenced them. . . .

Everything about the little settlement was poor and ugly and abused beyond belief. . . . The hair of every person there was black as a starling's wing, but as she spoke to each one in turn, Lydia saw that their eyes varied from the dark blue, almost violet color of the woman Callie's, to the light brown, amber of her husband Big Matt's eyes. . . .

Lydia was struck with the paleness of [the children's] faces, the thinness of their legs and shoulders. She wondered if they might not have pellagra, maybe even consumption.[10]

Mark is immediately deep into talk with Big Matt about the fire at the school and the accusations of the valley folk. "[N]o part in any burning, ever, in Thickety Creek or beyond. . . . I'm giving you my word that none of my folks harmed your schoolhouse."[11] Listening and feeling a bit as if she and Mark are on trial, Lydia suddenly realizes she must ask Big Matt about the bushwacking during the war.

"During the war, just before the fighting closed, some riders came to my mother's house—

He held up his big sinewy arm. "I'll ease your asking. No, it wasn't any Bludsoe that stole your stock, harmed your family, while the menfolks was off to war. . . .

It's gall to me to think you nursed suspicion of us all these years. . . .

I was of the mind, when you took that side of deer meat, that you took our good faith toward your family, too. I was wrong."

---

[10]Dykeman, *The Tall Woman*, 246–48.
[11]Dykeman, *The Tall Woman*, 250.

How strange, she thought, that now, just as her suspicions had been buried and she and Mark were finally free to be kindly disposed toward the Bludsoes, the Bludsoes had become suspicious of them, were withdrawing into a shell of their own.[12]

On the way down the mountain to their farm Lydia confesses to Mark,

"All these years, . . . none of us down here have ever really known what those folks were like. . . .
We've packed off on them everything bad we didn't admit of doing ourselves. The Bludsoes were bad! We didn't have to look for any wrong we might be doing. All my life I've heard tell how black-hearted were the Bludsoes. Now I know that they're just people, poor miserable people."[13]

Lydia pledges that she will do all she can to make things right. She convinces the community to send the Bludsoes a Christmas basket, but the gesture is rejected. Big Matt finds the basket when he comes home from hunting, takes it back down the mountain, dumps the contents on the porch of the store, and warns the valley people never again to take any charity up the mountain to a Bludsoe. " 'I understood why he couldn't take it' [Lydia says]. 'I was sort of proud of what he did.' "[14]

The last glimpse of the Bludsoes comes in the novel's final chapter. Tall-woman Lydia dies from typhoid, and the community mourns her passing. One of the mourners is Callie Bludsoe.

"I'm a stranger to you'uns, but I be no stranger to her that's laying in yonder. She saved a dog for my boy, Morgan, once. And just a year past, she come up on Stony Ridge and nursed me five days when I was abed. Any chore I could turn my hand to, I'd be proud."[15]

Like *The Hawk's Done Gone*, *The Tall Woman* creates unforgettable characters and a memorable world. The third-person narrator tells a tale that is believable. Lydia McQueen is one of the strong mountain women that people Appalachian literature. Like Mary Dorthula White, she treats the Melungeon characters in the story with respect and compassion. Lydia has little, but she is willing to share her possessions and her skill

[12]Dykeman, *The Tall Woman*, 250-51.
[13]Dykeman, *The Tall Woman*, 251.
[14]Dykeman, *The Tall Woman*, 257.
[15]Dykeman, *The Tall Woman*, 312.

at doctoring with her neighbors on the ridge. She refuses to adopt without thinking the strong prevailing prejudices of her neighbors on Thickety Creek, who would comdemn the Bludsoes for every bad thing that happens in the community. Instead, Lydia, with Mark's encouragement, evaluates them by observing them and by listening to what Big Matt has to say. As a reader, I can own Lydia's longings—to be a faithful wife and a good mother, to see her children educated, to wrest a living from the harsh mountain environment. I cannot forget the image of her plowing with her milk-cow Pearly the cornfield whose yield can stave off starvation. Lydia is certainly a tall woman who casts a long shadow in my memory.

Recently a student in an Appalachian literature class at Walters State Community College was emboldened enough to telephone Wilma Dykeman after a class discussion of *The Tall Woman*. "Are the Bludsoes really Melungeons?" the student wanted to know. Dykeman replied that they are indeed like Melungeons, people of the legend.

Mark McQueen, however, is not Melungeon. Instead he is an example of a brooding and dark outsider, orphaned and almost unwelcome even in a small Appalachian community.

4

"Ain't no telling what them folk will do!" Melungeons in Two Novels by Sharyn McCrumb

New York Times best-selling writer Sharyn McCrumb (1948–), born in North Carolina and now living at Blue Ridge in Southwest Virginia, writes about the mountains and towns of Appalachia because she knows them like the back of her hand. Her characters drive to Johnson City and Bristol, go to rock concerts in Knoxville, and talk about country music and Melungeons. McCrumb weaves the passions and the prejudices of the region into every book she writes. Her "ballad novels" use familiar Appalachian legends—ballads—in stories of suspense and intrigue. The primary characters in each one of the ballad series are Sheriff Spencer Arrowood and his deputies Joe LeDonne and Martha Ayers. These three have at least one major law enforcement problem to solve in each book. Another series, the Elizabeth McPherson novels, feature the adventures of a forensic anthropologist. Critics praise McCrumb's ability to cross genres and explore new ground and call her "versatile." She is known for giving the Appalachian region a memorable voice in contemporary fiction. McCrumb has written two books that feature Melungeon characters.[1]

She Walks These Hills

One of McCrumb's ballad novels, *She Walks These Hills* (1994), is a multi-layered narrative that uses the theme of journeys. It is built around the mountain story of Katie Wyler (fictional but based on a real person, Mary Ingalls Draper), a young woman captured by Indians, who manages to escape and *walk* from Pennsylvania back to Northeast Tennessee by

---

[1]For more about McCrumb, especially her philosophy of writing and her attitude toward her own works, including a revealing personal interview, a catalog overview of all her works, and several critical essays on aspects of her work, see the various links to her website online at <http://www.sharynmccrumb.com>. (As of April 2001, her former—not up-to-date—website was also still online: <http://www.geocities.com/SoHo/Square/8722/>.)

following the rivers and the mountain ridges. Many others in the
narrative are on journeys of their own: Harm Sorley, a sixty-three-year-
old mentally ill murderer, has escaped from prison, Northeast Correction-
al Center (NECC), in Mountain City and is heading home in the same
way as Katie Wyler; Jeremy Cobb, a history grad student at Virginia Tech
is backpacking to re-create for himself a part of Katie's journey; Martha
Ayers, the dispatcher in the Wake County sheriff's office is determined
to succeed as a deputy when given a chance—her journey toward voca-
tional fulfillment; Rita Sorley Pentland vows to return to the remote
mountain clearing where she lived when Harm left her to go to prison;
her daughter Chalarty is forced to go from denying and intellectualizing
her mountain heritage to acknowledging and cherishing it; and Sabrina
Harkryder—the Melungeon in the story—journeys from a pinched
adolescence to a bleak adulthood.

We are told of Sabrina's blood heritage the first time we meet her
after her hardscrabble Harkryder in-laws have called the sheriff because
Sabrina has threatened to kill her infant son, Dustin Allison Harkryder
(named after NASCAR driver Davey Allison). The baby's grandfather
says, " 'I told that boy not to marry her. She's got Melungeon blood.
Ain't no telling what them folk will do, I said to him.' "[2] Not only is
Sabrina threatening to kill her baby, but she has poisoned all the
Harkryder hounds by mixing antifreeze into their food. As Deputy
Martha Ayers approaches and hears Sabrina's story, we learn that the girl
got pregnant, dropped out of school to marry Tracy Harkryder, and has
pretty much been abandoned by him in the tumbledown trailer in Painter
(as in "panther") Cove.

> "[A]s soon as I started getting all fat and tired, he wouldn't give
> me the time of day! He was always off somewheres cruising with
> his buddies, staying out half the night. You know where he was
> the night the kid was born? At a damned Alan Jackson concert
> in Knoxville! . . . After the baby come, I had stitches from where
> they cut me down there, so I couldn't do nothing, and Tracy kept
> griping about how he'd been without his rights for such a long
> time. So he went out and found some bitch to give it to him. He
> told me last night. Said he'd be back today to get his clothes and
> his stereo."[3]

---

[2]Sharyn McCrumb, *She Walks These Hills* (1994; repr.: New York: Signet, 1995)
114.

[3]McCrumb, *She Walks These Hills*, 118.

Sabrina goes on to tell that she thought threatening to kill the baby might get Tracy to pay attention to her. However, her ploy doesn't work. As she says, " 'He didn't care, though. I reckon he loved them damned dogs better than us.' "[4]

Sabrina's story is laced throughout McCrumb's narrative. We see her again bruised and miserable at a high school football game, and then near the end of the novel she appears at the sheriff's office to report that her baby is missing. " 'Sheriff,' she said. 'That there convict [Harm Sorley] stole my baby. I want you to shoot him down like a dog.' "[5] Spencer Arrowood has no choice but to drive up to Painter Cove to begin searching for the baby. Sabrina is coldly silent most of the trip except for occasional angry outbursts: " 'I don't think Tracy would have bothered to take Dustin Allison if the damned trailer had been on fire. . . . It's not like anybody helps me or anything. I take care of him [the baby] round the clock, you know.' "[6] Spencer searches the cold and filthy trailer and asks Sabrina the usual questions while he waits for the search party of volunteers to arrive on the mountain.

One of the Harkryder women appears to talk with the sheriff. "Her lank hair was iron gray, and her face was quilted with fine lines around the eyes and mouth. She looked sixty; Spencer doubted she was much past thirty-five."[7] Her words to Spencer add to the sense of impending doom that the gray, cold day and the poverty of Painter Cove have already created:

> "When that Sabrina planted parsley in her garden plot, I told her she ought not to do it, because parsley in a yard invites death into the house, and she was pregnant then, but when I warned her, she just back-talked me, and went on planting. It was a sign; I knowed right then it was. That poor little baby. You won't find h'it alive."[8]

Spencer himself is the one who finds the baby's body.

> The sheriff stared at the log for nearly a minute before he realized what was wrong with it. . . . The bark on the top side of

---

[4]McCrumb, *She Walks These Hills*, 119.
[5]McCrumb, *She Walks These Hills*, 348.
[6]McCrumb, *She Walks These Hills*, 354-55.
[7]McCrumb, *She Walks These Hills*, 363.
[8]McCrumb, *She Walks These Hills*, 364.

the locust was damp, although it hadn't rained in the last twenty-four hours. . . .

[H]e saw what [the log] had been intended to conceal; a two-foot rectangle of broken soil. . . .

His fingers touched something that wasn't dirt, . . . the pale roundness of a tiny fist beneath his hand.[9]

When Spencer goes back to the patrol car, the search party is in a state of angry disbelief not because they know about the baby, but because Sabrina has stolen a car belonging to one of them.

Sabrina abandons the car after she manages to get it stuck in mud and meets up with Jeremy Cobb, who by this time is footsore, cold, and hungry. Although not dressed for the cold or the hard terrain, it is obvious that Sabrina could survive in the wilderness—like Katie Wyler. Jeremy tells Sabrina Katie's story and asks her what she thinks about the fact that Katie's fiancee, Rab Greer, apparently killed her when she returned from her incarceration with the Shawnees. Sabrina refuses to pass judgment on either Rab or Katie: " 'I think people can get caught between a rock and a hard place, and then there's no right answers without somebody getting hurt,' " she says.[10]

Of course this response is prophetic because by this time the reader may have guessed that Sabrina has murdered her own child just as Katie Wyler murdered her illegitimate child born in the Shawnee village after she was captured. Both Katie and Sabrina realized they would not be able to survive themselves with the very real burden of an infant and decided their personal survival supercedes the infants' rights to life. Readers don't learn of the infanticide outright until the very end of the novel when Sabrina has led Jeremy on his bleeding feet to seer Nora Bonesteel's house high on Ashe Mountain. Nora, who sees things that others do not, has had encounters with Katie's ghost since childhood and uncannily knows many things before they happen. Nora realizes that Sabrina and Jeremy have seen Katie and heard her voice even before Sabrina confirms it. " 'Yeah,' [says Sabrina,] 'I heard it. First we smelled smoke and heard a lot of yelling, then we heard somebody come up and tell us to run. It didn't bother me. I know about spirits and such. I'm Melungeon, you know.' "[11]

---

[9]McCrumb, *She Walks These Hills*, 372-73.
[10]McCrumb, *She Walks These Hills*, 394.
[11]McCrumb, *She Walks These Hills*, 423.

Nora, who has known for many years that Katie Wyler killed her baby so that she could escape from the Indians and begin her trek home, elicits the parallel truth from Sabrina.

> "I didn't exactly mean to! . . . I felt like a prisoner having to stay trapped up there in Painter Cove, missing my own people, and Tracy never paying me no mind. And it just kept crying all the time, day and night, crying. I thought if I could just get shut of this kid, things could go back to being like they was before, and I'd be free to leave. I could go back home to my mama, maybe even go back to school. I never thought I'd miss it but I did."[12]

This resolution is shocking and brutal. Katie was certainly in extreme circumstances. Sabrina is, too. However, many girls have married immature and abusive men to legitimize a pregnancy and made it through without killing their babies. The thing that seems if not to justify then to explain Dustin Allison's murder is the fact that Sabrina is Melungeon and, as we have already been told, " '[A]in't no telling what them folk will do.' "[13]

Readers are not told much about Melungeons or their heritage in this novel. There is an explanatory paragraph early when readers first meet Sabrina.

> The Melungeons were an olive-skinned people of uncertain origin who had lived in the northeast Tennessee mountains for generations. Depending on who you asked, they were a lost tribe of Indians, descendants of Portuguese explorers, or the offspring of runaway slaves. Nobody knew for sure, and mostly they kept to themselves.[14]

As a reader, I feel sorry for Sabrina Harkryder—she is between a rock and a hard place—but I cannot condone her actions, nor do I think that the apparent explanation is sufficient. I tend to fault her Harkryder in-laws as much or more than her Melungeon heritage. The other women in Painter Cove could/should have at least tried to mitigate her loneliness and supported her in her new roles as wife and mother. Even though the situation for them was far from ideal, they knew the code and had themselves survived under the same circumstances. But, of course,

[12]McCrumb, *She Walks These Hills*, 424.
[13]McCrumb, *She Walks These Hills*, 119.
[14]McCrumb, *She Walks These Hills*, 114.

they are Harkryders, if only by marriage. And once a reader gets into McCrumb's ballad novels, one knows Harkryders are beyond redemption.

Lovely in Her Bones

Lovely in Her Bones (1985) is one of McCrumb's Elizabeth McPherson mysteries. As such it is less layered and almost more formulaic, following Waugh's "rules for mysteries."[15] Readers get the clues to the resolution of two murders as the characters get them; we are just slower than whiz kid Elizabeth to figure out everything. Before the novel ever begins there is a note from the author acknowledging her real debts to persons from the fields of forensic anthropology and Appalachian studies who helped her in her research. She then goes on to say: "The Cullowhees are based on several groups of 'racial isolates' in Appalachia and elsewhere, and their social and political situation is consistent with the actual experiences of some of these groups."[16]

As I read, I surmised that McCrumb had read Jean Patterson Bible's book. This supposition has since been confirmed in an e-mail from McCrumb herself. She said that she also used material from the outdoor drama *Walk toward the Sunset* as a resource. The word "Melungeon" is never used in the novel, but the "racial isolates" phrase at the beginning is both a clue to her intent and her position on the issue of Melungeon origins at least when she wrote this novel back in the mid-1980s.

As the novel opens, Comfrey Stecoah, a representative of a group of people (perhaps a lost Indian tribe?), approaches one Dr. Alex Lerche, a forensic anthropologist at Virginia Tech. Lerche's research project is a complex chart that classifies skulls into racial groups by exact measuring of certain characteristics. Lerche has worked in the past with Plains Indians, but is eager for more data. Stecoah's group of people who live

---

[15]Rule 1. All clues discovered by the detective must be made available to the reader. Rule 2. The murderer must be introduced early. Rule 3. The crime must be significant. Rule 4. There must be detection. Rule 5. The number of suspects must be known, and the murderer must be among them. Rule 6. The reader, as part of the game of fair play, has the right to expect that nothing will be included in the book that does not relate to or in some way bear of the puzzle. Hillary Waugh, "What Is a Mystery?" in *Hillary Waugh's Guide to Mysteries and Mystery Writing* (Cincinnati: Writer's Digest Books, 1991) 6-8; cited in Kenneth L. Donelson and Alleen Pace Nilsen, *Literature for Today's Young Adults*, 5th ed. (New York: Longman, 1997) 142.

[16]Sharyn McCrumb, *Lovely in Her Bones* (New York: Ballantine, 1985) 5.

in isolated Sarvice Valley call themselves Cullowhee Indians and are seeking tribal status from the U.S. Government for the financial benefits that status would confer and are being threatened by a strip-mining operation. Stecoah offers to let the anthropologists dig up a graveyard and prove the groups right to tribal status by the skull measurements.

Stecoah arranges for the team of experts to camp in a valley Baptist church. Their time in the valley begins with a covered-dish supper and a lecture by Dr. Lerche. The dig itself is staffed by Lerche, two grad students in anthropology, two undergrads, some faceless diggers who drive in every day, and Elizabeth McPherson. Elizabeth's connection is not professional: although she is at this point mildly interested in anthropology, her real interest is Milo, one of the grad students. Elizabeth's task on the dig is to take the measurements of the skulls. Lerche and Milo set up a computer in a motel room in nearby Laurel Cove in order to have access to the figures already entered on Lerche's chart. Early on, the motel room is ransacked and the computer and all the relevant disks are destroyed. This alerts the team of workers to the fact that not every one of the Cullowhees is sympathetic with Stecoah's plan. Just as they are recovering from this destruction—a trip back to the university for another computer and for replacement disks puts them back in business—Lerche is murdered with a "play" tomahawk. Stunned, but undaunted, Milo, who is next in command, vows to continue in memory of the fallen leader. Shortly after Lerche's murder, Victor Bassington, the more disagreeable of the two undergrad students, dies mysteriously on his way from the dig site to the church to refill the water jug.

All work on the dig stops. Elizabeth and Jake Adair, the second of the undergrads, are confined to the church for safety's sake and begin talking. Elizabeth learns that Jake is a full-blooded Cherokee. Jake tells her among other things that the word "unaka" is the Cherokee word for "white man." This is the clue that unlocks the mystery for her. Elizabeth has taken a course in herb lore. As soon as she arrives in Sarvice Valley, she visits Amelanchier Stecoah, Comfrey's mother who is known as the "Wise Woman of the Woods." Amelanchier tells Elizabeth that the Cullowhees claim descent from the Unaka Indians, but sadly they have lost all their traditions, language, and folklore. This, coupled with the fact that the skull measurements do not match the data from the skulls of Plains Indians, shows Elizabeth that Amelanchier is the murderer. Elizabeth deduces correctly that Amelanchier knows that the Cullowhees are not Indians and fears that truth will come out from the anthropologic study and ruin their chances for tribal status. Elizabeth sends Jake to get tomatoes for lunch and, while he is gone, hikes through the woods to confront Amelanchier, who admits the crimes while feeding Elizabeth poison in a mug of tea. Milo and Comfrey arrive in time to rush Elizabeth to the hospital. Everybody still alive at this point in the novel lives happily ever after.

There are many references in this narrative to the realities of life for an isolated people group that stem from McCrumb's obvious research into that situation and other related subjects. During Stecoah's first visit to Dr. Lerche's office at the university, he says:

> "The trouble is can't nobody agree on where we came from. Some people want to think we're descended from the Indians and settlers of the Lost Colony, but I don't believe it. That was all the way across North Carolina on the coast. We're mountain people. My mother claims we're descended from a tribe called the Unakas who intermarried with some Moravian missionaries from Salem. Then there's folk who claim some of Daniel Boone's people left the party around the Cumberland Gap, and that they moved in with the local tribe, and that we're the descendants of that mixture. It doesn't matter a hill of beans to me, as long as we get the land."[17]

The characteristic mixture of possible phenotypes in Melungeon groups is described in the book as Lerche looks at the people who have come to the church for the covered-dish supper. "[H]e studied their features; green eyes, brown eyes, dark hair of every variation, every shape of face. The Cullowhees couldn't have been as isolated as they seemed."[18] This characteristic comes up again when Jake and Elizabeth are looking at old photographs of Cullowhees that are displayed in the church Sunday school room they are living in. Elizabeth, looking at a sepia photo of a bygone Sunday school class, exclaims, " '[T]hey're just as much of a hodgepodge as the ones today. Blonds, people with dark straight hair, people with dark kinky hair, light ones, dark ones.' "[19]

There is a reference to the tendency toward moonshining as a vocation, or avocation. "The Cullowhee Indians of Sarvice Valley had never been a particularly law-abiding group, and they were known for moonshining."[20] The idea is also present that "these people"—Melun-

---

[17]McCrumb, *Lovely in Her Bones*, 37.
[18]McCrumb, *Lovely in Her Bones*, 61.
[19]McCrumb, *Lovely in Her Bones*, 78-79.
[20]McCrumb, *Lovely in Her Bones*, 66.

geons in *She Walks These Hills*, Cullowhees in this one—can behave in strange and unpredictable ways.

> Pilot [the deputy sheriff] could well believe that there had been trouble in Sarvice Valley; the Cullowhees were an ornery bunch of folks, and trouble would be no stranger to that hollow of theirs. It seemed feasible that they had bashed somebody's head in for any number of reasons: poker game, drunk fight, that strip-mining business.[21]

Later Pilot explains the trait for mischief to the FBI man who comes to help with the murder investigation.

> "Take the Cullowhees, for instance. Those folks are so mean they must've been weaned on snake venom. Ain't a man in the valley that hasn't seen the inside of our jail two or three times. Summer's the worst. They get so likkered up they stab their own mothers." [Pilot goes on to narrate a well-known Cullowhee story.]
>
> "Bunch of Cullowhees got piss-eyed drunk at a poker game up here and killed some joker they claimed was cheating. He was a white man, too. Lord knows how he got in the game in the first place. . . .
>
> Well, they stabbed him in the belly, and went on with the game while he bled to death. And then they strung him up in chains behind a pickup truck and drug him down the highway to Laurel Cove. . . . there was about ten of them, a-sitting in the back of that pickup, waving like it was the Easter parade. . . . They got the driver of the truck by his license number, but he claimed not to remember who the others were. Never did charge anybody with the murder."[22]

The FBI man asks who the Cullowhees really are and Pilot gives this response:

> "People say they're part Portuguese or African or Inca. I've heard they're descendants of the Lost Colony." . . . [A second deputy adds,] "Nobody knows who *they're* related to, but the devil himself is related to *them*."[23]

---

[21]McCrumb, *Lovely in Her Bones*, 105.
[22]McCrumb, *Lovely in Her Bones*, 153-54.
[23]McCrumb, *Lovely in Her Bones*, 154.

Particular Christian sects are hinted at when Deputy Pilot Barnes comes out to Sarvice Valley to investigate Lerche's murder when he must use the Baptist church sanctuary for an interrogation room. As he looks it over he carries on an internal monologue. "He'd wondered if the Cullowhees were footwashers or snake handlers, but seeing the sanctuary he reckoned not."[24]

As noted in the plot outline, Elizabeth pursues her interest in herb lore by making a visit to Amelanchier Stecoah's log cabin quite soon after the diggers arrive in the valley. The old woman tells the young one stories about the origin of the Cullowhee people.

> "Most of the county was Cullowhee land in the old days. . . . Flat land you could farm, down on the creek bottoms. But then the whites came in wanting land, and they reckoned to steal it. . . .
>
> If we had been regular old Indians, why, there wouldn't have been no trick to it atall. They would have marched us out to the desert, like they did the Cherokees—but we were different. Here we was a-talking English, living in regular old cabins, and praying to Jesus, just same as them. There was only one difference."
>
> The old woman pressed her gnarled brown arm against Elizabeth's white one. "They called us people of color, and said we didn't have no rights. Got a law passed at the state capitol saying we couldn't vote nor hold office. Hell, we couldn't even testify in a court of law. . . . Then they started in with their lawyers and their judges, and they stole all the farmland away from our people—till all we got left is the ridges and the hollers. Now I reckon they want that, too!"
>
> "The law is gone, but the feeling stayed here right on." . . .
>
> Elizabeth shivered. Even in August it was not really warm on the mountain. The wind under the oaks bore the chill of autumn. Amelanchier sat still in her faded sundress, staring out at the mountains. After a while, she continued.
>
> "No, the feelings ain't gone. When my young'uns were little, we'd go into town and I could buy them a sody pop at the grill, but they'd have to stand outside to drink it."[25]

---

[24]McCrumb, *Lovely in Her Bones*, 114-15.
[25]McCrumb, *Lovely in Her Bones*, 140-41.

The old woman goes on to recount another sinister form of prejudice that Melungeons and other isolate groups endured. She asks Elizabeth a question and goes on to give the answer.

> "Why do you think I'm a root doctor? . . .
> The Cullowhees always had a root doctor because no town doctor would see our people. It was passed down from my gran'-daddy to me, because I was the seventh of his seventh child. Some things we can't cure, and folks dies. But we did what we could, which is more than the white folks would."[26]

There is no more information given explicitly until the end of the novel after Elizabeth has figured out that Amelanchier has committed the murders in order to suppress the fact that the Cullowhees are not Native Americans after all. Elizabeth asks the old woman,

> "Who are you really? Does anybody know?"
> "Only me. I'm the oldest one alive, so I remember when folks knew. My grandfather still had the whip scars on his back."
> "You were slaves then? Run away from plantations?"
> "Sold from the plantations," said Amelanchier in a steady voice. "Run away from the Cherokees. . . . [M]y people didn't go [on the Trail of Tears]. They run off and came back to the hills. Been here ever since. Most of 'em was half-breeds, mixed black and white." . . .
> "But why did you claim to be Indian?"
> "Because between 1830 and very recently, being anything else was not healthy around here. If they'd said they were black, they could'a been took back in slavery till the War between the States, and even after that they was worse off than the Indians." . . .
> "But everyone knows you weren't really Indian?" . . .
> "It was my gran'daddy, the Wise Man, who changed that. When I was a little bitty girl, he told folks that the best way to keep a secret is not to tell it out, so from then on, the children were told they was real Indians. When I go, the truth goes with me; I never told a one of my young'uns any different. I never knowed you could tell from the bones of the dead."[27]

---

[26]McCrumb, *Lovely in Her Bones*, 141.
[27]McCrumb, *Lovely in Her Bones*, 205-207.

Discerning readers can tell where McCrumb got her information by the slant she chooses to take on origins. One theory in Bible's book is that the Goins line of Melungeons that settled in Blackwater just below Newman's Ridge in Hancock County, Tennessee, and Lee County, Virginia, did descend from escaped slaves. The part about the Cherokees may be original to McCrumb, although her telling that the Cherokees did adopt many "white" practices including the owning of slaves in Georgia is entirely correct.

The whole plot of *Lovely in Her Bones* turns on the determination of the old woman and her disregard for both the lives of outsiders and the law. Brent Kennedy and others have commented on how Melungeons themselves suppressed true information about origins and history even within families to protect the younger generations as much as possible from the ravages of unfair laws and unscrupulous people. Amelanchier embodies these traits and practices. She knows the truth and refuses to tell it, for even as she is telling it to Elizabeth, she has laced the girl's mug of tea with deadly poison that would bring about Elizabeth's death. For people who have never suffered persecution, this seems an extreme position to take. For people inside the Melungeon story, it may make perfect sense.

Finishing this novel, a reader is left to decide for himself what he thinks. Because McCrumb is taking a shot at what she views as another abuse—the politics of gaining tribal status—no one in the novel really has the luxury of any time to reflect on the moral implications of murder as a justifiable act if it assures survival. Amelanchier only spends twelve hours in jail before a "hotshot lawyer from Atlanta" who specializes in minority rights is up in the mountains taking her case for free. It is clear that this fictional isolate group, like the Lumbees did in South Carolina, would gain the status they were seeking.

* * *

These two novels are very different from each other. In *She Walks These Hills*, McCrumb seems more serious. There are so many layers to the work, so many characters, so many threads, so many stories. The reader's experience is different, depending on which character she chooses to identify with. Any one of the people portrayed would be a good choice. Hamelin, Tennessee, is a "real" place. The time is now. The story is compelling. Sabrina, the Melungeon, is a minor character until the end of the novel when she is catapulted onto center stage. Her heritage seems to be the reason that she has no internal resources to fall back on. The years of marginalization force her into a corner from which she cannot escape.

On the surface, *Lovely in Her Bones* seems lighthearted. There are places in the story that made me laugh out loud as McCrumb takes potshots at Daniel Hunter Coltsfoot, the North Carolina Sheriffs' Association, and "hotshot lawyers" who represent persons whose minority rights are being infringed upon. However, simply reading through the list of references to Melungeon history and folklore that I presented above shows that McCrumb takes the isolate group in the novel and their plight very seriously. She is creatively and powerfully using information in the context of a good story. Sarvice Valley becomes a real place for the reader, and the bitterness of those who inhabit it wreaks havoc for the outsiders—the anthropology team, the FBI, and the local sheriff.

5

"The grace to face tomorrow": The Melungeon Line in Lee Smith's The Devil's Dream

Grundy, Virginia-native Lee Smith has been writing fiction for more than thirty years. Her father ran the dime store in town, and her mother was a teacher. On the "official website of author Lee Smith," she writes:

> I got hooked on stories early, and as soon as I could write, I started writing them down. I wrote my first novel on my mother's stationery when I was eight. . . . Even at that age, I was fixed upon glamour and flight, two themes I returned to again and again as I wrote my way throughout high school, then college.
>
> Decades later, I'm still at it. Narrative is as necessary to me as breathing, as air. I write for the reason I've always done so: simply to survive. To make sense of my life. I never know what I think until I read what I've written. And I refuse to lead an *unexamined life*. No matter how painful it is, I intend to know what's going on. The writing itself is a source of strength for me, a way to make it through the night.
>
> The story has always served this function, I believe, from the beginning of time. In the telling of it, we discover who we are, why we exist, what we should do. It brings order and delight. Its form is inherently pleasing, and deeply satisfying to us. Because it has a beginning, a middle, and an end, it gives a recognizable shape to the muddle and chaos of our lives.[1]

Smith's words add a bit to my definition of what makes good fiction. Yet her declaration that fiction is satisfying because it has form—a

---

[1] From "In Her Own Words," author Lee Smith's "foreword" to her "official website," accessed 3 November 2000 at <http://www.leesmith.com/herwords.html>. These "own words" of Smith also appear on her expanded "foreword" page (with illustrations), at <http://www.leesmith.com/words.html>. See also on Smith's website a brief "biography" and especially an article by Jeanne McDonald, "Lee Smith at Home in Appalachia."

beginning, a middle, and an end—fits rather well my ideas of what novels do.

The only one of Smith's many novels with Appalachian settings that has a Melungeon emphasis is *The Devil's Dream*. Recognizing the treatment of Melungeons in this book is more difficult than in other novels because the Melungeon material is woven tightly into the whole along with several other typically Appalachian themes. One of these themes is the tendency of Bailey family characters to a variety of ESP, the "sight," that is common in other works by Smith and in other authors as well. Sabrina Harkryder (*She Walks These Hills*) claims some "sight," saying she is Melungeon. However, Nora Bonesteel, who appears in five of McCrumb's ballad novels, has this quality, and she is definitely not Melungeon. So, in *The Devil's Dream* it's hard to know whether the "sight" that is particularly apparent in Rose Annie Bailey is an instance of Celtic mystery or a Melungeon marker.

The Devil's Dream is a saga (mid-1800s to the present) of a singing family that originates in the mountains of Southwest Virginia. There are three Melungeon characters: Jake Toney, the mysterious wanderer, one hundred percent Melungeon, who sires mercurial R.C. only to disappear "finely" and completely; R.C. himself, half Melungeon, who is the family patriarch and musical genius; and Rose Annie, one quarter Melungeon, the "Queen of Country Music," daughter of R.C. and his beloved Lucie Queen.

Another factor that makes analysis of this novel difficult is that there are sixteen different voices telling the story. Some of the book's sections are short, some long. (Katie Cocker's part—the longest sustained narrative portion of the novel—is almost one hundred pages.) Some of the first-person storytellers are more reliable than others. Five of the sections are told in third person by an unidentified narrator. We as readers believe these third-person sections because this is information we want to know, yet I doubt they are supposed to be written by the same person . . . although it's possible. So, when there is a remark about a Melungeon (or about anything else), we readers must filter the remark through more than one matrix. Relevant questions are (1) Who said it? (2) What for? and (3) Who's listening?

The facts about Jake Toney, the Melungeon progenitor in the story, come through Zinnia Hulett, the ugly, strawberry-birthmarked, jealous older sister of beautiful, selfish, and unpredictable Nonnie. Zinnia thinks she is telling us what we need to know about Nonnie, but in the process reveals even more about herself. We learn that the father of these two girls favors the younger one, gives her whatever she fancies, and covets an education for her. Zinnia takes up the thread of the story:

> But Nonnie, she didn't care nothing about that, all she wanted was a feller. Nonnie was just a fool waiting to happen.
>
> And one day, sure enough, she came back from going down into Cana with some of the neighbor people, looking like she had a fine mist of moondust laid all over her.
>
> "Well, who is he?' I axed straightaway, for I knowed immediately what was up. . . . "
>
> "Oh, Zinnia," she said, "I was just standing in the road talking to some folks when this man rode in on a gray horse, He was a man that none of us had ever seed before, and not from around here. He is real different-looking, real handsome, like a man in a song."[2]

Nonnie tells him her name and invites him up to the Huletts' cabin. Zinnia again, "[S]ure enough, here he come, and sure enough, Daddy run him off. He met with the man, whose name was Jake Toney, in private afore he run him off."[3] Nonnie is beside herself with anger, not being used to having her will thwarted, but Claude Hulett is adamant.

> "Now listen here, girls," he said, when Nonnie had finely quit fighting. "That man there is a Melungeon, and he won't be coming up here again. I knowed it as soon as I saw him," Daddy said.
>
> "A what?" Nonnie said, and then Daddy told us about the Melungeons, that is a race of people which nobody knows where they came from, with real pale light eyes, and dark skin, and frizzy hair like sheep's wool. Sure enough, this was what Jake Toney looked like, all right.
>
> "Niggers won't claim a Melungeon," Daddy told us. "Injuns won't claim them neither."
>
> "The Melungeon is alone in all the world."[4]

Nonnie is distraught for a few days, but, as soon as she goes back to school, she cheers up considerably. Zinnia smells a rat and decides to do a little investigating on her own.

---

[2]Lee Smith, *The Devil's Dream* (1992; repr.: New York: Ballantine, 1993) 56.
[3]Smith, *The Devil's Dream*, 56.
[4]Smith, *The Devil's Dream*, 57.

I can't say that I was surprised when I come riding around the bend there where that little old fallin-down cabin is, . . . and seed the gray horse and the little white pony hitched up in front of it. I got off my horse and tethered her back there in the woods and then walk kindly tippytoe over to the cabin, but I need not have gone to the trouble. For they were making the shamefullest, awfullest racket you ever heerd in there, laughing, and giggling and moaning and crying out, and then he'd be breathing and groaning at the same time, and then he hollered out, and then she did. . . .

You had better believe I told our daddy what was going on in that cabin![5]

Claude Hulett beats Nonnie, but it does no good. In the morning she disappears.

She had lit out in the dead of night on her pony, gone down to find her Melungeon at Missus Rice's boardinghouse, where he stayed, and I couldn't tell you what passed betwixt the two of them when she got there, but the next day he was up and gone before daybreak, alone. . . . Jake Toney left owing money all over town, as it turned out, one jump ahead of the law. He owed a lot of people due to the poker game he had been running regular in the back of the livery stable. Missus Rice was fit to be tied, as he left owing her considerable, also old Baldy McClain that ran the livery stable and was supposed to have gotten a cut on the game.

They *all* liked to have died when they found out that Jake Toney was a Melungeon to boot, which I told Missus Rice first thing when I went down there to get Nonnie. . . .

Well, we never seed hide nor hair of the Melungeon again, but Nonnie continued grieving him for weeks on end, and laying up in the bed all day long doing it. Then one day I looked at her good, and all of a sudden it come to me that she was going to have a baby.[6]

Father Claude, after consulting with the granny woman and the Baptist preacher, reluctantly agrees to an arranged marriage. The groom is Ezekiel Bailey who at forty still has the mind of a child.

---

[5]Smith, *The Devil's Dream*, 57.
[6]Smith, *The Devil's Dream*, 59.

"[E]verybody knows who she is and what she done, and won't nobody take a Melungeon's leavings around here neither, not to mention the child. This is the long and short of it," says Preacher Estep. "[This man] needs a wife the worst in the world. . . . He is in a fair way to come into quite a parcel of land over at Grassy Branch, . . . but he don't have no wife, nor no children to work it. He is a elder in the Chicken Rise church, too . . . and I don't believe this feller is too particular neither. . . .

I wouldn't see no reason to mention the Melungeon."[7]

Except for passing references, there is no more discussion of Jake Toney. What it means to have Melungeon heritage, however, plays out through the remaining 250 pages of the book.

The third-person narrator of a section titled "Nonnie and the Big Talker" tells that

R.C. Bailey, Nonnie's Melungeon baby, was born on February 14, 1881. . . . He was a colicky baby who had a high, thin cry like a cat mewing. Nonnie had been real curious to see whether he would look like Jake Toney or not. R.C. did have curly hair like Jake Toney.[8]

The next voice we hear is R.C.'s, who at seventeen has left home to work at a lumber camp near Holly Grove. and he is narrating his painful passage from adolescence to adulthood.

I was working days at that lumber camp out from Holly Grove, . . . and fiddling someplace nearabout every night. I could fiddle all night and work all day and never think a thing of it. I was wild as any young buck. . . . I was bad to drink back then. . . . I helt Mamma up in my mind as a flat-out angel in them days. . . . Why you could of knocked me over with a feather when she run off [with the medicine show].[9]

He tells about fiddling at a dance and sparking a "purty little redheaded gal."[10] Her regular boyfriend, Lonnie, grabs R.C. around the neck. When the girl protests, Lonnie grabs her instead. R.C. tells Lonnie to turn her

[7]Smith, *The Devil's Dream*, 59-60.
[8]Smith, *The Devil's Dream*, 66.
[9]Smith, *The Devil's Dream*, 83-84.
[10]Smith, *The Devil's Dream*, 84.

loose, which, of course, Lonnie does not want to do. In fact, when Lonnie demands that R.C. identify himself, suddenly the tables are turned. Lonnie starts laughing and says,

> "Oh so you are that Melungeon feller. . . .
> Shirley, this here is a woods colt that don't even know it. . . . My Grandma was Missus Rice that used to run the boarding-house in Cana, . . . and she tole it for a fact that yer mamma done tuck up with a Melungeon man that was staying up there in her boardinghouse, and yer mamma tried to run off with him too, but he wouldn't have her, and then she had his baby. Hell, it weren't no big secret at the time." . . .
> I couldn't work no more after that, [says R.C.] or do nothing afore I got to the bottom of it. . . . [T]he firstest one I went to see was Tom Kincaid that taught me to play the fiddle, and knowed me since I was a boy. . . . I told Tom what all that old boy had said about Mamma and the Melungeon, and his thin face got kind of a cagey look. . . .
> "I heard something oncet to that effect," he allowed finely. . . . "I am not telling you but what's the God's truth, you had best fergit this whole business, and get on back home and help yer pa. . . . Hit is best to leave well enough alone. Hit is best to keep yer goddamn mouth shut, if you foller me."[11]

R. C. refuses, insisting that he wants more information. Tom sends him up Cherokee Mountain to "ax" old Willie Malone. R.C.'s voice continues:

> Uncle Willie Malone told me what folks said about Mamma and the Melungeon, . . . an old voice coming from noplace, from the night and the mountain itself.
> "And now, if I was you, I'd fergit the whole thing, . . . [f]er yer daddy raised you as hisn, and used to trot you on his knee and walk you of a night and play with you by the hour, . . . they is not many men that had a daddy to set so much store by a baby as yourn done you."
> But I was young and hotheaded then, and three of four days drunk on top of it. I had heerd what I'd come to hear. . . . I went over to the camp and got my stuff and then I went over to

---

[11]Smith, *The Devil's Dream*, 84-85.

Grassy Branch and gathered up what I had left there, and told em I was leaving for a while. . . .

Best I can recall, my thinking run kindly along these lines. *Mamma is a whore, and I am a bastard,* and so by God I set out to prove it. It seemed like a great storm was raging in me. I fuggered I might as well get out there and fuck my brains out or do whatever the hell else I could think of, for it wasn't no pleasure in this life not nothing beyond it, nothing, nothing, nothing. . . .

I stayed gone for some several years, drunk moren not, beat up frequent, in jail a couple of times too. . . . Then come a pretty spring morning when I woke up in a woman's bed in Huntington, West Virginia, and didn't have no memory atall of who she was, or how I had got there, or where we was. . . . Then I heerd my mamma speaking to me, plain as that blazing sun. "Go on home now, son," she told me, and so I did.

I got back to find that Daddy had had a stroke and couldn't say a thing, nor move his left leg. . . . "I am home for good," I told them, and even though Daddy couldn't talk none, he could understand me. Tears came up in his old blue eyes. I hugged him as hard as I could. "You took good care of usuns," I told him, "and now I aim to take good care of you."[12]

R.C.'s narrative shows both his distress when he discovers the truth about his heritage and his sensitive nature. His "sign," or message from his mother, is an interesting occurrence. This message changes his life. There is also a hint of his musical genius (his sister Lizzie says "no boy could sing nicer or play a sweeter fiddle that R.C.").[13]

Ezekiel is the son of Moses Bailey and Kate Malone. R.C., though he is not a blood relative to either line, amalgamates traits from both. The Malones were a musical family; R.C. learns to fiddle from Uncle Willie, a kindred spirit. The spiritual sensitivity is the Bailey family trait. It is interesting that R.C., even though he is not a blood relative to either of the family progenitors, has both these characteristics in addition to the very real turmoil of being Melungeon.

The next voice is Lizzie's. She is a prissy young girl who has left home to become a nurse, disgusted by the family life of her Virginia childhood, which she claims "seems to me somehow clotted, messy, tangled, . . . I haven't the stomach for it—the babies, the mess, the sheer

---

[12]Smith, *The Devil's Dream*, 86-88.
[13]Smith, *The Devil's Dream*, 91.

work of feeding and clothing so many, the cooking, the eating."[14] In spite of her revulsion, in many ways she is a trustworthy narrator.

> [I was] fourteen when Daddy had the stroke and R.C. returned to us from whatever dark and mysterious realms of the spirit he'd travelled through in those lost years. . . .
>
> I am persuaded that R.C.'s anguish is habitual with him and has always been so, that it was not simply the result of our mother's abrupt departure. R.C. has been a person of extremes for as long as I can remember. Even as a boy, nobody laughed harder, or ran faster, or yelled louder—or sulked longer, or acted meaner, or was sweeter . . . or more tenderhearted! Yet he was quick to anger. . . .
>
> Let me put it this way—everyone felt more alive when R.C. came in the room. There was something about R.C. that put an edge on things. . . .
>
> "It was not so much the way he looked, although Lord knows he was good-looking—at least, the girls thought so! He had the curliest, prettiest fair hair, which never turned dark as so often happens, yet his once fair skin was now nearly swarthy. He had a big nose, high cheekbones, and a large mobile mouth. . . . R.C. was a young man of extremes. Often he seemed abstracted, brooding, lost in thought.
>
> "I believe he was a kind of genius, for he could build anything, make anything he chose to. . . .
>
> I believe, thinking now in retrospect, that R.C. could have gone anywhere and done anything he chose, and been successful at it, too—even if he never would be happy. The only time he was truly happy, I believe, was when he was actually playing music. The rest of the time he was driven by a great restlessness—yet I suppose we were lucky for it, as it led him into scheme after scheme, and we were the beneficiaries.
>
> "I will never forget the day, soon after R.C.'s return, when a man came by our house with a banjo. . . . The fellow sat down, at our request, and played a few tunes. . . . Then he handed the banjo over to R.C., who took it and played it instantly. . . . R.C. was fascinated with the banjo from that time on."[15]

---

[14]Smith, *The Devil's Dream*, 106-107.
[15]Smith, *The Devil's Dream*, 91-93.

Lizzie goes on to tell about Lucie Queen, how she falls in love with R.C. and marries him, about the Gibson guitar he buys her for a wedding present, about their babies, about their first musical performance in Cana when they needed to raise money to pay for the wagon's mending so they could get home. This performance was the beginning that led to so much more.

> "They played at square dances, play-parties, candy parties, house raisings, bean stringings, too. They played wherever any-body would pay them. . . . They did not play at many dances, since R.C. was enough our father's son to be uncomfortable with dancing, . . . and the family never missed meeting at the Chicken Rise church, not even when R.C. and Lucie had to drive most of the night to get back for it. . . . The act of public performance, which encouraged Lucie to be *more herself*, seemed to produce a brand-new Durwood (brother). . . .
>
> R.C., eccentric to his bones, was oddly less professional. Sometimes he sang with the other two and sometimes not, rising abruptly to pace round the stage whenever he chose. But instead of detracting from the programme, R.C.'s sudden mysterious movements added a sense of drama and unexpectedness to the proceedings. . . . [N]obody could fiddle like R.C. when the mood was on him! Or play the banjo, either. I suppose it goes without saying that R.C. was the presiding genius of the group. It was he who "worked up," as he called it, the songs; . . . it was he who found new songs for them to sing. Indeed, some of these turned out to be among the most requested—such as that haunting ballad "Preacher's Son," which R.C. picked up from an old man over at Bee, or his own "Melungeon Man," its title referring to a mysterious strain of folks scattered through the mountains, which some believe to be descendants of this country's first Roanoke Island settlers. Regardless of the origin of the Melungeons, that ballad captures such a feeling of *otherness*, of being outside, cut off from the rest of humanity, that I never heard them sing it without feeling a chill."[16]

Obviously Lizzie is not privy to the information about R.C.'s Melungeon heritage.

---

[16]Smith, *The Devil's Dream*, 103-104.

When Lizzie dies during WWI of "romantic fever" and is buried "quick" in foreign soil, R.C. takes it hard. But the real tests for R.C. are Lucie's passing, "I told [Ralph Handy] how R.C. never got over Lucie's death" says Katie Cocker years later,[17] and Rose Annie's running off with Blackjack Johnny Raines.

> "It [Lucie's death] has almost killed R.C." [relates Buddy's mother Gladys Rush]. "He's always been kind of funny anyway, and since this, you don't hardly ever see him. He just stays in the house. The first week or so after it happened, he wouldn't come out at all, and hollered out the door at the reporters that if they took one step closer, he was going to shoot them. I believe he would have, too."[18]

It's not only sister Lizzie who recognizes R.C.'s intensity and talent. One day Durwood's wife Tampa questions Lucie about his mercurial behavior and the third-person narrator reveals Lucie's thoughts, "How can she say she'd rather have one hour of R.C.'s undivided attention than a whole year with poor old broken-down Durwood? How can she say what it's like in the bed with R.C.? For a good woman like Lucie can't say those things."[19] R.C. even sees it himself, "I'm half crazy, anybody will tell you that."[20] Tammy Adele Burnette alleges, "The Baileys are all a little off, in my opinion. This goes for old R.C., who has always been either real smart or real crazy—often, you know, you can't tell the difference."[21] Ralph Peer, the RCA Victor representative presiding over the Bristol sessions, also sees the truth, "He realizes that R.C. Bailey is smart, a cut above most of the hillbillies, . . . and treats him with consequent respect."[22]

Finally the narrator can't resist putting in her own two cents' worth:

> "Alone among his carload of kin [driving back to Grassy Branch after their first recording session], R.C. understands the importance of this day, of this new recording equipment, of this

---

[17]Smith, *The Devil's Dream*, 286.
[18]Smith, *The Devil's Dream*, 186.
[19]Smith, *The Devil's Dream*, 119.
[20]Smith, *The Devil's Dream*, 112.
[21]Smith, *The Devil's Dream*, 158.
[22]Smith, *The Devil's Dream*, 121-22.

infant industry. It is always R.C.'s blessing—and curse—to understand a little too much about everything."[23]

We get a different perspective on R.C. when Rose Annie and Katie, the next generation, do most of the talking in the second half of the book. It is twenty or more years after the Bristol sessions, sweet Lucie is dead, and R.C. is as tormented as ever. His daughter Rose Annie tells the story:

> [Music] used to be his whole life. He don't have no more heart for it. . . . Daddy always ran the show when it was the Grassy Branch Girls, you know. It was him that thought of it being a sister act in the first place, and him that found the songs. Now he won't talk about those days at all. But he's still got that old record player from the Sterchi furniture store out in the shed, in what he calls his office, and you can hear him out there sometimes all night long, playing their old records—"Melungeon Man" in particular—over and over.[24]

R.C. does get almost the last word in the novel by refusing to come to Nashville to be a part of Katie's album of Bailey family songs.

> "Went out in the barn and locked the door behind him" [says Homer Onslow, Little Virginia's boyfriend]. . . .
> [Moments later the narrator tells us] R.C., in the barn up on Grassy Branch, puts the barrel of his rifle in his mouth and sets the needle over on "Melungeon Man" one more time. R.C. has been thinking about his mamma, whose love for the Melungeon marked his life and made him a man always outside the closed door, waiting there forever in the outer dark.[25]

So the reader follows R.C. from conception to death, watching his torment, recognizing him without ever really understanding him, benefiting from his genius without ever acknowledging its value, puzzling over the question of what it means to be Melungeon in one man's life. Rose Annie is a different story altogether. She, too, leads a truly tormented life although she never ties it to being Melungeon. She knows that she is different, and says so over and over. It takes the readers a while to catch on, because we think perhaps Rose Annie is just delicate,

---

[23]Smith, *The Devil's Dream,* 123.
[24]Smith, *The Devil's Dream,* 130.
[25]Smith, *The Devil's Dream,* 306, 309.

or spoiled, or both. One of the most interesting voices in the novel is
Rose Annie's own:

> "I swear, sometimes I don't have no control over what I do.
> . . . I can't seem to do much better, no matter how hard I try. I
> do go to church, and I read the Bible and *The Upper Room* and
> *Good Housekeeping* and the *Reader's Digest*, I try real hard to be as
> good of a wife and mother and citizen as I can (Buddy is in the
> Toastmasters), but things get away from me somehow. I'll be
> washing the dishes one minute and crying in the garage the next.
> It is like a black cloud comes up out of noplace and smothers me
> down to the ground."[26]

This sounds like a 1950s version of R.C.—another person of extremes.
But only two pages into Rose Annie's narrative, we begin to suspect that
the situation may be out of control.

> "[Buddy] knows all about my nervous breakdown, but he
> doesn't know anything about the baby, of course. Nobody did
> but Daddy and Aunt Freda, and Freda's dead now. . . .
> Buddy is real good to me and I know it. I can't imagine what
> would of happened to me if he hadn't come along and married
> me when he did. It saved my life, I reckon, and God knows I'm
> grateful, and I try to be the best wife I can, as I said, but I swear
> there's this black empty place right down inside me ever since
> Johnny left. . . . Seems like I remember everything that happened
> to me, and everything that happened to the rest of my family too.
> Seems like I am a walking memory, sometimes. . . . Oh Johnny.
> *Johnny, Johnny, Johnny*, I see him everywhere I look, I reckon this
> is the problem. . . . [W]hen I stand here and look out this win-
> dow, it is like I am looking at myself and Johnny, at a hundred
> little mes and Johnnys all up and down this valley. I can't get
> away from me and Johnny. Maybe I'd go crazy if I did."[27]

Rose Annie goes on to tell about growing up with her cousins—
Georgia, Johnny, and Katie—and what life was like in the 1930s. She is
quick to explain that though they grew up like cousins, almost like
brother and sisters, that Johnny was really no blood relative, being
Virgie's son by a man who was no more than a voice in the night.

---

[26]Smith, *The Devil's Dream*, 129.
[27]Smith, *The Devil's Dream*, 131-34.

"It was Johnny [she says] that taught me everything I knew, and try as I might, I can't remember a time in my childhood that he wasn't there. 'Rosie' he called me. Cousin, brother, heart of my heart, best friend—'Johnny is my best friend,' I told them all as soon as I learned to talk, and they laughed and laughed. . . .

Oh they all took care of me to some extent, I suppose, for I was the littlest one and sick a lot as a child. . . . I had light, light hair, sort of like it is now, I reckon, and real pale skin; they would not let me out in the sun without a hat for I sunburned so easy. . . . They all doted on me, Mamma and the boys—Daddy too. They spoiled me something awful . . . [b]ut I was a colicky baby, so they said, born early, and real nervous. . . . But always, from the first day I remember there was Johnny who stood in his special place between me and the world, protecting me, giving the world to me bit by bit so it wouldn't scare me.

For I scared easy. . . . "[28]

Rose Annie has an imaginary friend, her "little girl":

"Sometimes I did catch a glimpse of her, just ahead of me on the road to Holly Springs, for instance, going around the bend, I'd see her blond hair or her blue dress so plain for just a minute. Or she'd be out in the schoolyard playing with the other children, as I walked over the hill—then I'd look again, and she'd be gone. . . .

Over time, I came to love that little girl as much as I feared her, and she has been with me ever since, just out of sight. . . .

The only person who ever knew about her was Johnny, and she didn't scare *him* at all. He used to laugh about her, and one day he stood right out in the middle of the road and hollered at her to show herself, but she did not. Johnny could make me laugh about her too. But he did not laugh *at* me, you understand, he never laughed at *me*, but at *her*, and this kept me safe."[29]

However, Rose Annie is not safe for long. She succumbs to Johnny's good looks and the heat of their lust fueled by long familiarity and real affection. One day when the two of them go out in the mountains to dig ginseng, Rose Annie's innocence is shattered.

[28]Smith, *The Devil's Dream*, 136-37.
[29]Smith, *The Devil's Dream*, 139.

"Johnny looked like an Indian, with his big dark eyes and that floppy black hair which he wore too long. Johnny had brown skin and high cheekbones and a sticky-out Adam's apple.
. . .

[H]e came over and took my hand and drew me to the edge of the craggy knob itself. He stood right behind me, so close I could feel his breath on the back of my neck. . . .

His breath on my neck went all over my body, and though he did not put his hands on me that day, or kiss me, this is when it began, that part of it.

I felt like I was on fire all over. I had not felt like this before, ever, nor would I again. . . .

So you see the problem. I had it all, everything there is, I think, when I was just a little girl, and it has ruined me for men ever since. Or for *life*—I might as well say it. Johnny ruined me for life by making me feel so much *then*. . . .

For we were on fire in those years, and just as determined to let no one know, and we got away with it too, so that to this very day no one knows the extent of it, nor when it started nor how long it went on."[30]

Rose Annie's relationship with Johnny permeates her whole life, the way only a first love can. She tells us more.

"In the same way that Johnny stood between me and the world, he stood between me and God. . . . I made a god out of Johnny Rainette, and I've been cut off from the other one ever since. . . .

[A]s time when on, me and Johnny got crazier and crazier, and the crazier we got, the more we did it. It was almost like we were trying to get caught. Rainy days in the hayloft in the sweet-smelling barn, with the horses below, rustling and sighing in their stall, the rain on the pitched tin roof, and my little-girl ghost peeping in at us between the wide boards. Or out in the woods, we'd make sure nobody was around and then we'd drop in place like we'd been shot.

The last time my family ever had a stir-off up here on the old place, why, right down there, it was—Johnny and me did it outside not a hundred yards from where my daddy stood

---

[30]Smith, *The Devil's Dream*, 140–42.

fiddling in the field. Not a hundred yards! Something broke in me that night, and it has not gone back right ever since."[31]

Immediately after this night, life spins out of control for Rose Annie. Her Uncle Durwood and her mother Lucie die within three days of each other. Johnny crawls into her room through the window to comfort her, and they fall asleep only to be found in the morning by Freda. "One thing I remember thinking is how crazy it was to be found like this, when we were *doing nothing*, and yet all those other times. . . . "[32] However, one of those times bears fruit, for Rose Annie is pregnant.

"We were going to run off and find somebody that would marry us as soon as Johnny got his two-week paycheck from the mill. But instead of that, I told Freda. I still don't know why I did it. I told her on a Wednesday afternoon, two days before we planned to run off. Then before I know it, Daddy was driving me and Freda to Bristol in the dark of night. . . . He took us to the train station and threw my stuff out on the platform. . . .

The train came and Daddy put us on it. I was so glad to see my little girl among the others. She wore a hat, which hid her long blond curls, but . . . I knew she was with me, and she would stay close by me in the months to come, when she was the only one I could really talk to. . . .

[T]hen there was a tiny little baby, my own tiny baby girl, she came too soon, though, she was in a tent, I never got to hold her, she never had a name. . . . I was very sick then and I stayed in the hospital a long time having my nervous breakdown and my little girl stayed with me all the while, and she watched out for me then too, and spoke right up to the mean ones. . . . When I got back to Grassy Branch, Johnny was not there and nobody mentioned him. . . . Everybody was real nice to me. . . . Then Buddy Rush got out of the army and came around. . . . I've always somehow had this idea that Johnny might come back here sometime looking for me.[33]

Of course, that is just what does happen. Rose Annie hears Johnny on the radio singing "Five Card Stud" his country hit, calls the station to make sure her ears are not lying to her. Then it's only a matter of time.

[31]Smith, *The Devil's Dream*, 143–45.
[32]Smith, *The Devil's Dream*, 150.
[33]Smith, *The Devil's Dream*, 151–53.

We get this story from Gladys Rush, Buddy's mother, who is naturally partial to Buddy but who is also starstruck. She tells the tale while she pages proudly through her scrapbooks full of pictures of many of country music's great singers. Rose Annie and Johnny run off to Nashville and are billed as the king and queen of country music. Gladys is fascinated by the drama of Rose Annie's glamorous life in Nashville, and in her mesmerized condition, even when she takes Buddy Junior and Sugar to visit Rose Annie in Nashville misses the telltale signs of the deterioration of the fairy-tale marriage and of Rose Annie's advancing mental distress.

> "As for Rose Annie, that visit was an eye-opener for me. I went over to Tennessee prepared to hate her, but I couldn't hate her any more than I could when she was married to Buddy and laying in the bed. I thought she would be *changed*, I guess, since she had become the Queen of Country Music and all, but the only thing changed about her was the size of her bosom on that album cover. In the flesh, she was the same Rose Annie as always, with something about her that makes you want to hug her and tell her it would be all right. She looked young as ever, and pretty as ever in a frail kind of way like a wildflower. . . .
>
> I don't know why I thought that, but you know how wildflowers are—they die if you try to transplant them or bring them inside. Her hair was still as pale and flyaway as dandelion fluff, and the color still came and went in her cheeks. Her eyes were that cornflower blue—oh, it was not possible to stay mad at Rose Annie."[34]

Are these the Melungeon blue eyes?

Finally even Gladys has to admit that things are not right. Johnny is missing performance dates. One newspaper story tells that Rose Annie was picked up by the police in Florida incoherent and bleeding after Johnny has locked her out of their motel room. Gladys says she hopes things will be resolved when it is time for the children's Christmas visit. However, things are not resolved. One day near Christmas a young girl comes to the mansion on Hickory Lake and tells Rose Annie that she is going to have Johnny's baby. The girl leaves crying and Rose Annie sits on the sofa with her little girl and the .32 Johnny gave her for protection. When Johnny comes in drunk, she shoots him.

---

[34]Smith, *The Devil's Dream*, 198.

This section is masterfully told in Rose Annie's confused and crazy voice. We get the story in disjointed snippets as she talks to the police officer who has come to arrest her. She is decorating a blue Christmas tree as she talks—it is certainly a blue Christmas she's facing without her Johnny and without her sanity.

Subsequent references to Rose Annie are in Katie's strong no-nonsense voice. Katie, who has come to Nashville to try to make her way in the music business, pulls no punches.

> "The first thing you do, of course, is call up whoever you know, but when I tried to call Rose Annie I got a recording that said, This number is no longer in service at this time. . . . When I went out to get some supper, I passed a rack of newspapers and saw immediately why I couldn't get Rose Annie on the phone. 'BLACKJACK JOHNNY SHOT BY WIFE' pretty much said it all. I bought a couple of newspapers and a couple of beers and some nabs and went back to my room and read all about it. It was just tragic for Rose Annie, to have left Buddy Rush for him and have it turn out this way. I was sure he'd deserved shooting, since she'd shot him. I never thought otherwise."[35]

Later when Katie meets Ralph Handy she says "Then I went on to tell about Rose Annie, who was out at Brushy Mountain State Prison. . . . I told him how I went to see her as often as I could."[36] Rose Annie is slated to be a part of Katie's family history album; Katie announces this fact at her press conference at the Opryland Hotel:

> "Rose Annie is definitely coming too. They're releasing her from Brushy Mountain State Prison just to cut this album, that's one reason we're going to cut it live.—I don't know. I just don't know. I'd sure like to have 'Subdivision Wife' on here if she wants to sing it— . . . "[37]

When Rose Annie arrives, . . . for a minute nobody recognizes her. . . .

> Rose Annie has gotten old all of a sudden, the way women will at their age who don't take care of themselves, with wispy gray hair hanging down in her face, hunched shoulders, veiny blue hands sticking out the sleeves of her old coat. Katie wonders

[35]Smith, *The Devil's Dream*, 269.
[36]Smith, *The Devil's Dream*, 286.
[37]Smith, *The Devil's Dream*, 13.

where Rose Annie could have possibly gotten that awful old coat. Rose Annie will be up for parole next year but she might have to live in a rest home, this is what they've told Sugar, as she suffers from depression. Her spirit has been broken, as you can see. Still, the loveliest smile comes over Rose Annie's face as she recognizes Katie, and her beautiful eyes, still cornflower blue, are perfectly clear, a girl's eyes in an old woman's face.[38]

Never once in the novel is it mentioned that Rose Annie has Melungeon blood. One wonders whether she knows. She accepts her father's intensity and acknowledges his attachment to "Melungeon Man," but she doesn't ever seem to be aware of why he likes that particular song so much out of all the family's repetoire. Personally, I think Rose Annie has Melungeon eyes. They are mentioned twice as being light "cornflower blue" and as being striking and memorable. I know about that, for I recently looked into a pair of Melungeon blue eyes at the Fall Festival in Sneedville, Tennessee, just at the foot of Newman's Ridge, and I will never forget that experience. Such eyes are ageless and unforgettable.

It is possible that Rose Annie is meant to be simply fragile, prone to depression, and unable to control her behavior. It is not normal to abandon your children or to shoot your husband in cold blood in the living room. On the other hand, Melungeons are known to be "unpredictable." Big Matt Bludsoe (*The Tall Woman*) kills his own son for telling a lie, and as Tracy Harkryder's grandfather tells Spencer Arrowood in *She Walks These Hills*, "Ain't no telling what them folk will do."[39]

---

[38]Smith, *The Devil's Dream*, 307, 308.
[39]Sharyn McCrumb, *She Walks These Hills* (1994; repr.: New York: Signet, 1995) 114.

6

Still Dealing in Death:
A Melungeon in Kinflicks,
by Lisa Alther

Lisa Alther (1944–) was born and raised in Kingsport, Tennessee. Her father was a physician there (now retired). Her grandfather moved from Clintwood, Virginia, to Kingsport in 1918 to found the town's first hospital in the boatyard area along the Holston River.[1] In a talk given at the Kingsport Public Library she related how her reading of Brent Kennedy's *The Melungeons* opened her eyes to her own heritage.[2] She and her father realized that they have ancestors in common with Kennedy and that they are in fact of Melungeon descent. Alther now lives in Vermont, but was in Appalachia in the fall of 1999 filling the Wayne G. Basler Chair as writer in residence at East Tennessee State University. Several of her novels are set in Appalachia.[3]

Kinflicks, her first novel, gets its title from the home movies and snapshots that an adoring mother took to chronicle the lives of her children. The main character, Ginny Babcock, grew up in Hullsport, Tennessee, the fictional equivalent of Kingsport. As a highschooler in the late 1950s and young adult in the 1960s Ginny tries everything that was going on in that era—she is a cheerleader and flag girl who dates a football star, girlfriend of a motorcycle thug, and an intellectual at an Eastern women's college. She then revels in a homosexual liaison with the editor of the college newspaper, tries commune life in New England, marries Ira Bliss— insurance salesman and pillar of small-town Stark's Bog, Vermont, and has an affair with a Viet Nam deserter named Hawk. The novel alternates between chapters that chronicle Ginny's life and chapters that detail the

---

[1]Rick Wagner, "Writer Sets Sights on Region Again," *Bristol Herald Courier*, 20 September 1999, A:1, 12.

[2]Lisa Alther, "The Melungeon Melting Pot," talk at the Kingsport Public Library, 19 October 1999.

[3]*Kinflicks* (1975); *Original Sins* (1980); and *Five Minutes in Heaven* (1995). For more on Alther, see her autobiographical essay, "Border States," online at <http://rhombus.net/artvt/artvt/p_altherbio.htm>.

weeks she spends at the bedside of her terminally ill mother. In her introduction to the 1996 paperback edition, Alther writes:

> How could a person satisfy at once both the need for safety
> and security and the need for change and adventure? . . . I
> decided to invent a character . . . who would careen from one
> relationship to another seeking such a balance. . . . This was the
> origin of the picaresque flashbacks in which Ginny alternates
> between a security that leads to suffocation, as with Ira Bliss, and
> adventures that lead to disaster, such as those with Clem Cloyd.
> . . . Mrs. Babcock [Ginny's mother] embodies the virtues of the
> traditional woman, virtues that have left her feeling deprived and
> resentful in the face of death. . . . Thus, I began to see Ginny's
> struggle to find alternatives to her mother's mode as, in part, a
> rejection of her mother's martyrdom.[4]

Alther readily admits that the book is autobiographical and that it
chronicles her own efforts to answer the questions that Ginny and her
mother pose both consciously and in the events of their lives. She says
that the themes in *Kinflicks*, "the concept of androgyny and the necessity
for each person to develop both the masculine and feminine sides to his
or her psyche in order to achieve sanity,"[5] have continued to surface in
her writing. She asserts that she writes (and reads novels, too) to discover
how to live and that her books are what she wanted to read when she
was younger.[6]

Alther is currently working on a historical novel about the origin and
evolution of Melungeons, which will be partly set in Southwest Virginia,
East Tennessee, Eastern Kentucky, and Western North Carolina.[7] It will
be interesting to see how she weaves the themes mentioned here and the
historical research she is doing into this new book. Over lunch one day
in December 1999 she and I discussed her growing-up experiences which
she claimed had nothing to do with being Melungeon. However, the
longer we talked the more she began to realize that her own experiences—of not really knowing who her ancestors were, of leaving the
mysterious family behind on the mountain ridges and in the valleys, of
her grandmother's refusal to talk about family history, of the insistence
that some progenitors were Tidewater aristocrats—fit the paradigm for

---

[4]Lisa Alther, *Kinflicks* (1975; repr.: New York: Penguin, 1996) ix-x.
[5]Alther, *Kinflicks*, xiii.
[6]Alther, *Kinflicks*, xiv.
[7]Wagner, "Writer Sets Sights on Region Again," A:1.

persons with Melungeon heritage who have passed, almost without a trace, into white society in Appalachia. Alther's father's vocation of medicine made it possible for the family to live very comfortably and to have access to both middle-class social amenities as well as prestigious educational opportunities (Alther herself went to Wellesley). This new novel will be very important in the body of Appalachian literature that features Melungeon characters because, like Brent Kennedy's nonfiction book, it will be the first work of fiction written by someone who is consciously on the inside of the legend.

Kinflicks has two different strands that deal with Melungeons. The first is a Melungeon character, Clem Cloyd. Clem's family runs the farm where Ginny grows up that is a part of the "estate" (a big plantation-style house that Ginny Babcock's grandfather Mr. Zed built and the adjacent dairy farm). As the first person narrator, Ginny writes:

> I had always known Clem. We were inseparable throughout childhood, riding our ponies all over the farm and swimming in the pond and building forts in the woods. . . . Clem as a little boy was short and slight, with a tangled mat of black hair that hung in his dark serious eyes. He was an ideal subject for a Save the Children ad. His family was part Melungeon, members of a mysterious, graceful, dark-complexioned people whose ancestors were found already inhabiting the east Tennessee hills by the first white settlers. Admirers of the Melungeons claimed for them descent from shipwrecked Portuguese sailors, from deserters from DeSoto's exploring party, from the survivors of the Lost Colony of Roanoke Island. Detractors portrayed them as half-breeds, riffraff from the mating activities of runaway slaves and renegade Indians. The truth was anyone's guess. And in any case, the Cloyds themselves couldn't have been less interested. Their forebears having endured various minor persecutions due to being labeled "free persons of color," the present-day Cloyd family longed to forget all about their obscure origins and get on with the business of living. All that remained to mark them as Melungeon was their gypsy-like good looks.[8]

Ginny and Clem are best friends as children, as Ginny tells it. "[I]n a secret pact in which we pricked our index fingers and mingled our

---

[8]Lisa Alther, *Kinflicks*, 107-108.

blood, we were married."⁹ The two children share important growing-up experiences. They witness the death of a fawn and try to rescue a frog from the mouth of a large black snake. By the time the children are ten, however, Clem is put to work on the farm by his father and Ginny must seek other companions. She begins playing with some girls from Magnolia Manor, a nearby housing development; their favorite pastime is playing house in the bomb shelter that is in the Babcocks' basement. One afternoon the girls decide to have a party and to invite boys. Ginny invites Clem, much to the other girls' dismay. (Are they sensitive at ten or eleven to his being Melungeon or is it instead the fact that his clothes and his very body smell like manure?) Spin the Bottle is rejected as an amusement in favor of a game called Five Minutes in Heaven where "each couple vanished into the chemical toilet cubicle while the others sat outside and timed the tryst (and in my case wondered what the couple inside could possibly be finding to do with each other for five minutes in a dark closet)."¹⁰ Clem and Ginny, not sure what exactly they should be doing in the dark, have a conversation about what is happening on the farm, are admonished to "finish" by the waiting group outside. Clem does lean over to kiss Ginny. " 'There!' he said proudly, wiping his mouth with the sleeve of his work shirt. ' . . . Well, in'nt that what we're *supposed* to be doin in here?' "¹¹

This prepuberty experience is the beginning of a significant change in Ginny and Clem's relationship. Ginny's narrative continues:

> From then on, Clem Cloyd was my archenemy. Both he and I began playing football with the boys in Magnolia Manor. We always tried to be on opposite teams so that we could smear each other into the dirt. . . . Sometimes after he had tackled me, he would lie on top of me longer than necessary, his chin resting on my stomach and his dark eyes looking slyly up at me over my shoulder pads. At such times I would wrap a leg around his hips and gouge him with my cleats until he rolled off me in pain.
>
> This went on until his accident, at which time he supposedly ceased to be a factor in my existence. He was disking a new field on a hillside when the tractor tire hit a buried boulder and reared up like a startled horse. The tractor rolled over on him, crushing one of his legs.

---

⁹Alther, *Kinflicks*, 107.
¹⁰Alther, *Kinflicks*, 111.
¹¹Alther, *Kinflicks*, 111.

I visited him once in the hospital. He lay swathed in white linens, his injured leg suspended from a pulley arrangement and encased in a full cast. We had nothing to say to each other. . . .

From then on Clem Cloyd was very much on the periphery of my life. He limped around school in his orthopedic motorcycle boots which had a four-inch sole for his injured leg; his dark greasy hair hung in his scowling face. He wore tight blue jeans, which had pegged legs and were studded down the leg seams and around the rear pockets with bronze upholstery tacks; and a faded dark green T-shirt; and a red silk windbreaker Floyd [his older brother] had brought him from Korea. . . .

To compensate for his injured leg, which was now somewhat shriveled with its foot twisted inward, his entire body alignment had altered. He dragged the injured leg, and the shoulder on that same side hunched down and forward. Because of his deformed gait, he preferred, whenever possible, to roar around on his dark green Harley motorcycle, which he'd bought with the prize money he'd won in the state fair with his show steers. The Harley had jeweled mud flaps and two huge chrome tail pipes; . . . he sometimes wore a molded plastic helmet of metallic green (the color of the cycle), which was decorated with a large Confederate flag decal. Other times he wore only yellow-tinted goggles and no head covering, so that his pomaded pompadour quivered in the breeze. Unfortunately, his thug image was undercut by the fact that he reeked of manure. From his barn chores, his body and all his possessions were permeated with the acrid odor, and the less kind students at Hullsport High, to be funny, sometimes held their noses after he had walked past.

Before long, I was flag swinger for Hullsport High and Clem was the town hoodlum.[12]

As a flag swinger, Ginny is among the elite in high school. Her boyfriend is football hero Joe Bob Sparks. Coach Bicknell thinks that Ginny and Joe Bob are seeing too much of each other, so Ginny gives Joe Bob hand jobs on the sly during study hall in the school darkroom and sets out to prove to the coach that they are not going steady by finding someone else to date. She picks the most conspicuous person she can find, Clem Cloyd. On their first date they ride up and down Hull Street on the Harley, Ginny's arms tightly clasped around Clem's waist, and get a

---

[12]Alther, *Kinflicks*, 111-13.

cherry 7-UP at the Dew Drop in full view of Joe Bob in his friend Dolye's Dodge and Coach in his black DeSoto.

The second date is a different story. " 'Last time we done hit *your* way,' [Clem] shouted over his shoulder. 'Tonight we do hit *mine.'* "[13] They race through the night to a Prohibition-style speakeasy[14] on the motorcycle as Ginny thinks about how inappropriate her wardrobe is for riding on the back of a Harley.

> The Bloody Bucket was a country nightclub run by Clem's brother, Floyd Cloyd. By day Floyd was the industrious janitor at the state school for the blind and deaf in Knoxville, in the basement of which he reputedly ran the largest still in the eastern part of a still-strewn state. By night he crept around town in a black hearse with a false floor delivering his bootlegged liquor to all the upstanding citizens of the dry town of Hullsport. . . . On the nights when he wasn't making deliveries, Floyd opened up his nightclub, dubbed the Bloody Bucket [and] sold his famous home brew by the drink to those who ventured in. . . .
>
> According to the popular imagination, the Bloody Bucket was the scene of poker games with stakes of many hundreds of dollars, of knife fights, of lascivious floor shows and wanton prostitution, of racial integration and every other vice known to modern man. . . . Because it was so irresistibly appealing, we, the uninitiated, naturally reacted publicly to its presence on the outskirts of our town with scandalized outrage. . . . [N]o law enforcement agency had ever been able to surprise Floyd Cloyd with liquor in his possession.[15]

This description plays on at least two of the common conceptions of Melungeons: that they make and consume quantities of moonshine, and that their amusements are rowdy and immoral. The other trait that appears here and in other passages where Clem speaks is his mountain dialect. No other characters in *Kinflicks* except Clem's father, Maxine, and Mr. Zed's mountain kin, use the Appalachian vernacular.

Contrary to Ginny's expectations at the Bloody Bucket, Floyd as proprietor is decked out like a riverboat gambler, "elegant in a white

---

[13]Alther, *Kinficks*, 116.

[14]It might seem that a speakeasy type club is too much of an anachronism for a novel set in the late 1950s; however, towns in Upper East Tennessee were dry into the late 1980s. Alther's portrayal is accurate.

[15]Alther, *Kinficks*, 117.

shirt and brocade vest,"[16] but the other men are wearing green work clothes while the women have bouffant hairstyles and wear heavy makeup. Ginny is surprised by two things—one, that the only person interested in her presence is Floyd (because he thinks it will be an excuse for the local lawmen to shut him down); and two, that the singer with the pickers on the raised platform, "dressed in a tight black straight skirt and a low-necked rayon jersey and ballet slippers, [is] Maxine 'Do-It' Pruitt, [her] best friend from the first to the fifth grades."[17] Ginny gawks at her former playmate jolted for a moment out of her narrow preppy rut:

> Maxine's hair, which had been a dirty blond in the fifth grade, was now strawberry blond and was teased into cascades of ringlets that made it look as though her neck would inevitably snap under the excess bulk. She had also been transformed from a stringy lanky kid into a warm soft voluptuous young woman with huge breasts that were molded by her bra into bulletlike projectiles. I had to hand it to Maxine: She was a professional, something I would never be.[18]

Ginny continues by describing her first experience with corn likker:

> I made the mistake of sniffing deeply and was almost anesthetized by the vapors. . . . The liquid burned my mouth, and I could have sworn I felt it corroding my esophagus inch by inch as it descended into my poor unwitting stomach. The vapors ascended into my sinuses and foamed and fizzed like Drano in a drain.[19]

Not only was Ginny's initiation into the mysterious pull of sexual intercourse in the bomb shelter in the basement of her parents' house, but the loss of her maidenhead takes place there, too. Both times Clem is her partner. Intercourse with Clem causes her eventually to break up with Joe Bob. Clem begins to call her "woe-man" and introduces Ginny to a whole range of sadomasochistic literature and paraphernalia. However, the pleasure of orgasm eludes her; she cannot see what all the fuss is about.

One night Ginny, at the Bloody Bucket with Clem, has an eye-opening conversation with Maxine, who asks:

---

[16]Alther, *Kinflicks*, 118.
[17]Alther, *Kinflicks*, 118.
[18]Alther, *Kinflicks*, 119.
[19]Alther, *Kinflicks*, 120.

"How come you to stop that flag swingin stuff over at the school?"

"I don't know. I got tired of it. It's kind of dumb, don't you think?"

"Shit, if I could be flag swinger, do you think I'd hang around this dump?" Her green eyes flashed. I looked at her with surprise. "And how come you to take up with ole Clem here when you had that Joe Bob Sparks hunk?"

"Clem's not so bad."

"Clem's not so bad, but he's no Joe Bob Sparks."[20]

Ginny, who thinks she has found real authenticity by renouncing flag swinging and Joe Bob, is astounded that Maxine longs to be middle class and popular.

Although Ginny doesn't realize all the significance of the event when it happens, her interlude with Clem ends abruptly because of a near-disastrous motorcycle accident (that her worried parents have been both predicting and dreading all during her dalliance with Clem). Ginny as the retiring Persimmon Plains Tobacco Festival Queen is obliged to be present at the festival to crown her successor. Clem shows up saying, " 'Let's go fuck, queenie.' "[21] They climb on the Harley and start off on the narrow, winding road between Hullsport and Persimmon Plains, which is still wet from rain the night before. Going way too fast, Clem loses control on a curve; Ginny grabs for him but falls off the bike, her yellow chiffon skirts catching in the rear wheel. She slides on her side across the asphalt and then off the road and down a cliff. Clem is not allowed to visit during her long convalescence, nor is Ginny allowed to come home from her Eastern women's college to see him at Thanksgiving. Then, just before the Christmas holiday she gets his letter announcing that he and Maxine are engaged. Clem's letter states a fact that is borne out in the remainder of the novel: that because they have shared so much over so many years, their lives can never be totally separate.

Ginny reconnects with Clem and Maxine when she comes back to tend her ailing mother. Mrs. Babcock has idiopathic thrombocytopenic purpura—she is bleeding to death, surely a symbol for the way she poured out her whole life for her husband and children. Shortly after her arrival in Hullsport, Ginny decides to stay at the small cabin original to

---

[20]Alther, *Kinflicks*, 134-35.
[21]Alther, *Kinficks*, 141.

the farm instead of in the big empty house. On the way to the cabin in the Jeep she passes the Cloyds' small, mean dwelling.

> After a mile, she came to the Cloyds' tenant house, which was shingled in maroon asphalt tiles and clashed hideously with the orange-red clay of the front yard. Behind and below the house were the dark brown barns and white silos and spotless gray-cinderblock milking parlor. . . . She decided not to find Clem and announce her arrival. . . .
>
> What would Clem be like now that he had to be up at four A.M. for milking and could no longer prowl the streets on his Harley until early morning? Ginny had seen him at the Major's funeral—looking intensely uncomfortable in a dark suit and starched shirt. But she had only exchanged greetings with him and received his condolences. The major had praised Clem's running of the farm. Some sort of metamorphosis must have occurred. The Clem Ginny had known could never have endured such a purposeful life. . . .
>
> She tooted the horn gently in the old tattoo her family had always used to indicate to the Cloyds that it was Babcocks going past to the cabin, not vandals and thieves.[22]

Another day coming home from the hospital she meets Clem and gets a clue to the very transformation she has suspected:

> It was late twilight as Ginny passed the Cloyd house. She tooted. Through the fuzzy gloom that made everything look out of focus, she saw a figure down the hill waving its hand. She stopped and backed up and got out. It was Clem, walking toward her smiling.
>
> "Heard you was comin," he said. "Otherwise, I wouldn't of knowed it was you." He nodded at her peasant dress. He was in a dirty sweat-stained T-shirt and jeans and manure-caked high-top work shoes. He looked hot and tired. . . .
>
> "I hear you're doing good things with the farm."
>
> "Highest production per head in the state. Got me $18,000's worth of prize sperm in the freezer," he said with a proud smile, wiping beads of sweat from his upper lip with the back of his hand.
>
> "That's great. Did you hear my mother is in the hospital?"

---

[22]Alther, *Kinflicks*, 68.

"Yeah, I did. I'm real sorry. She's done had a bad year, ain't she? Pray God she'll be out soon. Is she bad sick this time?"

Ginny looked at him quickly. Pray God? Was this *the* Clem Cloyd, star of Hullsport low life? "Uh, well, I don't know exactly. She's had this before and has snapped right out of it. I don't see why she shouldn't this time. . . . "

"Why don't you come in for a while and say hi to Maxine? . . . "

Maxine looked much as she had during Bloody Bucket days, only more so. . . . She dwarfed Clem, who was still slight, though wiry and toughened by all his physical labor. His face, on the other hand, usually tense and sneering and unhappy in high school, had softened and relaxed. With a start, Ginny put her finger on the big change in Clem: He no longer limped. . . . He'd had surgery or something? . . .

Three small dark children with Clem's Melungeon features squirmed shyly at their places. This didn't seem the time to be asking about Clem's leg.[23]

This passage illustrates several important characteristics imported into this novel from Melungeon lore. The description of the house is congruent with the commonly held beliefs that Melungeons live in the rudest of structures and that they do not own good farmland. Successful though he is, Clem works for the Babcocks, and the contrast between the dairy buildings and the Cloyd house underscores this servant/master relationship. The dialect is evident again in Clem's speech. A clue is also present that Christianity is a significant thing in Clem's life. We see this in Clem's father very early in Alther's narrative when he insists on quickly killing the faun that the mowing machine has injured in the hayfield saying, "Got to put hit out of hits misery. Just die slowlike anyhow. Can't function no more like the good Lord meant."[24] Clem's invoking a prayer to God is a red flag for Ginny and an important point for readers to note as well. The next day in real time, but many pages later in the novel, Ginny sees the Cloyds' lights on and decides to stop.

"How about some soup beans and corn bread?" Maxine asked. "There's lots left."

---

[23]Alther, *Kinflicks*, 167-68.
[24]Alther, *Kinflicks*, 110.

Ginny hadn't eaten all day and had given a pint of blood [for a transfusion for her mother]. "I'd love some if you've got it. I'm starved. . . . Clem, tell me to shut up if this is rude," Ginny said between bites, "but what's happened to your leg?"

Clem and Maxine smiled serenely. "Hit's well," he said.

"I noticed. But how come? Did you have an operation or something?"

"No, the Lord has made me whole."

"Oh, brother," Ginny said with a grin.

"But he *has*, Ginny. I pledged my life to Jesus after our wreck, an my leg growed out and straightened hitself." . . .

Ginny stared at him with disbelief. . . . the leg looked sound and normal. The healing episode was apparently true.

"Well, do you belong to one of the churches at the circle, or what?" Ginny sputtered.

"We got our own ministry, me and Maxine. We meet up at the springhouse, a couple dozen of us, ever Friday night. . . .

"We'd love to have you come Friday, wouldn't we, Maxine? . . . You wouldn't have to join in. You could just watch." . . .

"Hit could change your life. Like hit done mine," Clem assured her. "But even if hit don't, what have you lost? A couple of hours maybe."

"Do you preach, or what?"

"We don't have no set schedule. We do whatever the good Lord instructs us to."

Realizing how deeply offended Clem would be if she refused, Ginny accepted. "What time?"

"Seven-thirty, Friday."[25]

It is interesting that Clem's meetinghouse and place of ministry is the springhouse. Before refrigeration, a springhouse on a farm was an important part of food preservation. Having a spring, with its cool water bubbling out of the earth itself, was a real asset for a country family. This particular springhouse had been Clem and Ginny's playhouse when they were children (where Clem kept his most cherished possessions). Ginny was the only other person Clem allowed to have access. It was also a trysting place (where Clem stashed his pornographic books and displayed his posters) for some of their sadomasochistic rituals when they were dating. To have the "meeting" occur there is an interesting use of place

---

[25]Alther, *Kinflicks*, 260-62.

to symbolize something important and to reinforce the momentous nature of the change that has occurred in Clem's life. As the cool, refreshing water flows through the channel in the stone floor, the "living water" of John chapter 7 comes to mind, and the importance of this springhouse earlier in the novel makes Alther's use of it as a church/chapel particularly noteworthy. What happens at the meeting is predictable if one has any inkling about Melungeon/mountain religion in East Tennessee.

> That night Ginny climbed the path to the springhouse alongside Clem. . . . The door was still chained and locked, but hanging on it was a crude hand-lettered sign that read "Holy Temple of Jesus." . . .
>
> Half a dozen people stood chatting outside. . . . they treated Clem and Maxine with a respect bordering on deference, and kept referring to them as Brother and Sister Cloyd. . . .
>
> Brother Cloyd began introducing her around as an old friend. She was well aware that Clem was counting on her not to divulge to his brothers and sisters in Christ the fact that he and she had "known" each other in the true biblical sense on the floor of their Holy temple not ten years earlier. . . .
>
> Inside, lined up across the stone floor, were several rows of crude benches that faced a raised dais. Ginny noticed that the furniture Clem had made when they were kids remained: the bookshelves where he had kept his pornographic paperbacks now held tattered hymnals. The small table she had perched on the last time she had been here, right before leaving for her freshman year at Worthley, had been converted into an altar. . . . Hanging on the wall above it was a simple wooden cross. And the stream continued to gurgle along in its stone channel, giving the place a refreshingly damp cool feeling on the hot summer night.
>
> Ginny sat on a bench in back and tried to make herself as inconspicuous as possible. . . . She was still stunned by the transformation in Clem. Not only that his crippled leg had regenerated itself—she was getting used to that major miracle. Primarily she was amazed by the transformation in Clem's manner. She remembered him as a sour, antisocial, borderline-pathological boy. And now here he was at the door of his springhouse, greeting his parishioners—transformed into a warm, self-confident man. . . .
>
> Three men were on the front platform unpacking their instruments—a bass fiddle, a guitar, drums. Another man who had just

come in carried a large black box to the altar, set it down reverently, and backed away. . . .

Maxine was standing on the podium in front of the men with the instruments, just as she had stood on the platform at the Bloody Bucket all those years ago. . . .

[Ginny] had fully expected to find the evening tedious . . . ; what she had *not* expected was to be caught up in the flood of emotion surging through the room. She had not expected to find herself clapping with cheerleader-like enthusiasm. And she had especially not expected to launch into a version of the Hullsport High chicken scratch in front of her bench. Nor had she expected to be watching with sympathetic comprehension when a woman dancing in the aisle next to her fell to the floor and began twitching spasmodically and babbling.

Most of all, she had not expected to see Clem walk up to the dais and light the wick sticking out of a Dr. Pepper bottle filled with kerosene. The hard-driving gospel music continued. . . . Two parishioners were now speaking in tongues, and several more were shouting to Jesus fervently and snapping their bodies at the waist like whips. Clem called out over the din in a calm voice, "Remember, brothers and sisters. Only those anointed by the Spirit. Don't misread the signs, brothers and sisters. If you do, you'll get hurt. The devil is lurkin here tonight jes waitin for a chance to deceive. So don't misread your state of grace."

Then Clem slowly ran the fingers of one hand through the flame from the Dr. Pepper bottle. . . .

[He] walked calmly to the mysterious black box and unlatched it. Reaching in, he pulled out a snake. Ginny gasped. She could see even from the back of the room that the snake, patterned in varying shades of brown, was a copperhead. Every Southern child, Ginny and Clem no exceptions, grew up terrorized by copperheads. . . .

She stopped clapping, stopped mouthing words to the unfamiliar gospel songs, stopped doing the chicken scratch, and gaped in fascinated horror as Clem took the copperhead gently in his two hands and held it up to his face. With one little finger, he turned the copperhead's head—and its fanged mouth—until he and it were gazing into each other's eyes. There was a faint smile on Clem's dark Melungeon face. . . .

Clem reached in the black box—a celestial snake pit apparently—and casually took out another copperhead. This continued until five copperheads and two diamondback rattlesnakes were being passed around, and until Ginny was in a state of nervous collapse in the back row.

Eventually, all the snakes found their way to Clem. He ended up holding two in his hands, with two more wrapped around his arms and one hanging around his neck. A rattlesnake lay on the podium, and he caressed its pale belly with his stockinged foot. The second rattlesnake lay at striking distance just behind him, positioned on an open Bible on the altar, its tongue darting in and out rhythmically. . . .

[T]he music stopped abruptly. All eyes focused on Clem. He cleared his throat and said quietly, "They says this here can only be done with music. They says the rhythm of the music hypnotizes the snakes. Well, ah don't hear no music now, friends. The Lord does *what* He want to *when* He wants to. I ain't tamin these here serpents, brothers and sisters. You know that. The Lord is. He's here among us right now. He could kill me any second by turnin one of these devils loose. But He ain't, cause He's usin me as a channel to display to you His power over Satan." Ginny glanced around nervously, prepared for anything now—to see God even.

"These serpents is deadly," Clem continued. "Don't kid yourselves, brothers and sisters. They're powerful. But they ain't as powerful as the Lord! Behold the power and the glow-ry of your Lord!" He raised the snakes in his hands on high. Emotion of some sort—awe? terror?—surged through the room like a gust of wind. Ginny felt it grip her stomach.

Then Clem dumped all the snakes back in to their box and fastened the lid.

Next he turned around and started preaching, quoting the gospel according to St. Mark:[26] . . . In a quiet eloquent voice, Clem simply pointed out that everyone present had either witnessed or participated in all these things, except for their visitor, who was attending services for the first time. He considered this fact—that all the brothers and sisters had witnessed and participated and that no one had been hurt—a sign of God's approval

---

[26]"And these signs will accompany those who believe: In my name they will drive out demons; they will speak in new tongues; they will pick up snakes with their hands; and when they drink deadly poison, it will not hurt them at all; they will place their hands on sick people, and they will get well." (Mark 16:17-18 NIV)

of their undertakings. The state had a law against what they were doing. They might be thrown into prison at any moment because of their faith. . . . The true believers in any era had always been hounded and persecuted abominably. But their souls flourished as their flesh suffered.[27]

Fantastic as this narrative of a meeting of snake handlers may seem, it is very close to Mattie Ruth Johnson's description of what church was like when she was growing up in Hancock County in her book, *My Melungeon Heritage*. People who believe in the literal truth of Mark 16:17-18 still practice their faith in the hills and hollows of Appalachia. It has not been Ginny's growing-up experience of Christianity; her parents took her to the upper-middle-class Episcopal church on Church Circle in Hullsport. Yet, Ginny, even though she feels uncomfortable and fearful and a bit dazzled by the performance at the springhouse, must admit to Clem and to even to herself that "*something* had been going on. Clem's leg had regenerated itself, and the copperheads hadn't struck, the flame hadn't singed."[28]

Unlike Ginny, her mother is less skeptical of the supernatural power of God.

She had grown up in the rural South surrounded by every form of religious perversion. She had been raised in the Southern Baptist church, deserting it for the Episcopal church largely at the insistence of Wesley [her husband]. . . . Although she admired the dignified language of the Anglican prayer book, found solace in the antiquity of the rituals, she still nurtured in her heart a fondness for the fervid fundamentalist sects of her homeland—the faith healers and snake handlers, those who saw visions and rolled in aisles and spoke in tongues. . . . But she suspected she lacked the one element essential to faith healing—faith in that form of healing.[29]

Mrs. Babcock has replaced the comforting faith she remembers from her childhood with church practices that were more socially acceptable to the middle-class circles in which she moved as an adult, but in the process she has lost the authenticity. Ginny, who never knew the Baptist or the Pentecostal traditions except as something other people did, has

[27] Alther, *Kinflicks*, 358-63.
[28] Alther, *Kinflicks*, 363.
[29] Alther, *Kinflicks*, 411.

nothing; her church memories are only of emptiness and low expectations. When Clem invites her to be saved saying "Ginny, I almost killed
you ten years ago. . . . I'd purely love to make hit up to you by givin you
a *new* life in Christ,"[30] she resists even though

> she knew she was ripe for conversion, . . . she recognized in
> herself all the symptoms of Incipient Conversion Syndrome: She
> was severely demoralized in her personal life; all the various
> traditional ties and beliefs had failed her, were failing her. She
> knew that if she didn't watch out, she'd be fashioning copper-
> head necklaces with the best of them.[31]

Conversely, because of her positive childhood experiences, Mrs. Babcock
agrees to having Clem come to her hospital bedside after a service when
he feels "the power upon him."[32] Ginny, having witnessed only the
effects of the miracle of Clem's restored leg and the glossolalia, the
dancing in the spirit, the snake and the fire handling in the springhouse
church service, is skeptical of any positive outcome but willing to let him
try to be the agent of healing.

> Clem walked in the door the next night dressed in green
> work pants and a fresh white shirt. . . .
> After greeting them, he invited them to pray. It was a simple
> little prayer, which asked that God's will be done, but that that
> will include healing Mrs. Babcock. Then, his eyes tightly shut like
> a child making a birthday wish, he placed his supercharged
> hands on Mrs. Babcock at different spots—her head, her heart,
> her incision.[33]

Although Ginny and her mother allow themselves to feel a little
hopeful, the healing does not occur. Instead, the following day Mrs.
Babcock takes a turn for the worse. It is interesting that Alther leaves a
loophole for Christianity to be neither a vehicle for healing Mrs. Babcock
nor an option for Ginny at the conclusion of the novel. She says—as
quoted above—that healing may not come because faith is lacking. It
seems that here in order for faith healing to work, faith must be present.
Yet, in scripture Jesus himself used miracles to *bring* people to faith; the

---

[30] Alther, *Kinflicks*, 363.
[31] Alther, *Kinflicks*, 363.
[32] Alther, *Kinflicks*, 410.
[33] Alther, *Kinflicks*, 411.

twentieth-century Babcock women turn that around. They choose healing, but not wholeheartedly; therefore, they are neither surprised nor disappointed when Clem's prayer avails nothing . . . unless, of course, it avails *everything* because death, which for believers means being with God forever, is ultimate healing. There is a hint that this interpretation is possible. When Mrs. Babcock's retina hemorrhages, her eyes must be bandaged, and Ginny obligingly takes up her mother's encyclopedia-reading project.[34] One entry she reads to her mother is the one for "yantra." A yantra is an object used in yoga. Ginny admits to her mother that the yoga she did with Hawk has not given her any answers she sought. Her mother then offers:

> "My conclusion from nine years of encyclopedia reading, . . . is that all the great world religions have been training systems to instruct adherents in how to die."
> "Oh, come *on*. There *has* to be more to life than death!"
> "*Why* does there? . . . "
> Mrs. Babcock formally acknowledged that she was dying. This last month in the hospital was merely the graduation ceremony. The process had been under way for years.[35]

So, in light of this passage, it is entirely possible that Clem's prayer does bring this healing of the most profound and ultimate sort.

One other aspect of Clem's character cannot be ignored: he has a thing about death. Once he goes through the near-death experience of the tractor accident, he constantly searches for what he calls the Ultimate Orgasm, death itself. He both longs for and fears this experience. This quest makes it impossible for him to find satisfaction in a physical orgasm. His sadomasochistic fantasies are a part of his paranoia. Ginny reflects toward the end of the novel that Clem "had spent his adolescence pursuing death and had escaped it only by divine intervention."[36] One example is his behavior on the way home from the Persimmon Plains Tobacco Festival when he flirts with both ecstasy and disaster.

> The road signs read "65 mph—Speed Checked by Radar." But only Clem went more than forty on that road. . . . he tore

---

[34]When all three of her children left home, Mrs. Babcock had set out to read the entire set of multivolume encyclopedias the family owned, and, as she languishes in the hospital terminally ill, she has reached the final volume.

[35]Alther, *Kinflicks*, 412.

[36]Alther, *Kinflicks*, 359.

along it that day in his best form, leaning out and speeding up on the curves. His body and the cycle were one, satyrlike. The only problem was me [Ginny], clinging to him from behind in my yellow chiffon gown. My arms were wrapped around him at hip level, and I could feel his cock stirring as he hit sixty-five on a curve.

He started shouting into the wind, "Do hit! Do hit to me, you mother fucker! Go ahead! Kill me if you can!"[37]

This scene ends, of course, with Ginny's maiming. Clem walks away unscathed. When Ginny reconnects with the "new" Clem, calm, warm, self-confident, she thinks that there has been a change in him more profound than simply the healing of his deformed leg. However, at the end of the snake-handling church service, she ponders her responses and thinks, "Clem had *not* changed after all; he was still dealing in Death, still trying to subdue it to his command."[38] This Melungeon trait of reckless disregard for safety and sanity strikes a familiar chord, and old man Harkryder's voice reverberates in my consciousness: "Ain't no telling what them folk will do."[39]

The second major emphasis in *Kinflicks* that is important in an analysis of Melungeon markers is the references to Ginny Babcock's ancestry. As Alther unabashedly says in her introduction, the book is very autobiographical,[40] and she goes on to say "although each of my novels is ostensibly quite different from its predecessors, I realize that the themes introduced by *Kinflicks* have preoccupied me ever since."[41] Alther, like all writers, is free to use her imagination, but she must, after all is said and done, write what she knows. Ginny's tie to an Appalachian heritage is through her mother. We get hints through the narrative about Ginny's grandfather, Mr. Zed, his coming to Hullsport, and his founding of both the factory and the new family dynasty. Mr. Zed, mountain through and through, originally lives in the small log cabin where Ginny chooses to stay as she ministers to her mother and does serious thinking about her own life.

The cabin, built of chinked logs and covered by a dull green tin roof, had a patchwork history of occupation. It had been built

---

[37] Alther, *Kinflicks*, 142.
[38] Alther, *Kinflicks*, 363.
[39] Sharyn McCrumb, *She Walks These Hills* (New York: Signet, 1994) 119.
[40] Alther, *Kinflicks*, x.
[41] Alther, *Kinflicks*, xiii.

around 1800 by the original settler of the farm—one of the motley breed of horse thieves and adventures and deserters who had crossed the Blue Ridge Mountains, fleeing the civilized coastal regions of Virginia and North Carolina for the mountainous backwoods of Kentucky and Tennessee and southwest Virginia. By the time her grandfather, Mr. Zed, eluded his destiny as a coal miner and bought the farm, the cabin had been deserted for decades. Mr. Zed rebuilt the cabin and lived there with his wife and his small daughter, Ginny's mother, while his pseudo-antebellum mansion was under construction. When Ginny's mother and father were first married, they had lived in the cabin. Ginny herself had been born there. Shortly after Jim's birth, her grandparents had traded her parents the mansion for the cabin. After her grandmother's death, Mr. Zed had spent the rest of his life in virtual seclusion at the cabin, trying to figure out how to undo what he had spent his lifetime doing—founding Hullsport and establishing the factory.

Hence the kudzu. The kudzu vines served a double purpose; First, they held up the red clay sides of the bowl, which were always threatening to collapse into the pond; and secondly, they were an experiment with far-reaching implications in the deranged mind of the aging Mr. Zed. Kudzu was being highly touted at the time by the agricultural extension agents as the wonder vine of the century. Not only did the high-protein foliage make nutritious cattle fodder, *but* the plant spread so voraciously that only a few starter plants were required to take over an entire hillside. . . .

[Mr. Zed] would plant it, under cover of night, at selected spots around the factory and the town. The vines would silently take hold and begin their stealthy spread. Before Hullsporters were even aware of their existence, the grasping tendrils would choke out all life in the Model City. The site would be returned to Nature.

Word got around town to humor the old man as he crept around furtively planting, and scowling at the smokestacks and holding tanks, and shaking his fist at the encroaching superhighways and shopping malls and housing developments. "Senile," they would say, shaking their heads sadly. "Mr. Zed's done gone mental."

To Ginny, when she would walk up to visit him, he would shake his wild crop of tangled hair and say plaintively, "I never should of left Sow Gap, honey. I was a miner's son. I had no bidniss tryin to be nothin else. Lord God, I done made a mess. Virginia, honey, don't you never try to be what you ain't."[42]

This last sentence should be written in all caps, for it definitely is a very important theme in the novel. It is the long way to say "Don't put on airs" or "To thine own self be true." Ginny, of course, spends 500 pages trying to be herself and not knowing exactly what that entails. Both Mr. Zed and his daughter (Ginny's mother) have really mastered the art of deception about their origins and their true identities. Both of them die realizing that deception has been a serious mistake. Ginny, following them, seems to be an even slower learner.

> "But what *am* I?" [Ginny]'d ask him reviewing her history of being born in a farm cabin in Virginia with a rural Southern mother and an industrialist father from Boston, and with refugees from the coal mines for grandparents; growing up in a fake antebellum mansion in a factory town in the New South with a dairy farm out her back door; being christened "Virginia" by her mother in a burst of geographic chauvinism, and "Babcock" by her father, which name emblazoned the walls of a hall at Harvard. Being a human melting pot, to what one god—social or economic or geographic—was she to direct her scattered allegiances?[43]

Ginny remembers all these things as she enters the cabin where she was born, puts away the groceries, knocks down the spiderwebs, and dusts the floors. She also remembers a visit from a cousin.

> [A] few months before her grandfather's death, her cousin Raymond had arrived for a visit. Raymond was tall and painfully thin with black bags under his eyes and hollows under his cheekbones. His coloring was almost albino, like a crayfish from an underground stream. He talked very little, mostly sat hunched over wheezing. Black lung from the mines, her grandfather explained later.
> "I tell you the truth, Raymond,' " Mr. Zed said, shaking his bushy white head angrily, "I declare, I rue the day I left Sow Gap!"

---

[42]Alther, *Kinflicks*, 70.
[43]Alther, *Kinglicks*, 70.

"You're plumb crazy iffen you do," Raymond gasped. "Sow Gap like to have killed me. Can't do nothin no more cept sit around tryin to breathe."[44]

We never hear anything about the Major Babcock's blue-blooded New England family. However the references to the Hull family are numerous. One day during her stay in Hullsport, thinking familiar objects may comfort her mother, Ginny stops at the big house on her way to the hospital to gather up ancient family photos and the cherished Hull family clock with its steepled roof and etched glass door.

Taking down the photo of her Great-grandmother Hull, her mother's grandmother, Ginny scrutinized it. Her mother had always said that Ginny looked so much like her. She was Ginny's age in this photo, in her late twenties. She wore a high-necked lace blouse with a pin of some sort at the throat. . . .

She stared hard at this great-grandmother whom she'd never met. Dixie Lee Hull. She had been a legendary cook, right up until the day she had cut her finger on the recipe card for spoon bread and had died of blood poisoning. . . .

The most remarkable thing, Ginny reflected, was that she contained within each of her cells the tiniest fraction of a germ of nucleic acid from the very body of the woman in this cracked yellow photo, delivered to her via the intercession of her mother and grandmother. Traced back twenty generations, or six hundred years, Ginny calculated that she would find herself directly related to some 1,048,576 people—probably the entire population of northern Europe at that time, which was where her forebears had come from. . . .

Ginny wondered what one picture her descendants would seize on to remember her by. This was probably one of the only pictures ever taken of Dixie Lee Hull. To have it done, she would have had to take a day out from her spoon bread baking, put on what was probably her only fancy outfit, and travel to Big Stone Forge by wagon. It must have been a big deal.[45]

By this time, you are probably saying, "Wait a minute; I thought you said the Ginny's family could be Melungeon." I did suggest that. The thing to remember here is that the Hull family left the ridges, the hollers,

[44] Alther, *Kinflicks*, 73.
[45] Alther, *Kinflicks*, 242-43.

and the coal mines behind. They succeeded in town; in fact, Mr. Zed founded the town of Hullsport. Neither he nor his wife looked back in their busy middle years to their humble beginnings (although he apparently had regrets about denying his heritage when he was old as his comment to Ginny and his conversation with Cousin Raymond attest). According to Brent Kennedy and to some of the narratives on the Melungeon Homepage, not only do Melungeons who make it "out" never look back and usually embrace religiously a Northern European heritage, some actually destroy or alter all official (birth certificates, marriage certificates, etc.) and personal (baptismal documents, photographs) family records.

Another clue that Ginny herself is of Melungeon heritage is her admission to Eddie Holzer that she is part Cherokee Indian. "My great-great-great-grandmother was a Cherokee squaw. That makes me one thirty-second part Cherokee Indian. Up against all that Anglo-Saxonry."[46] Melungeons are considered by all, themselves and outsiders alike, to be a mixture of European (or Mediterranean) and Native American.

According to Ginny, Mrs. Babcock, obsessed with both death and her ancestry, wrote up numerous epitaphs, obituaries, and memorial services for herself and dragged her three children through many graveyards to make tombstone rubbings of forebears. This could certainly be seen as a quest to establish legitimacy for herself and her progeny. However, the most telling section on family history is the narrative about one trip to Sow Gap Mrs. Babcock took as a five-year-old that is etched in her memory.

> The trip, a hundred and fifty miles of rugged foothills, had taken two days in the shiny new Ford. The deeply rutted road looked like a hog wallow. Every couple of hours they got bogged down, and her father had to pry the auto out of the mud with logs and boards. Twice he had to go in search of farmers with mules to drag the car out. There were rivers to ford, mountain gaps to cross. Parts snapped on the auto and had to be fabricated out of scrap iron in farmers' junk heaps.
>
> Throughout the trip, her mother, in her flowered hat and white gloves and silk print dress, kept repeating, "Honey, you must never be ashamed of your origins. Your people are hard-working God-fearing folks. Hardy pioneer stock. A little backward maybe, a little slow. But hard-working and God-fearing."

---

[46]Alther, *Kinflicks*, 315.

These sermonettes had first suggested to the little girl that there might be something wrong with her origins. All kinds of questions started assembling themselves in her brain: Apart from this mud-bound marathon of a trip, why had she and her parents never been back? Why had they left in the first place when all their relatives were there? Why hadn't she seen her grandparents since she was five, her aunts and uncles and cousins?

They had arrived just as her grandfather's coffin was being lowered into the ground in a family plot on a hillside. Off into the distance rolled ridge after ridge of mountain, rising up abruptly from deep valleys. And directly below was Sow Gap—consisting of a handsome red brick courthouse on an unpaved street, surrounded by a couple of sandstone churches and several frame stores. There she had stood in a ruffled chiffon dress with ribbon ties, surrounded by cousins she had never met in neat dresses made of flour sacks. . . .

That night at supper, in a room packed with relations, Uncle Reuben demanded of Mr. Zed, "Why ain't you never been back afore, Zed? It like to killed Pa, you runnin off like that without nary no reason."

In indirect answer, Mr. Zed regaled the assembly. . . . His cousin Zeke had been running for sheriff on the Democratic ticket. Mr. Zed had been a Republican and hadn't liked Zeke anyway, and so had refused to work for his election. . . . [Zeke] had come gunning for Mr. Zed, who had to gallop off into the woods on his horse and hide in a stream bed for a couple of days. . . . "Now Zeke's dead, I figure it's safe for me to visit." . . .

Mrs. Hull told that night about teaching at the state reform school for girls in the next town, while Mr. Zed was working in the mines. One afternoon as she was leaving, her students surrounded her buggy intent on turning it over. She had fought them off like Cyrano de Bergerac with a long hat pin.

Her young daughter sat listening and staring in disbelief at her dignified parents—her father in a dark suit and starched collar, and her mother in her silk print dress and costume jewelry and well-coiffed hair, her mother who now had two maids and spent most of her time rushing off to meetings of church groups and civic clubs in a flowered hat and white gloves. . . .

On the train home, . . . the little girl demanded, "How come we moved away?" She had loved the family dinners, crowded with her flamboyant aunts and uncles and cousins, in contrast to the lonely Hullsport dinners in the echoing formal dining room with just the three of them.

Her parents laughed with embarrassment, as though the answer should have been self-evident. "For *you*, honey," Mr. Zed replied. "To give you opportunities we ain't never had."[47]

It is clear from these quoted passages that there is real ambivalence about leaving the past and the ancestry behind. The voice on Wayne Winkler's documentary tape echoes in my mind, the voice that alleges "Our ancestors thought they were giving us a gift, the gift of a white racial designation."[48] Leaving didn't work for Mr. Zed or for Mrs. Babcock. Nor has Ginny put the data together in any sort of meaningful way as the novel ends. She chooses abruptly not to return to Ira, indicating to him that she will file for divorce and for custody of her daughter Wendy. Clear about what she is rejecting, she is not as clear about what she is affirming. She does realize as she reflects on her mother's death that

> [d]ying was apparently a weaning process; all the attachments to familiar people and objects had to be undone. . . . Her mother had to work on doing without them because she must have suspected that she was about to leap into a realm where she would have none of these familiar comforts to orient her, where unresolved earthly attachments would only have flayed her to bits. . . . And, presumably, . . . she ended it all of her own accord, springing away free at last from the bruised body that had served her well and then had failed her abysmally.[49]

Ginny decides that death by suicide is the solution for her. She will outwit Death by taking her own life. On the heels of this decision while lying down for a nap, Ginny has a fantasy daydream that passes her whole life before her eyes.

> [S]he was standing at the bottom of a down escalator in a huge department store. . . . Joe Bob in his Gant shirt and chinos grabbed her hand and made her run with him up this down escalator. After decades of effort, with sweat pouring down their

---

[47] Alther, *Kinflicks*, 413–15.

[48] "Sons and Daughters of the Legend," audiotape of a radio documentary compiled by Wayne Winkler, WETS-FM, Johnson City TN.

[49] Alther, *Kinflicks*, 498–99.

faces they reached the top, where the Major was waiting. But just as Ginny reached out to embrace the Major, Clem, in his studded jeans and red silk windbreaker, grabbed her hand and dragged her down the up escalator. They ran and they ran, like chipmunks on an exercise wheel, Clem lurching and hobbling on his bad leg. Her mother was waiting at the bottom. . . . As she was being carried under the moving steps, down into the guts of the department store, she reflected that, after all that effort, she hadn't made any progress.[50]

R. C. Bailey's song "Melungeon Man" comes to mind.

Melungeon man [woman?] don't know where he's goin'
Melungeon man don't know where he's been,
He's just lookin' for the grace to face tomorrow
In a world outside the world of other men. . . .

Melungeon man, didn't know what he started,
Melungeon man, didn't know how it'd end.
'Til his soul finds a home, he'll have a seizure to roam,
Knowin' he's just another Melungeon man.[51]

R.C., tormented and unhappy after his Lucie dies, succeeds at suicide by putting a gun in his mouth. Although her several attempts at suicide fail ("degenerate into burlesque" is how Alther puts it), Ginny at the end of the novel is truly looking for the grace to face tomorrow.

She wrapped her mother's clock in her faded Sisterhood Is Powerful T-shirt and packed it in Hawk's knapsack with her other scant belongings. She left the cabin, to go where she had no idea.[52]

[50]Alther, *Kinflicks*, 499-500.
[51]Words transcribed from the CD of the music from the performance of *The Devil's Dream* at Barter Theater, Abingdon VA, 1996.
[52]Alther, *Kinflicks*, 503.

7

Inside Out: Melungeons, Centerpiece in Jesse Stuart's Daughter of the Legend

Jesse Stuart ranks among the most preeminent Kentucky writers. During his lifetime (1906–1984) he published more than sixty volumes of poems, stories, fiction, biography, autobiography, and essays. He spent many years as a teacher and school administrator and proudly affirmed that being an educator was close to his heart: "First, last, always, I am a school teacher. I loved the firing line of the classroom."[1] *The Thread That Runs So True* (1949), an autobiography that details some of his teaching experiences was selected by the National Education Association as the "best book of 1949."[2]

Born in a one-room log cabin in W-Hollow, Greenup County, Kentucky, Stuart was the second of seven children. His father and mother were virtually illiterate, but evidently valued education, for young Jesse was the first in his family to graduate from high school in his twentieth year (May 1926) even though he had had to miss school often to help his father on the farm. One of his high school teachers, Mrs. R. E. Hatton, encouraged him to write both fiction and poetry and introduced him to Scottish poet Robert Burns.

---

[1]J. Coady, "State's Poet Laureate, Jesse Stuart, Dies," *The Courier Journal*, 19 February 1984, A:21, as cited by Jamie Ballard in his "Jesse Stuart," accessed 15 February 2000, at <http://www.english.eku.edu/services/kylit/stuart1.htm> (also at <http://www.post325.org/stuart.htm>).

[2]"Jesse Stuart Biographical Sketch," accessed 11 February 2000, at <http://www.morehead-st.edu/projects/village/bio.html>.

[Editor's note. There is a perplexing piece of Stuart archives in the Gilbert Coble Collection of Jesse Stuart at Indiana State University Library. In a "miscellanies" box is a copy of a leaflet produced by E. P. Dutton & Co. with pictures and a brief autobiography of Stuart. In the sentence "My mother's family are Indian and English" the words "are Indian and" have been crossed out with green ink and replaced with "is," making the sentence read: "My mother's family is English." The perplexity arises of course because we don't know who "corrected" the pamphlet. This intriguing Stuart artifact is described online at <http://cml.indstate.edu/rare/rbooks/stuart.html>.]

After working as an elementary teacher, a farmhand, and a factory laborer, Stuart went on in the fall of 1926 to Lincoln Memorial University in Harrogate, Tennessee. He accelerated his program by attending summer school and graduated in three years. His LMU years provided the background for *Daughter of the Legend,* for, while he was a student there, Stuart dated a Melungeon girl.[3] Stuart knows his topic well; it is easy to discern in the novel that "Oakhill" is Sneedville, Tennessee, and that Sanctuary Mountain is Newman's Ridge. Whether he got most or all of his information from the girl he knew at LMU is speculation. However, Jacqueline Burks in her master's thesis quotes from a letter that Stuart wrote in which he says, "I didn't do any researching for my book. I just knew the people."[4] Wilma Dykeman, in the introduction to the edition of *Daughter of the Legend* recently published by the Jesse Stuart Foundation, comments on Stuart's enthusiasm for his topic and his narrative style.

> I remember well the morning he sat at the breakfast table with my husband, James, and me and told us about a Melungeon girl he had met when he was a student at Lincoln Memorial University in Harrogate, Tennessee. . . .
> I suppose he wanted to share his interest in the Melungeons with us because we lived in Tennessee and had been interested for a long time in these mysterious, misunderstood people. . . .
> By the time Jesse Stuart met the girl whose heritage fascinated him, the Melungeons were gradually becoming part of the society beyond their stony hills and deep valleys. It was only natural that these strange people, at home in a rugged, picturesque and harsh setting, would seize Stuart's imagination. . . .
> Jesse Stuart was a storyteller. Erudite complexity, subtleties of irony, and stylistic experimentation held little interest for him. Like bards of old and tellers of tales around the winter hearth or during long lazy summer evenings when there was not imported entertainment, Stuart carried listeners-readers along by sheer narrative zest. He saw the whole human comedy being played

---

[3]Jacqueline D. Burks, "The Treatment of the Melungeon in General Literature and Belletristic Works" (M.A. thesis, Tennessee Technological University, 1972) 47.

[4]Jesse Stuart to Mrs. Horace Burks, quoted in Burks, "The Treatment of the Melungeon," 47.

out in the region he called his own, and he shared it respectfully and exuberantly.[5]

In his preface to *Daughter of the Legend*, John H. Spurlock mentions the fact that Stuart published three newspaper articles about Melungeons during the 1930s, which make up a rough outline of what became the novel:

> In these articles, Stuart spoke of Newman's Ridge and the Melungeon villages of Ewing, Virginia, and Mulberry Gap and Sneedville, Tennessee. He presented the five popular theories of that day regarding the origin of the Melungeon people, the same as those appearing in this novel. He described the physical beauty of the Melungeon men and women, their lifestyle, religious beliefs, fondness of hunting and fishing and the love of freedom, which their reclusive lifestyle allowed. Stuart's articles included an account of a local legend regarding a Melungeon couple, Halley Mullins and her husband Skinny—both of whom became characters in this novel.[6]

Daughter of the Legend, an anomaly in the Stuart canon because it is not set in Kentucky, is an interesting mixture of fact and fiction. Set in fictional Cantwell County, Tennessee, the novel, written in the early 1940s when Stuart was in the Navy serving in the Naval Writers' Unit, but not published until 1965, is a love story detailing the relationship between the protagonist/narrator Dave Stoneking, a young lumberjack from Wise County, Virginia, (another heavily Melungeon area) and Deutsia Huntoon, a beautiful Melungeon girl who lives on Sanctuary Mountain. Dykeman calls the novel "a prime example of romantic plot and characterization wedded to realistic observation of nature's bountiful diversity and universal human experiences in the corner of Southern Appalachia Jesse Stuart claimed as his own."[7] Stuart explores the mystery of the origins of the Melungeon people, their lifestyle, many facts of their history, and the very real prejudice they endure from their white neighbors. The details he uses are accurate when compared with factual accounts in both the popular press and in scholarly articles.

---

[5]Wilma Dykeman, "Introduction" to *Daughter of the Legend* by Jesse Stuart, ed. John H. Spurlock (Ashland KY: The Jesse Stuart Foundation, 1994) xi-xiii.
[6]John H. Spurlock, "Preface" to *Daughter of the Legend*, viii.
[7]Dykeman, "Introduction" to *Daughter of the Legend*, xiii.

Young Dave falls in love with Deutsia the first time he lays eyes on her and determines to marry her in spite of the obstacles he encounters. He spends an idyllic winter with her on the mountain—building their first and only house, providing other Melungeon families with sturdy furniture he can build, learning the ways of the mountain people that he becomes one with by virtue of his marriage. The fairytale is shattered by the birth of Dave and Deutsia's son because the young mother dies in childbirth. Undecided for a few days after her death, Dave, who has experienced reconciliation with his former logging partner Ben Dewberry during their vigil beside Deutsia's deathbed, walks out of the novel with only his clothes and his tool kit, the same way he walked in. He says,

> I knew it took women to care for an infant. I knew more about cutting timber than I knew about how to care for a baby.
> . . .
> "He must never leave his people," Daid [Deutsia's mother] said a dozen times a day. . . .
> Maybe [she] knew already that if he stayed with them and was raised in the tradition of the Melungeons, he would be hurt less than if I took him with me. Maybe Daid was afraid I would take him among my fair-complexioned people where he might feel prejudice. Could I take my son to my father's home? . . .
> All my better judgment pointed to my leaving our son with Deutsia's family. I know that I had had my one love and that I would not marry again. I was broken in body and spirit. I knew that I would leave Sanctuary Mountain and go back to the land of my own people.[8]

So, the novel ends. Dave leaves his heart behind with Deutsia in her grave and his son behind to grow up in the Melungeon culture. Even though the fact is never overtly stated, the boy must be dark-skinned, as legend predicts that boy babies having Melungeon heritage will be—else why would Dave not take the child with him?

Stuart's choices of names in this saga are noteworthy. Cantwell County is a place where things can't go "well" because of the rampant prejudice and the existing double standard. Sanctuary Mountain provides a safe haven for Melungeons to live as they have for generations and to be close to the natural world that is so much a part of their culture and

---

[8]Jesse Stuart, *Daughter of the Legend* (1965), 224-25. References to *Daughter of the Legend* are to the 1994 edition, as cited at n. 5 above.

their daily round. Many of the characters' names are related to names in nature. Deutsia probably comes from *deutzia*, the name of a genus of shrubs that has pink or white flowers. Deutsia's father's name is Bass. Dave's friend Ben has the last name of Dewberry—a dewberry is related to and resembles a blackberry. And, Ben's fiancée is called Fern Hailston. The beloved teacher at the mission school is Miss Rose. One of Deutsia's brothers is named Cress; another is called Force. The family name of Huntoon, of course, suggests hunting, but in addition, a *toon* is a tree in the mahogany family that has fragrant, dark red wood and flowers that yield a dye. This could possibly be a tie to Melungeon blood, touted as mysterious and much mentioned in the story. If Dave had pricked Deutsia's finger and sucked some of her blood, he would have become a true Melungeon and would not have had any difficulty getting a marriage license. (According to the narrative, this strategy was actually used by another white boy who married a Melungeon girl.) The ties to the natural world are very strong in the story as well as in the names— plants and animals, the signs of the weather, snake handling, the gathering of herbs as a cash crop—all these dominate Stuart's narrative.

It is worth mentioning that the narrator, young lumberjack Dave Stoneking, is an outsider. His love for Deutsia renders him a sympathetic and finally even an empathetic observer/participant in life on the mountain, but he never really belongs. Is he a version of Jesse Stuart himself—perhaps in love with a beautiful young woman, yet in the end wise enough to realize that the cultural differences between the white mountain people and the Melungeons create a gap too wide to bridge? Dave has an interesting role in the Melungeon society on Sanctuary Mountain: he is cast as the outsider who because of his superiority (due perhaps to education?) knows what the people need and who consciously works to better them. This concept of the outsider as a savior or do-gooder is directly related to the missionary movement that impacted Appalachia in the late nineteenth and early twentieth centuries. According to Ron Eller's lecture notes for his course in Appalachian history at the University of Kentucky, "missionaries imposed a . . . vision of Appalachia as an area in need of assistance from outside agencies, . . . had to insist on the reality of the mountaineers' neediness,. . . . [and] often resorted to reinforcing myths and legends about the illiterate, uncouth, unsaved mountain people."[9] Stuart seems to have adopted this model in

---

[9]Ron Eller, "Lecture Notes for History 580," accessed 16 February 2000 at <http://www.uky.edu/rgs/appalcenter/lec12.htm>. This page appeared briefly also at <http://www.uky.edu/rgs/appalcenter/eller2.htm>, but currently may

a minimized way. He has an Appalachian mountain boy who is an outsider to Melungeon culture doing "social work" and thinking about ways to make life better for the marginalized group. It is difficult to say whether Stuart's use of the model is intentional or unconscious. Dave Stoneking certainly functions as the enlightened person who brings new and better ways of doing things to Deutsia's people.

The first instance of this is midway through the novel when Dave tells Deutsia what a good furniture builder he is. He has noticed on his first visit to the Huntoons' "shack" (the word Stuart uses for all the log cabins/houses that the Melungeons have built on the mountain) that there is very little furniture and that what there is looks very simple and plain.[10] As Dave and Deutsia's plans to marry unfold, he says, "I can make about anything with wood. I can make very good furniture. . . . Making furniture is my hobby. I wish you could see the furniture in my home in Virginia that I made for my mother."[11] After the couple moves into the house he builds for them and they arrange their meager belongings, Deutsia is enchanted:

> "This is the prettiest place on this mountain, Dave," Deutsia said. . . . "I'm proud of our home."
> "Maybe this house will inspire our people[12] to make better ones."
> "Sure it will," she said. "They'll be trying to build one like ours. You wait and see. They'll ask you why you built a place like this. . . ."
> "It's well anchored against the wind here," I said. "The big chimney will help hold us, and the logs are well notched."[13]

When Dave declares that his first indoor task will be to make some good chairs, he then asks Deutsia what pieces she would like next; she lists a cedar chest and a walnut bed. He is eager to begin and allows that he has spotted the trees, already dead and thus well seasoned, he will use. He describes the process:

---

not be available at either site.

[10]Stuart, *Daughter of the Legend*, 101.

[11]Stuart, *Daughter of the Legend*, 109.

[12]It is interesting to note here that Dave by using "our" is already outwardly identifying with the Melungeon people. His words in a sense belie his inner attitudes.

[13]Stuart, *Daughter of the Legend*, 133-34.

Before the great snow had melted and gorged the mountain streams, I had finished our chairs. I had made two rockers and six straight-backed chairs. While I worked, Deutsia would cook meals for us and we'd eat at our little table together. After we'd eaten, I'd go back to my whittling, planing, and sandpapering, and putting arms and legs together. . . . [Deutsia] would hold the pieces while I bored small holes with brace and bit to pin the pieces together with wooden pins or bored holes to fit rungs into the legs.

When the snow had melted, leaving drifts here and there, I went with my ax to the dead, seasoned black walnuts and wild cherries that I had found on the mountains. I chopped these trees down, trimmed their branches and topped them. And then I chopped two straight dead cedars that would split easily. I got Bass's mule and dragged these logs to the house so I would have plenty to do when another snow fell.[14]

During the winter, Deutsia's prediction is borne out. Dave and his old logging buddies Bert and Hezzy are asked to build a coffin for a prominent member of the Melungeon community. His excellent work on the coffin, his own house and furniture, the cedar bathtubs he makes for himself and for the Huntoons' Christmas gift, as well as the set of chairs he makes for Daid secure his reputation as a wood-worker. Dave tells of his growing "business":

Hunt Mallicote came to our shack to trade me some red fox skins for a gunstock he wanted me to make for him from black walnut. Cliff Lochees came to get me to make a coffin for his little girl who was burned to death. . . . Wolf Altwahs came and wanted to trade wine and animal pelts for beds and baskets. The Leffertsons, Nahans, Cades, Coves, Coyes, Doves, Tacketts, Treadways, Snowwaters, Dees, and Greenwoods came to see our house and to trade with us. They brought wine, rugs, nuts, roots, barks, and animal pelts to trade for chairs, tables, and beds. So many came that if I had taken all their orders, I would have had to work two years ahead, and I wouldn't have had any time to hunt and fish with the Huntoons. My reputation had grown.[15]

---

[14]Stuart, *Daughter of the Legend*, 136.
[15]Stuart, *Daughter of the Legend*, 191-92.

As he lives on the mountain with Deutsia, Dave thinks about his own
life. He often seems to come to the conclusion that the ways he knows
are very good if not better than the life patterns on the mountain. One
example of this is his decision about the necessity of buying kerosene for
their lamps when he is preparing to go down to Oakhill for supplies.

> The first thing I wrote on the list was kerosene. . . .
> When Sylvania and Skinny ran out of kerosene on the
> mountain, we did without oil for our lamps. I'd been in many of
> the cabins on the mountains and I'd seen the dark smoke stains
> on the paper.[16] They had come from pine torches used to light
> the cabins. We kept pine torches ready but had never used them,
> because we didn't want to smoke our walls. I was a little
> different from the Melungeons. I was more afraid of burning our
> house down. Kerosene was a necessity as far as I was con-
> cerned.[17]

Dave announces in this passage that he is different. The context, of
course, is the issue of kerosene for the lamps and the danger of fire from
the practice of burning pine knots, but I think his declaration may be
more far-reaching than he knows.

At Christmas Dave adopts the role of Santa Claus. This whole
scenario of the Christmas celebration points out how very different Dave
is from the Melungeon men. If Dave in fact is an extension of Stuart
himself in that relationship with the Melungeon girl, we can gain
important insights into Stuart's attitudes about Appalachia's Melungeons.
On Dave's regular trip to town for supplies he buys many gifts for
Deutsia and her family and carries them up the mountain packed on his
back (sans sleigh and reindeer).

> When I poured out what I had brought home, it made a heap
> larger than what the old pack peddlers used to bring to our
> house. Deutsia came over with a smile on her face. She sat down
> on the floor very awkwardly and began to examine packages in
> the stack. . . .
> "Dave, you're strong to have carried this much. Candy,
> cheese, cigarettes, nails, saws, files. . . . material for our window
> curtains! . . . Outing flannel, pink, white, and blue! Dave, you're

---

[16]Cabin interiors were wallpapered with newspaper.
[17]Stuart, *Daughter of the Legend*, 137-38.

so different from our men on this mountain. You do things the right way. And you're so nice to me. Oh, and what is this?"

"A dress for you."

"I've never seen anything so pretty! How beautiful!" Then Deutsia examined the spools of thread and the assortment of needles I'd brought along.

"Soap, and towels, and washcloths," she said. She held a bar of the soap up and smelled of it. "Smells so good. Smells so much better than the soap I make. What are we going to do with all these things?"

"Open that last flat package, Deutsia. You'll see."

"Christmas wrapping paper and colored twine and ribbon," she sighed. "Honest, you've thought of everything!"

"Yes, Christmas is getting close on us," I said. "We want our first Christmas together on this mountain to be a great one. We want it to be a Christmas your folks and we will remember!"[18]

So, Dave has said he is different; Deutsia has seconded the statement. The truth of the difference is underscored in the actual Christmas celebration. In addition to the bounty he has brought from the store in town, Dave uses his woodworking skill to make many presents for his in-laws.

I had made two cedar water buckets for Daid and Bass. These were really simple to make. But I had made a cedar pitcher and bowl, for Daid and Bass too, just like the ones I'd made for Deutsia and me. Then I made two cedar dough trays, one for Deutsia and one for Daid. I made each one two feet long, hollowing them from the cedar log into things of beauty.

Then I did something else that I hoped might spread over the mountain and make living conditions better for everybody.[19] I'd not seen any signs of where anyone bathed in winter. In Daid and Bass's home, I didn't see a washtub with soap and bath towels around as we used to have in the smokehouse at my home in Wise County. Now I'd ripped pieces from my cedar log with my ripsaw. Cedar wood is soft, pliable and easy to work and I tongue-and-grooved those boards until they fit so snugly they were almost leak proof. I made two cedar bathtubs, one for us and one for the Huntoons.

---

[18]Stuart, *Daughter of the Legend*, 154-55.

[19]It feels as if there is certainly a note of condescension here.

I made each tub alike and the same size. I made one end of the tubs square so they would sit flush in the corner of a room. One end I slanted, like the end of a small boat. I bored a hole and made a stopper for a drain which could be opened or kept closed. I thought the Huntoons might like my idea. . . . I carried the bathtub, which weighed about a hundred pounds, very close to the Huntoon shack. . . . After hiding the tub, I hurried back.

Deutsia had arranged the presents and put them in my sack. I laid the big sack across my shoulder and then I picked up a large basket that had two water buckets, the cedar bowl and pitcher and the dough tray that Deutsia had wrapped in colored paper and tied with colored string.[20]

When Dave and Deutsia arrive at her parents' cabin on Christmas morning after breakfast, the Huntoons scramble to choose a tree off the mountainside, to cut it and bring it inside. A couple of the children gather natural decorations like red dogwood berries, smooth rhododendron leaves, shiny sprigs of laurel and tangles of honeysuckle vines. Daid and Alona pop corn and string the puffy white kernels. Then Dave empties the sack, and Deutsia arranges the presents under the tree. Daid and Bass both remark on the difference having Dave in the family makes.

"Say, I never saw anything like this," Bass said. "That many presents and all wrapped in that pretty paper with fancy ribbons and strings! What's going on here? We're changing on this mountain! I wish all our neighbors could see this."

Tears welled up in Daid's eyes. "I am so glad you married our Deutsia," she said. She laid her hand on my shoulder. "You're so respectful to a woman. You look out for everything."[21]

At the beginning of the Christmas dinner Dave surprises them all, and possibly even himself, by asking permission to pray over the food. He has brought not only lavish store-bought presents, the hand-fashioned cedar bathtub (implying perhaps that the family doesn't bathe often enough?), but he finds himself imposing his particular brand of Christianity just as the "outsider" missionaries from the north brought their brand of religion into the hills and the valleys. He says,

---

[20]Stuart, *Daughter of the Legend*, 156-57.
[21]Stuart, *Daughter of the Legend*, 159.

"Would you mind if we say a few thankful words to God for all these things we have? Let's all hold hands around the table."

Little Cress and Alona thought it was strange to hold hands around the table. Bass and Daid had surprise written on their faces, too. But we held hands, and I said, "I'm not very good, God, at asking a blessing, but we have so many things to be thankful for. We've got Sanctuary Mountain to live on and we've got homes up here, fires to sit before, beds to sleep on and roofs to cover us. And, God, from the looks of this table, the Huntoons have plenty of good grub for this Christmas dinner. God, we thank You that we are all alive, that we are able to talk and laugh and to give presents to one another. Thank You, God, for so many wonderful things you have given us and for all this food before us. Amen."[22]

Another practice that points out the differences between Dave and his Melungeon family by marriage is the prevalence of tobacco use among all the members of Deutsia's family. Surely we are much more sensitive to the dangers of tobacco use than were people in the 1920s–1930s when this book is set, in the 1940s when it was written, and even in the 1960s when it was published. However, there seems to be more than a little condescension in narrator Dave's description of the Christmas celebration.

"A box of cigars," Bass said. "I'll try one of these factory-made cigars right after dinner. I'll be getting up in the world."

"And store-bought cigarettes for me," Pribble said. "I won't have to crumble the weed into pieces of any kind of old paper when I roll my own. Store-bought cigarettes."

"And for me, too!" Force said.

I had never known people who like to smoke or chew tobacco like the Melungeon men. And many of the women smoked clay pipes. . . .

Little Cress went to the living room and fetched Bass' box of factory-made cigars. He tore into the box, took out a long cigar and admired the little gold paper band around the center. Then he bit the end off that he put into his mouth, struck a match under the table, lit his cigar and blew a big cloud of smoke toward the ceiling.

---

[22]Stuart, *Daughter of the Legend*, 163.

"It tastes wonderful," he said. "Boys, have one." He passed the cigars over to Pribble and Force. Each took a cigar, bit off the end and struck a match under the table and lighted it just as their father had done.

Daid opened a pack of cigarettes, took one from the pack, and since I was sitting close I lighted it for her. Then Deutsia, Meese, and Alona took cigarettes from the package and began to smoke. The Huntoons were a happy family. They had love for each other and they were as free as mountain winds. I thought of my home in Virginia. My father and mother didn't believe in smoking and they certainly didn't believe in drinking. We lived better than the Huntoons, but we never had as much fun as they had. Now the kitchen was filled with smoke, for everybody was smoking but little Cress, and if he had asked for a cigarette, I believe Bass and Daid would have given it to him.[23]

Bass, enjoying himself immensely, lights up a second cigar and remarks on how different Dave is one more time.

"Daid and I have a wonderful son-in-law," he said. "We love you, Man! You've jined us from the heart and we are with you all the way. We love you in this family and our people all over this mountain love you."

"No man like you has ever married one of us," Pribble said. "Our people have heard of you over on Black Water."

"Yes, over among the Clinch Mountain ranges," Force said. "Melungeons we met over there ast about you. They wanted to know why you married a Melungeon and accepted the problems of our people."[24]

The difference is so clearly stated—it is impossible to miss the point.

One final example shows once again Dave's belief that he knows a better way and that by changing long-standing practices the Melungeons can raise their standard of living and perhaps even break down some of the crippling prejudice. Dave relates:

I had found my place in a world I loved. The Melungeons accepted me and no longer feared me as an outlander. I showed them how to pack their animal pelts, their roots and barks, and

[23]Stuart, *Daughter of the Legend*, 160-61, 165-66.
[24]Stuart, *Daughter of the Legend*, 166-67.

told them where and how to ship them. They walked across the mountains twenty miles to ship them from Rose Hill, the nearest railway station.

I did as much for the Melungeons as I could, for they were my people. I couldn't stand to see them cheated by the people who wouldn't sell us a marriage license. As the winter days wore on toward spring, I was thinking about a place for them to sell their wild strawberries, huckleberries, raspberries, blackberries, and wild honey. . . .

I would fight for all the Melungeons. I would fight to the bitter end against the barriers that encircled us. I would fight to break the barriers, for soon we would bring a child into the world, and I wanted him to have the freedom that I had enjoyed in my youth.[25]

There are two other instances, in addition to the comments about his former way of life in Wise County, where Dave appears to set himself slightly above the Melungeon people he has chosen to join. One is the recurring assertion that Melungeons are happy hunters and gatherers. The first description of this predilection comes from Ben when he is trying to convince Dave not to go with Deutsia:

"They're a strange people. . . . You can't get one to move down into the valley where the land is fertile. They won't work. Oh, they'll tend a few patches. But all they want to do is hunt and fish."[26]

The love for hunting and fishing comes up again and again from Bass, from Pribble and Force, from Deutsia herself.

I'd hunted a lot myself, but I'd never known people in my lifetime to hunt like the Huntoons. . . .

I often wondered when I was working on the logs if Deutsia wouldn't be as happy hunting with her people in the woods during the day and beneath an October moon at night as she would be settling with me behind the smooth-hewn walls of a log house. I wondered if she would be as happy with me as she had been when she hunted with her father, bothers, and sisters.

[25]Stuart, *Daughter of the Legend*, 192.
[26]Stuart, *Daughter of the Legend*, 70.

When this work is done and Deutsia and I have a home of our own, I thought, we will take to the mountains to hunt with Bass, Pribble, Force, Cress, Alona, and Meese. We will go because I know how Deutsia loves the life they are living.[27]

Dave is also puzzled by the Melungeon men's lack of skill with wood-working tools and their resistance to working for him as he builds his house,[28] even though he will pay them in cash. He says,

Pribble didn't know anything about sawing down a tree. I had to show him and then he rode the crosscut saw. . . .

Pribble moaned and groaned, for he didn't like to work, but I held him until we got the trees cut down. . . . Not one of the Huntoon men helped me, for they were always in the woods with their dogs and guns. They hunted by day and they hunted by night. And when they weren't hunting they were fishing. Once Bass went out to help me, but he was awkward with an ax and I didn't like his work. I told him nicely that I would rather finish the logs by myself so that when he had time from his hunting he could help me do the things that it would take more than one man to do, such as rolling the foundation stones in place and putting the logs upon each other. Bass was pleased, for he wanted to get back to the woods and the rivers. . . .

Often [Deutsia] came to the woods where I was working to look at the logs. She'd ask me how I could smooth the sides of a log with an ax until it looked as if it had been sawed by a mill. She couldn't understand how I could do it, for it had never been done on this mountain before.[29]

The second, almost imagined, slight is the description of Brother Dusty, the Holiness preacher who can barely read:

"I'll take my text," he said, "from the sixteenth chapter and the eighteenth verse of St. Mark." He bent over his opened Bible and began to read, stumbling slowly over the words as a barefoot boy stumbles over rocks when he first pulls off his shoes in the spring.[30]

---

[27]Stuart, *Daughter of the Legend*, 130-31.
[28]Stuart, *Daughter of the Legend*, 127.
[29]Stuart, *Daughter of the Legend*, 127-29.
[30]Stuart, *Daughter of the Legend*, 78.

The centerpiece of the novel is, of course, Deutsia herself, the daughter of the Melungeon legend. Dave has already met her when the novel opens, and he brings the reader up to date by describing her.

> She was standing alone across the street from Little Tavern. I'd started to the tavern to buy a soda but stopped still in my tracks at the sight of her. I wondered how any woman in the world could be so beautiful. Her hair was as golden as a poplar leaf ripened by early October's sun. It fell loosely down her back almost to her knees. I'd never seen hair that long and as October-poplar-leaf-golden as hers. She looked at me with soft blue eyes shaded by heavy lashes. Her eyes were as blue as the petals of mountain violets. Her sun-tanned face had the smoothness and color of a ripe hickory nut stripped of its shell. She was tall and slender, straight as a sapling, with slim ankles and shapely nut-brown legs. . . .
>
> "My name is Deutsia Huntoon," she said. Her lips parted, revealing two rows of perfect teeth, as white as corn grains before they begin to harden in the husk.[31]

From this description it is obvious that there are many things about her that make her beautiful, but again and again her eyes are mentioned.[32] Dave never becomes accustomed to their mesmerizing look. It is the same for anyone who, like me or Ted Anthony, has met a "Spanish-eyed" Melungeon: once we look into those remarkably pale blue or green eyes, we never forget them.

One of Deutsia's obvious qualities is her affinity for and knowledge of nature. She knows where the bees water;[33] she is clever about finding fox paths;[34] she leads Dave over ridge and rill to an unmarked bee tree.[35] Dave delightedly declares that she "knows every flower that blooms and she knows where they grow. She knows every little stream on this mountain and she knows every kind of tree, vine, and briar. She knows the birds and where they build."[36] When the two lovers get stranded on the mountain by a thunderstorm she leads Dave to the shelter of a cave and

---

[31]Stuart, *Daughter of the Legend*, 2-3.
[32]Stuart, *Daughter of the Legend*, 7, 16, 20, 145, 199.
[33]Stuart, *Daughter of the Legend*, 44.
[34]Stuart, *Daughter of the Legend*, 46.
[35]Stuart, *Daughter of the Legend*, 49.
[36]Stuart, *Daughter of the Legend*, 50.

finds mountain teaberries for their breakfast. On the day of her wedding she gathers all kinds of wildflowers—Queen Anne's lace, goldenrods, sourwood boughs, pine boughs, milkweek blossoms, ironweed tops, butterfly weed, blue violets, and wild lettuce, mountain teaberries, sawbriars with blue berries, and phlox—to decorate very tastefully the living room where the ceremony will take place. " 'We must get it right,' she said. 'Make it look as pretty here as in this mountain world where it grew.' "[37]

Besides her family, the biggest influence in Deutsia's life is Miss Rose, a teacher who was one of the Presbyterian missionaries.

> "We liked her better than any teacher we ever had," Deutsia said. "She brought leaves, blades of grass, and wild flowers into the schoolhouse and asked us to name them."
> "Did she know their names?"
> "You bet she did," Deutsia said. "That's how I learned them. I don't believe there was a tree, plant, or flower that grew on this mountain she didn't know." . . .
> "Where did she live while she was here?"
> "She stayed with us."
> "Was she like the people down in the valley?"
> "No, she loved us, helped us, taught us, and we loved her. . . . She never went back from this mountain after she came up here," Deutsia said. "She died at our house and is buried in our graveyard. . . . She did more for us than anybody we've ever known. She taught the old people to read and write. She didn't want a school down in the valley. . . . I never went to another teacher. . . . I went to the eighth grade, which was as far as I could go on the mountain."[38]

As Deutsia's pregnancy advances there is discernable foreboding. Her disposition as well as her body is changing. The novel moves toward its climax, and we as readers sense that things are moving too fast toward a bad end.

> Now Deutsia was beginning to change shape. She was shy when people came to visit us. Often she would go into the kitchen and stay until the visitor left. . . . [S]he was shy with me and wouldn't let me hold her and kiss her. I noticed for the first time the somber autumn mood in her face that I had first noticed

---

[37]Stuart, *Daughter of the Legend*, 121.
[38]Stuart, *Daughter of the Legend*, 169-70.

in Daid's face. As the days passed and our baby grew, Deutsia's mood became as somber as the mood of winter's dark trees that stood leafless and barren in the wind. . . . In summer when I met her, she was happy. And now in the bleakness of winter, after she had felt life within her, she had grown depressed.[39]

The parallel to Mildred Haun's story "Melungeon-Colored" is hard to ignore. All the signs in both narratives point to disaster. "As the days of April swiftly passed into May, Deutsia acted more strangely than ever. . . . Once I went over to talk to Daid . . . [who] only said, 'I understand. I understand.' "[40]

Dave hopes for the best and tells himself that Deutsia will feel better once the baby is born, but we don't really believe him. So we are not at all surprised when one night in the midst of the worst storm imaginable the labor begins. Dave goes for Daid and Bass and sends a neighbor to bring Fern Dewberry, the county nurse. The midwife who often attends the Melungeon women is on another call, and they all doubt Fern will risk her life on such a night to climb up the mountain. Even though Fern and her husband Ben (Dave's old friend) do manage to get to the house, the sense of foreboding does not lift; the birth is a desperate struggle. The baby, a boy, is healthy, but Deutsia hemorrhages.

> The bed was red. . . . Her blood once so highly condemned, was spilled in childbirth. So much blood was spilled that warm salt water could not replace it. . . .
> It was all over. They'd done their best. It was midnight and my beautiful Deutsia had breathed her last breath on Sanctuary Mountain. . . .
> I felt myself leaving the room and Ben and Bass trying to hold me. But I went out into the wild storm that was raging. . . .
> Now thirty-six years have passed, but I can still remember when I ran from our house into the dark night. The weight of the storm clouds pressed heavy upon me when I looked toward heaven, where no stars looked down. . . . My loss was so heavy I didn't think I could bear it. I believed, and I know this is true now, that a man has only one great love in his lifetime. My love was my beautiful Deutsia Huntoon.[41]

[39]Stuart, *Daughter of the Legend*, 171-72.
[40]Stuart, *Daughter of the Legend*, 206.
[41]Stuart, *Daughter of the Legend*, 218-22.

The story ends on this despairing note. Dave is bitter because Deutsia had no access to the medical care that might have saved her life. Dave who has nurtured hope throughout the narrative that there could be reconciliation between the townspeople of Oakhill and the Melungeons on the mountain, feels bitterness and anger. His leave-takings—of Deutsia in her family's cemetery and of their son, Huntoon, with Daid and Bass—close the book on the Melungeon chapter in his life. We know when he leaves that he, who has told the story eloquently and sympathetically, will stop fighting for mercy and justice. After fighting for less than a year, Dave's spirit is broken. And, yet, the Melungeons whose plight he has exposed, had suffered for many years. Is Stuart suggesting that the problem of racism in Appalachia is too overwhelming to solve?

The ending of this novel only serves to underscore one of its main points, and annoyed as I get at Stuart's platitudes and sometimes conde-scending tone, I have to admit that his chronicle of the indignities and injustices that the Melungeon people suffer is distressing and accurate. It is apparent that the privileged whites of Cantwell County are not above using Melungeons when it suits them. Many buy their liquor from Sylvania and Skinny, the Melungeon couple who make high quality moonshine and also serve as middlemen for other Melungeons who operate stills on remote hillsides. However, if any Melungeon man is caught with any liquor in his possession, he is immediately clapped in jail without a trial.[42] The jailer likes to have Melungeons incarcerated because he uses them as janitors and tells them that by serving the county they can reduce their sentences.

The prejudice of the valley people is detailed time and again in this novel. The first hint comes when Dave meets Ben Dewberry's girl, Fern Hailston, at Little Tavern. Ben introduces Dave and says he is looking for Deutsia Huntoon. "Just as Ben said the word 'Deutsia,' the smile left Fern Hailston's face; it seemed to grow as cold as her hand had felt to me."[43]

Next is the issue of illegal manufacture of whiskey; moonshining is a legitimate enterprise for whites but not for Melungeons. " 'If you live in the valley and make whiskey,' [Deutsia] said, 'you don't go to jail. If

---

[42]Very early in the novel we are introduced to Don Praytor who was caught with a half-pint of moonshine and who has languished in jail for eight months and has never been tried for any crime. Stuart, *Daughter of the Legend*, 10.

[43]Stuart, *Daughter of the Legend*, 5.

you live up on the mountain where I live and if you are even found with whiskey on you, you go to jail.' "[44]

Another instance of racial discrimination is limited access to what meager entertainment Oakhill offers. When Dave suggests to Deutsia that they could go to the movies for a date, Deutsia replies, " 'I don't go to the theater. . . . I don't like the balcony seats. . . . We can't get the best seats; . . . they are for the valley people.' "[45]

Furthermore, Melungeons are not welcome at Little Tavern in Oakhill, and after Dave has married Deutsia he's not welcome there either. He goes into town for supplies and decides he will get some lunch at Little Tavern before he walks back up the mountain; however, the proprietor refuses to serve him.

> "Sure you used to eat here. But that's when you belonged to us and not to them. That was before you betrayed your people. Now you see what I mean, don't you? . . . [Y]ou thought you'd slip back here. . . . No trouble, Lumberjack!" he said with a forced grin as he backed away from me. "Don't start anything. You don't have a chance."
>
> He is right, I thought. I don't have a chance. . . . I knew where Spooly had gone. He'd gone over to the cash register to get his gun. . . . I was already out and on my way. . . .
>
> I can spend my money in the stores, I thought. I could spend a thousand dollars buying items to make living easier in the valley or up on the mountain. Yet I couldn't sit down in Little Tavern and eat. . . . It simply didn't make sense.[46]

This is exactly the point Darlene Wilson and Charles Stallard make in their essays on the Melungeon Home Page.[47] As late as the 1960s, Melungeons were *sometimes* welcome to spend their money in the stores in Wise and Coeburn, Virginia, but they were made to feel like second-class citizens even then. Stuart is recounting reality here.

Early in the story Dave is walking on Sanctuary Mountain looking for Deutsia's home. He comes upon Don Praytor, the man who at the very beginning of the novel is in jail for having just one pint of whiskey in his

---

[44]Stuart, *Daughter of the Legend*, 10.
[45]Stuart, *Daughter of the Legend*, 42-43.
[46]Stuart, *Daughter of the Legend*, 148-49.
[47]As at <http://melungeons.org/mel_uos2.htm> and <http://www.melungeons.org/mel_uos3.htm>, both accessed 22 August 1999, but currently both offline.

possession. Don warns Dave by telling him about the prejudice he will experience by continuing to date or by marrying Deutsia.

> "Dave, we don't know who we are. But we do know that we are human beings . . . we know we're a race hated and despised. We know it's hell to be a Melungeon. . . .
> "If you marry Deutsia, you will be Melungeon," he said. "You will be one of us. And you will always regret it. You're different. You have life with freedom before you. And you'd better hold to it. You will have trouble all your life if you marry Deutsia!"[48]

Another warning from a person who knows the discrimination from the inside comes to Dave from Deutsia's father Bass.

> "If you marry Deutsia, you will have to love her. . . . It will be a test of your love for her, because when you marry her you'll be one of us, and people are not kind to us. If you do not know about us, and all the barriers against us, you'd better think this over before you jump from the frying pan into the fire. . . .
> I ask you these questions because you are an outlander and a stranger, and I want you to know the facts about us. . . . I hope she doesn't get a husband that is prejudiced against her and her people."[49]

The incident at Little Tavern is mild compared to what ensues when Dave and Deutsia go to the courthouse to get a marriage license. They are told that there is a law that prohibits the clerk from issuing them a license.

> "Dark races and white races don't mix here. There's a law against it, thank God."
> He hit the table with his hand. I looked at Deutsia as she tried to turn her face from me. Tears were streaming down her sad face. "You can't get a license here," [Mr. Woods] said.
> "I thought this was a free country!"
> "Don't argue with me," he warned, his voice contorted with anger. "Don't argue with me if you want to go out of here alive. You may be a big strong man but I have the difference right here in my desk." He pulled the desk drawer open until I could see

---

[48]Stuart, *Daughter of the Legend,* 64-65.
[49]Stuart, *Daughter of the Legend,* 108.

he meant business. I saw the long, bright shining barrel of a .38 Special.

"Only one white man ever got a license here to marry a Melungeon. He was so ugly he couldn't marry one of his kind, so he cut the woman's arm he was to marry and drank some of her blood and swore he had Melungeon blood in his veins. . . . We issued the low-down a marriage license."[50]

Extremely upset by this turn of events, Deutsia confesses to Dave that she did not sleep the night before, fearing just such an eventuality. The wedding does proceed, but without the license, at the Huntoons' home on Sanctuary Mountain.

Dave appoints himself to work for justice. The day he walks down to Oakhill for supplies and Christmas gifts, he determines to talk to the local judge about the unfair application of the "law" to the Melungeons. Here is what happens in Dave's own words.

Ever since I had met Don Praytor in the county jail, there was something I wanted to ask Judge Palmer. . . .

"Judge, why is it when a man from Sanctuary Mountain is caught drinking, possessing or selling illegal moonshine whiskey he has to lay in jail six months before he is given a trial?"

"To answer you briefly, quickly and to the point, it is none of your affair," he said. . . . "Just how well do you know the people who live on Sanctuary Mountain? I know you're not one of 'em for you don't have the looks!"

"I am now," I said. "I married one. . . .

"Judge, . . . the law says that a man shall be given a fair and a just trial. I'm not a lawyer but I know there's a law against holding a man too long in jail before he's given a trial."

"Would you mind leaving before I have you arrested?"

"No, I don't mind going. Be sure to speed up the trials for the men on Sanctuary Mountain."

I turned around and left his office in a hurry. . . . When I got to the foot of the stairs, Bud Mahan[51] came with his broom. "I heard it," he said in a low voice. . . . Nobody on earth ever

---

[50]Stuart, *Daughter of the Legend*, 114.
[51]Bud is a Melungeon serving time because he can't pay his fine for being caught with a half-pint of moonshine in his possession.

talked to old Judge Palmer like you did. I'll bet he'll do some thinkin' after this."[52]

This incident certainly does point out an annoying and apparently recurring form of prejudice against the Cantwell County Melungeons. In addition, it is just one more example of what almost seems to be a "messiah complex" with Dave. How can Dave Stoneking, a young outsider armed with only righteous indignation, without any kind of political, social, or economic weapon, really think that one harrangue in the office of a judge who is known to be prejudiced and unfair will change anything?

Besides the obvious abuse in the legal system, there is prejudice in education. The Melungeon children are not allowed to attend school in the valley. Dave mentions the problem when he speaks to Judge Palmer and defends the Melungeons:

> They are educated in their way. . . . They don't have book education because they've been denied schooling in the valley and the missionary teachers, outsiders called Presbyterians who believe Melungeons are God's children too, walk up that mountain and teach them up to the eighth grade in pitiful log-shack schoolhouses while valley children can go to high school and then on to college. No, they're not educated in books. . . .[53]

Later in the novel Deutsia explains to Dave what educational opportunities are available for children growing up Melungeon. "She told me about the schoolteachers the superintendent of Cantwell County schools had sent upon the mountain. They hated to come and the only reason one ever would was because he couldn't find a school any place else. . . . And then Deutsia told me of the teachers they had sent since she had quit school. They had had as many as five teachers in one year because the teachers didn't like to board in one of the shacks, and they didn't like the people."[54]

Rose Fox—who was mentioned earlier—who taught at a Presbyterian mission school on the mountain and maintained that the Melungeons had the right to have a school near where they lived. This woman was loved by all. She was buried in a Melungeon cemetery.

---

[52]Stuart, *Daughter of the Legend*, 140-44.
[53]Stuart, *Daughter of the Legend*, 143.
[54]Stuart, *Daughter of the Legend*, 168-70.

"Our people chiseled a big rock and put her name on it and
these words: 'Rose Fox, without malice in her heart for anyone
and the best-liked teacher that was ever on this mountain to
teach our children, sleeps here.' Each spring the school children
take baskets of wild flowers and decorate her grave on Decoration Day."[55]

This is, of course, a reference to the Presbyterian mission school in
the Vardy community across Newman's Ridge from Sneedville. The
school, which did go up to eighth grade, was a successful educational
enterprise during the first half of the twentieth century. The poor access
to education during these years in Hancock County—the Cantwell
County of Stuart's story—did have the results that the novel delineates
so clearly. Many adults, like Brother Dusty the Holiness preacher, could
not read well. Book learning was not highly valued, definitely less valued
than other pursuits such as hunting and fishing. Poor educational opportunities and the somewhat negative attitude of the people toward education was due in part to the legacy of the laws in Virginia, Tennessee, and
North Carolina, passed in the 1830s, that denied "free persons of color,"
some of whom were Melungeons, access to public education. Stuart, an
educator who did with some difficulty complete high school and college,
perhaps imposes his own values onto his narrator Dave Stoneking and
also onto Deutsia. After all, the prototype for Deutsia was a girl he met
at Lincoln Memorial University, a Melungeon girl who obviously had
made it off Newman's Ridge through high school and to college.[56]

---

[55]Stuart, *Daughter of the Legend*, 169.

[56]Being an educator myself, I linger here on this point. I have noticed in Appalachian fiction and in Appalachian life there are certain characters/persons who
pursue education and then are profoundly changed by it. They sometimes go
back to their mountain homes and kin and sometimes do not. Whether they
return or not, these persons are so radically reoriented in terms of ideology and
practice by their educations that they cannot reintegrate into mountain communities. They have trouble sorting out their values—deciding what is really important
to retain from the culture in which they were raised. The change seems to me to
be regrettable—these characters in fiction sometimes end up being at odds with
what is clearly the good in the story. The character Miles Bishop in Denise
Giradina's *Storming Heaven* illustrates this pattern. After college he becomes a part
of the establishment, works for the coal company, and hence *is* a part of the problem instead of part of the solution. Another example is Lizzie Bailey in *The Devil's
Dream* who goes to nursing school, adopts outside ways, and never does return
to Grassy Branch. In *Daughter of the Legend* there is even another layer. Dave

Another significant social service denied to Melungeons is good medical care. Although Dave is shocked and dismayed by Fern Hailston's apparent disdain for his choice of Deutsia Huntoon as an appropriate girl to date, he learns from Deutsia herself that Fern is unusual among valley people.

> "She's a good nurse. She's the only person that will climb the mountain to deliver babies for our women. Mountain paths never get too steep for her to climb and the night never gets too dark for her to go."[57]

The need for good medical care seems very urgent to Dave as Deutsia nears the end of her pregnancy. In spite of her reassurances about how natural having babies is, he wants her to have access to both a physician and a *hospital*. Both Dave and Deutsia exhibit their prejudices.

> "[Y]ou ought to go to a hospital to have our baby."
> "I think that's funny," she said. . . . "Imagine taking me to a place I'd never been before to have our baby. . . .
> "I'm not going. Women on this mountain would laugh at me for generations to come. What would the *women in the valley*[58] think of a Melungeon going to the hospital to have her baby? . . .
> "But look how Melungeon women have their babies. . . . They never have a doctor. Miss Fern is all they have. Sometimes we don't get her. . . .
> "Nearly any woman on this mountain can deliver a baby."
> "But I don't want any of these women to deliver our baby," I said. "If you won't go to the hospital, I'm bringing a doctor up on this mountain."
> "Doctors won't come up here, Dave, you know that."

Stoneking, an Appalachian native but an outlander to the Melungeons, adopts the missionary role. He wants to be sympathetic to their plight and even stands up for them, but his veneer of caring seems pretty thin; his air of superiority comes across clearly. Dave knows better ways of doing things and wants his "fellow" Melungeons to recognize their ineptitudes and misconceptions and consequently to change their practices.

[57]Stuart, *Daughter of the Legend*, 16.

[58]Italics mine. Deutsia argues here that not only would the Melungeon women ridicule her, but the women in town, in the valley, would think she was putting on airs.

"If I pay one enough, he will come. . . . I'm going to try any-way."[59]

This interchange is, of course, both telling and prophetic. It shows where both Dave and Deutsia stand on the issue. It once again illustrates Dave's attitude. The interchange is prophetic in that we as readers begin to catch Dave's fear. He has perhaps become enough of a Melungeon to read the signs. He has a sense of impening doom. We readers of stories know enough to heed. Dave does walk down the mountain to Oak Hill. He declares to himself, "I would get a doctor for her, if money would bring one."[60]

Dave tries Dr. Pratt first. When Pratt realizes that Dave is asking him to climb Sanctuary Mountain his face clouds and he says,

> "I can't stand the walk up there. . . . Women up on that mountain never did have a doctor when their babies were born. . . . I can't make that trip. . . . Go down and see Dr. Clifton. He's a younger man than I am. . . . I have patients waiting to see me, Young Man. I can't go."
> "I'll give you a hundred dollars if you will."
> "I wouldn't go for a thousand."[61]

Dave, hoping for the best but fearing the worst, does go to Dr. Clifton and receives the same disappointing rebuff.

> As I walked back up the mountain, I was as mad as I'd ever been in my life. For the first time, I felt badly toward Deutsia because she wouldn't go to a hospital. I was not only mad but I was deeply hurt and felt for the first time that my fight was a useless one. The county clerk wouldn't issue us a license to marry but we'd married anyway. And now Deutsia was going to have a baby and I couldn't get a doctor. If we can marry without a license, I thought as I walked up the mountain toward our shack, we can have our baby without a doctor. I knew that we would have to.[62]

As Dave fears, the baby's birth is their undoing. But not even Fern Dewberry, competent nurse that she is, can save Deutsia whose Melun-

[59]Stuart, *Daughter of the Legend*, 201-202.
[60]Stuart, *Daughter of the Legend*, 203.
[61]Stuart, *Daughter of the Legend*, 204-205.
[62]Stuart, *Daughter of the Legend*, 205.

geon blood is spilled for all time. As Deutsia is dying, Dave wonders whether he can forgive the people of Oak Hill who personify those who unfairly discriminate against Melungeons and withhold the things that should be theirs by virtue of their membership in the human race.

There is one final element of this novel that demands attention. In addition to the very clearly articulated themes—his manifesto for equal rights for Melungeons, his outrage at the indignities these people have suffered—and to the compelling story line, Stuart has seamslessly woven in the Melungeon elements, many facts, legends, and bits of lore. One of the most interesting is his description of a typical worship service at the Holiness Faith Healers Church on Sanctuary Mountain, which is similar to both Alther's recounting of Clem's congregation in *Kinflicks* and Mattie Ruth Johnson's honest recounting of the church services her family attended on Newman's Ridge in *My Melungeon Heritage*.

> The pines had been cut away, except for a few on which lanterns hung, and around the cleared enclosure that was the churchhouse were walls of the thickly studded trees. . . .
>
> Two of the boys played a snappy tune on their guitars, almost like a fast square dance tune, while the people that faced us, and many of the congregation sitting on the benches, sang "Feasting on the Mountain." In front of the choir, the preacher stood with a rough handmade table before him, his hand upon his opened Bible. Down beside him were the wire cages like the ones I'd seen at the shacks on Sanctuary Mountain. . . .
>
> The preacher stood at the table before us, dressed in his faded clean-washed overalls and blue work shirt with his sleeves rolled to his elbows and his shirt collar unbuttoned. There was a beard on his face and when he opened his mouth, he showed two rows of discolored front teeth. He was a tall man but bent over like a wind-whipped oak on the mountaintop, and his eyes looked down at us like a hawk's eyes when they look over a flock of chickens.
>
> "I'll take my text," he said, "from the sixteenth chapter and the eighteenth verse of Mark. . . . 'They shall take up serpents; and if they drink any deadly thing, it shall not hurt them; they shall lay hands on the sick, and they shall recover.' " . . .
>
> The choir rose from their log seats; the young men with the guitars looked at each other, one nodded a signal to the other and then there was a fast plucking of strings, a wild outburst of many-tongued discordant voices singing, "I'll Be a Holiness until I Die." I know that this was a dance tune, for my feet began to

move, to pat on the pine needles, and I looked about me and other feet were doing the same.

[A] big dark-complected man with a deep booming voice like a mountian wind surging down into a hollow [yelled], "I'm saved and sactified and I can't sin no more! . . . Glory be to the God that gives us power to heal the sick and the afflicted, that gives us power to handle the serpents and if we are right with God, they won't bite us! Blessed be the name of the Sweet Jesus that gives us power to handle fire and won't let it burn us! Send us the Light, Sweet Jesus!"

"Amen, Brother Cliff," Preacher Dusty said to the big man, who was still standing, his body jerking as I'd never seen a man jerk before.

"The serpents and the fire will test you, Brother Cliff," a tall woman screamed as she arose from her seat. . . . "If you ain't right with Jesus, the serpent will send his fangs into ye and turn loose his venom and the flame will wither yer flesh . . . scorch and burn it. . . . Ah, the devil is in ye when the serpent will fang ye and the flames scorch ye. . . . Ah, it's the sign that ye ain't right with Jesus!" She danced a tune, her head thrown back, her face toward the pine-bough ceiling. Her eyes were closed, her mouth was open and she mumbled words that I couldn't understand.

Now Brother Dusty was walking between the rows of seated people, looking straight ahead at something I couldn't see. His hands were spread before him and he, too, was mumbling words I couldn't understand.

"What are they saying?" I asked Deutsia. . . .

"They are talking in the Unknown Tongue," she said. . . .

[T]he big woman, with her eyes closed, sprawled on the ground, her body jerking and her lips and eyelids twitching. There she lay before Deutsia and me, her dress high upon her body, showing her big legs, her cotton bloomers and her red outing petticoat. She stared vacantly toward her heaven in the sky as she mumbled her unknown words. . . . [S]he jumped up and started running in circles, shouting "Glory to Sweet Jesus" as she ran.

Maybe she started the others; I don't know. It seemed that everybody arose from his seat but Deutsia and me. People—men, women, and boys—grabbed each other and started swinging as I'd seen them swing in figure eight of an old square dance. But dancers never piled upon the floor and kicked and moaned and said words no one could understand as these people did. . . .

Small children held babies in their laps while their mothers and fathers shouted and rolled. I saw little girls and little boys run madly through the crowd, stepping on men's hands and women's tangled hair, screaming as they went. . . .

I've been to many a church in the mountains, I thought, . . . but I have never seen anything like this. . . . I heard a scream among the people and wild screams among the tenor-voiced children. I got up and saw Brother Dusty with a big rattler around his neck. He was patting the rattler's head while it flicked out its tongue to catch and listen to the sound of the confusion. . . . Brother Dusty turned this way and that to show the rattler to all the people.

"Sweet Jesus gives me the power," Brother Dusty said. . . .

I wondered if only Brother Dusty would handle a rattlesnake, fondle it and coddle it and let it listen to his congregation, let it wrap itself about his neck as if it were a necktie. This giant rattler must have been heavy about his neck; it looked him in the eyes with its cold, black, hard lidless eyes and put wild fears into the small children who looked up at it. But the rattler didn't scare Brother Dusty. All eyes of the shouting people turned toward him, but not the eyes of the people lying on the floor jerking. Their eyes were closed and their jerks came easier. Many had jerked until they could move no more, and they lay on the pine-needle floor lifeless and exhausted. . . .

I saw many men and women, with rattlesnakes around their necks and in their arms. And they were fondling them with no more fear than I would have had if I'd handled a piece of rope.

"These're Sweet Jesus' children," Brother Dusty said "There ain't no part of the devil in 'em. Not a chip from the devil's tree o' sin in 'em. Not a drop of th' devil's blood! Yes, we've had people bitten by the serpent but the serpent knows the ones that's got devil in 'em. He knows the facts, People, for he can smell th' devil in a man a mile away, and he can taste the devil in 'em when he bites!" . . .

I turned my eyes toward the table that Brother Dusty had used for a pulpit and saw women who didn't have rattlers to prove their faith standing with flaming pine torches, holding the flames to their hands, the rich heavy smelly pine smoke going up in dark heavy spirals toward their faces.

"The flame can't sear this flesh," one screamed, but I know the flame was searing her flesh the way she twitched. . . .

The children didn't fear the flames; they feared the ugly writhing snakes. They would gather close to watch these women stick the flames to their hands. With one hand these women held the pine torch and applied the flame to the other hand. That evening was something I would never forget. . . .

"What's the matter, Young Man?" Brother Dusty said as he stood before me with his rattlesnake too near for my comfort."

"Don't get that rattler close to me."

"Be saved tonight, Young Man," he said. "It's the devil in you. You're possessed with seedy, vile sin." . . .

"What about you, Honey?" a woman said to Deutsia. Deutsia didn't answer her, but with her soft hand she stroked the rattler's gray-black head.

"That snake acts as if it knows you," I said to her. I got up from the seat and began to back away. . . .

We finally broke clear of those caught up in the spirit of the meeting, but faced another crowd of people standing at the rear. Many had their hands and faces bandaged.

"What's wrong with these people, anyway?" I asked.

"Burnt hands and bitten by rattlesnakes, she said. "They had devil in 'em."[63]

This long description is as interesting for the ways it is different from similar passages in other novels about Appalachia as it is for the vivid picture it conjures of a Holiness meeting under the stars on an October night. One difference is that the writer actually gives us the words from the Gospel of Mark rather than assuming readers know what the passage contains. Another interesting feature is the way Stuart uses analogies to the natural world in his descriptions of what goes on. Brother Dusty looks at the congregation as a predatory hawk sizes up a flock of helpless chickens just before the kill.[64] The big dark-complected man has a voice like a mountain wind surging down into a hollow."[65] Dave mentions the habitat of a rattlesnake in the wild by contrasting it with the din of the meeting, which is "the sound of the confusion, a greater sound of voices than a rattler ever hears when left alone free to roam his mountain world

[63]Stuart, *Daughter of the Legend*, 76-85.
[64]Stuart, *Daughter of the Legend*, 78.
[65]Stuart, *Daughter of the Legend*, 78.

among the rocks and wild huckleberry vines."[66] Seeing the snakes, Dave recoils in terror remembering his logging days when, as he relates, "Too many had almost got me in the timber woods."[67]

Dave says there was a lot to see, and he is correct. All the hallmarks of a Holiness meeting save the drinking of poison (usually strychnine in snake-handling circles) are present—people are being slain in the spirit, handling snakes, applying fire to their flesh, speaking in tongues, and dancing in the spirit. We can even discern that Brother Dusty is a "shoutin' preacher" by the exclamations of "Ah!" that precede many of his statements.

Deutsia says once they are away from the outdoor "churchhouse," "This is the last revival meeting before the rattlesnakes go to sleep. That's why I wanted you to see it, Dave."[68] This comment follows two earlier ones told to Dave in a loud whisper while they are still in the midst of the service, "I don't belong to this church. . . . I don't belong to any church."[69] This declaration effectively makes her an outsider among her own people. Her dedication to Melungeons in prison (she takes them food and drink whenever she is in Oak Hill on a summer Saturday night) and the largest funeral Dave has ever seen in his life when Deutsia dies intimates that she is special, almost otherworldly, almost an angel or even a Christ-like figure. Later in the novel, in springtime just before the birth of the baby Dave and Deutsia are out for a walk and the religion issue resurfaces. Dave after seeing two blacksnakes mating says,

> "Now that the snakes are out, the spring revivals will soon start."
> "Yes, it'll soon be time for everybody to get religion again," she said. "But my religion is to be out under the moon and stars at night and to hear the wind blow. Religion to me is terrapins, mating snakes, and wild spring flowers blooming on the mountain."[70]

Deutsia is not expressing anything like the Holiness doctrine that her family and many others of the Melungeon community espouse. Dave makes no comment in response to her statements about her affinity for the natural world. Her remarks do not imply that there is a god involved

---

[66]Stuart, *Daughter of the Legend*, 81.
[67]Stuart, *Daughter of the Legend*, 83.
[68]Stuart, *Daughter of the Legend*, 86.
[69]Stuart, *Daughter of the Legend*, 85.
[70]Stuart, *Daughter of the Legend*, 198–99.

in nature. If she worships anything it is the life force in the flora and fauna of her mountain world. She does not seem to see this force as malevolent or capricious, for she does not fear storms but instead finds natural shelter when a storm catches her on the mountainside. It is difficult to know how to put all this together except to say that Stuart seems to be setting some limits: even though Dave Stoneking can marry the girl he loves and become one with her people, he (and perhaps also Stuart) cannot buy into the reckless and supernatural practices of the snake-handlers. As Dave notes after he attends the church with Deutsia, "I rolled and tossed on my bunk, thinking of . . . what a strange church it was . . . and this snake religion. That worried me more than the blood in Deutsia's veins."[71]

Daughter of the Legend carefully notes and outlines the various theories to explain Melungeon origins. The passages seem somewhat didactic; however, the information is correct and complete. Don Praytor, a Melungeon himself, is one character who talks to Dave about possible theories.

"We're called Sons and Daughters of the Legend. . . . We've heard we're a white, Indian, and Negro mixture. You'll never know what kind of blood Deutsia Huntoon has in her veins. I've even heard we're descendants of a people that once lived in a city called Carthage, that was destroyed by the Romans in 146 B.C., and that some of the people fled from that ancient city to a country called Morocco, where they mixed with a race called Moors, and later some of these migrated to Portugal and then on to South Carolina and then to Sanctuary Mountain. Dave, we don't know who we are. But we do know that we are human beings. We know we are here even if we don't know how we got here. And whatever we are and whoever we are we know we're a race hated and despised. We know it's hell to be a Melungeon."[72]

A long speech for an unlettered man to make.

Early in the novel Ben Dewberry, Dave's long-time friend and logging partner, does his best to enlighten Dave about Deutsia and her people.

"There are four theories about how they got here and who they are. You remember Sir Walter Raleigh's Lost Colony? There

---

[71]Stuart, *Daughter of the Legend*, 90.
[72]Stuart, *Daughter of the Legend*, 64.

was never a trace of it found. It's believed they were captured by the Cherokee Indians and brought to this mountain and here they mixed with the Indians. . . .

"And here's another theory, . . . that a Portuguese ship was wrecked on the Carolina coast, and the sailors rigged up a raft and reached shore, migrated inland, were accepted by the Cherokees and took Cherokee wives. Many say that it was a Spanish ship instead of a Portuguese. . . . But these are theories they don't like to believe."

"What are the theories they like to believe?" I asked. . . .

"Many people believe the Melungeons are a mixture of poor mountain whites, Indians, and Negroes," Ben continued. "And here is what they say. That during the Civil War, Cantwell County fought for the Union almost to a man, and that many escaped mulattoes from the Deep South were smuggled to Cantwell County, where they found refuge upon Sanctuary Mountain and mixed with the poor whites. . . .

"And the last theory is that there is not any Indian blood in the Melungeons, . . . but just a mixture of escaped slaves and trashy whites. And this is what the majority of people believe."[73]

Stuart here gives accurate information about the possibilities. However, he is not unbiased; he comes down just to the left of Walter Plecker, Virginia's infamous Registrar of Vital Statistics, who maintained throughout his tenure in office that there were only two races—colored and white—and the Melungeons, by gosh, were colored. By having Ben Dewberry state that "the majority of people" believe that Melungeons are a mixture of escaped slaves and "trashy" whites, Stuart is undoubtedly stating the theory that was most prevalent among people he knew in the 1940s when the novel was written. Stuart does admit, if the letter quoted earlier is accurate, that he did no research. No one today, even if she believed this last theory to be the case, would state it in such imflammatorily biased language.

Dave ponders all this information and adds his own ideas one night when he cannot sleep.

I thought of Spain, and the things I'd read about Spain and the Spanish people in my advanced geography, my favorite subject in school. . . . I'd read where the Spaniards were dark and

---

[73]Stuart, *Daughter of the Legend*, 71-72.

handsome and that there were mountains in Spain, there were guitars and music and much dancing, fighting, and fun. And I read where the Spaniards drank wine with their meals. . . . Could it be, I thought, that the blood of the Spaniards flowed in Deutsia's veins?

Could she have come from the Portuguese? I wondered. I remembered a picture of a dark-complected man with bearded lips I'd seen in my geography when I studied about Portugal. I read that the Portuguese had once been, like the Spaniards, a powerful nation of seafaring people, that they took their ships to almost every port in the then known world and did a lot of trading. And it could have been, I thought, that one of their ships had wrecked on the Carolina coast and that the Portuguese had come ashore and had migrated westward to the mountain ranges, had taken Cherokee Indian wives, and caused all this trouble two-hundred years later when I'd met one of their beautiful descendants in Cantwell County. Could it be that Deutsia had that seafaring blood in her, just a spark of that ancestry left, that made her roam the mountain and know the rivers?

Maybe it was the Indian in her, I thought. The Cherokee blood that made her roam the mountain, know the trees, the birds, almost every variety of plant and flower that grew on the mountain, the plant roots that were good to eat and those that were poisonous, the nuts and berries that were good to eat and where to find them, how to fish, hunt, course the wild bee to his tree.

Maybe some of her ancestors were savages in the vast dark continent of Africa. Maybe they had known the fear of the cobra, a snake more deadly than the rattlesnake, in the dense jungle where the wind was hot and smothery to breathe; maybe they had known the scorch of the torrid sun, which had darkened their flesh; maybe they had known the jungle trails and all the fears of the wild beasts that infested the jungle; maybe they had chanted unknown words while they danced to the beat of the jungle drums. Maybe blood from these savages was in Deutsia's veins.

And there must be something of my own ancestry in her, I thought, when I remembered her hair. For I'd read in a history book about the blond hair of the Anglo-Saxons. Roman soldiers took young girls they had captured on this isle back to Rome to sell into slavery, but when the people of Rome saw their golden hair they wouldn't sell them as slaves. When I read about the Anglo-Saxon girls that escaped slavery in Rome, I wanted to think your Roman boys two thousand years ago fell in love with these golden-haired girls, married them and were kind to them, taught them the Roman language and the ways of the Roman people.[74]

If Dave Stoneking speaks for Stuart, and even if he doesn't, we can see an attempt to legitimize what Dave is about to do (his marriage) with historical precedent—the scholar's method brought to a backwoods problem.

The bit of Melungeon lore that is most often recited in both fictional and factual narratives is the story of Mahala Collins Mullins, the huge lady moonshiner. This story is told in *Daughter of the Legend*. The character is named Sylvania and her husband is called Skinny. Dave's logging buddies, Mort and Hezzy, discover Sylvania's wares by accident and then visit her shack every weekend for a new supply of whiskey. Skinny and Sylvania take money or plunder in trade. They serve the Melungeons in two ways—by stockpiling hard goods they would otherwise need to buy in town and by buying Melungeon-manufactured corn likker. Sylvania's libations have an excellent reputation not only among the Melungeons, but also among white residents of Cantwell County who make the trip up the mountain to Sylvania's shack. When Mort and Hezzy get done telling Dave about this legendary woman, Dave has a question:

> "Wonder how Sylvania gets by with the law?" I said. "I saw a man in Cantwell County jail from this mountain yesterday. He was jailed because the sheriff found a half pint on 'im."
> "Sheriff can arrest Sylvania all he pleases," Hezzy said. "But he couldn't get her outen the shack. Skinny said his wife hadn't been outside his shack fer thirty-six years. Said she couldn't get through the door."[75]

This is, of course, a version of the same story that Brent Kennedy and so many others tell about the huge woman who seems to grow with each retelling. In order to put the whole tale into the confines of his story, Stuart must tell about the woman's death. Dave is enlisted to help Mort and Hezzy build her coffin from oak and line it with cedar. Skinny

---

[74]Stuart, *Daughter of the Legend*, 90-91.
[75]Stuart, *Daughter of the Legend*, 30-31.

declares, "I want 'er put away in a nice box."[76] Because she was too big to get through the cabin door, several strategies are considered to get her body out: the people talk about tearing down the house, sawing the door bigger (no small task when the house is a log cabin), or burying her under the floor. The method that wins out is dismantling the chimney.[77] Six men bear the huge coffin inside through the opening. It takes fourteen to carry the black oak casket out to the graveyard and twenty to lower it into the grave. Stuart's details add a little more to the legend of this remarkable woman.

Many valley people attend her funeral, some out of curiosity, others with genuine sadness. Bert Prat and Lonnie Pennix were Cantwell County sheriff and deputy respectively during Prohibition when anyone in the valley who got liquor, got it from Sylvania. She is respected by whites and Melungeons alike as an honorable practitioner of a respectable trade.

> "There was never a better woman than Sylvania. When she sold you a gallon of moonshine, you got a gallon of unadulterated moonshine and not two quarts of moonshine with a quart of water and a quart of carbide all stirred up. I don't know what we'll do without her. We won't have no market fer our corn up here."[78]

Sylvania's death serves one other function; it allows Stuart to include details about customs surrounding death and burial. The Melungeon custom of "Decoration Day," when families pay respects to their dead by decorating their graves is mentioned in connection with the death of Miss Rose Fox, the missionary teacher. However, when Sylvania dies, Dave gets to see the situation for himself.

> "Now we must take a quick look at the Sanctuary Mountain graveyard," Bass said to me. "I want you to see where we sleep up near the sky where the wind is allus blowin' over." . . .
> "[W]e came to the Melungeons' city of the dead. Each grave had a little house built over it and the house was painted white. Since the Melungeons didn't have money to buy paint, they used

---

[76]Stuart, *Daughter of the Legend*, 172.

[77]See chap. 8, below, on James Aswell's Tennessee Writers' Project stories for a complete discussion of the Mahala Mullins story, her moonshining, and her death and funeral.

[78]Stuart, *Daughter of the Legend*, 183.

a white clay for paint. Here were acres of little houses, row on row and close together, with little paths between. The place was clean and well kept with a pine tree here and there. What surprised me was that the Melungeons took better care of the little houses that covered the graves of their dead than they did the shacks where they lived.[79]

This description matches others in various books and dissertations about Melungeon practice around death and cemeteries.[80]

As was discussed at some length in the opening pages, Melungeon phenotypes have been much the reason for prejudice in many cases. One of the things that most startled Will Allen Dromgoole, a Nashville journalist who wrote about Melungeons in the late nineteenth century, was the fact that a single Melungeon family could have members with several different phenotypes. Detractors, of course, used this variation to suggest that Melungeon women were promiscuous and had children by many different men. Dromgoole was also scandalized by the fact that a dark-skinned woman might be seen suckling a fair baby, or vice versa. This proclivity for variation in phenotypes is mentioned several times in *Daughter of the Legend*. Deutsia herself has blond hair, dark skin, and the famous Melungeon eyes. However, there are other phenotypes prevalent among the people of Sanctuary Mountain. Dave, the narrator comments on this early in the novel when he says that the Melungeon girls are the most beautiful in Cantwell County.

> [Y]ou will find the tall, straight girls, dark-complected, light-complected, girls with charcoal-black straight hair and charcoal-black wavy hair, girls with long ripened-wheatstraw-colored hair and long October-poplar-leaf-golden hair, girls with shapely bodies, small waists, thin ankles, and long hands with fingers that taper like marigold leaves.[81]

Don Praytor's children are another example.

---

[79]Stuart, *Daughter of the Legend*, 179-80.

[80]Phyllis C. Barr, "The Melungeons of Newman's Ridge" (M.A. thesis, East Tennessee State University, 1965) 30-31. Jean P. Bible, *Melungeons Yesterday and Today* (Rogersville TN: East Tennessee Printing Co., 1975) 105-107. Mattie Ruth Johnson, *My Melungeon Heritage: A Story of Life on Newman's Ridge* (Johnson City TN: Overmountain Press, 1997) 106-108, 122.

[81]Stuart, *Daughter of the Legend*, 42.

Mrs. Praytor had come from behind the window curtain, had leaned her dark face against the windowpane and was looking straight at me. Her dark face reminded me of the dark gloom of an autumn day when a cold rain is stripping the last leaves from the trees on the mountain. The children were all different. There were four fair-complected ones; two of the four had reddish hair and two were blonds. The fifth child had charcoal-black straight hair that fell about her shoulders and her face.[82]

A third example, to drive Stuart's point home for sure, is given about halfway through the novel: "And then Ben Daniels came and brought his wife Nettie, his dark-complected son and his fair-haired apple-cheeked daughter."[83] Pat Elder explains this phenomenon as follows:

Generally, children can never be darker than is the darker parent. Talespinners viciously wanted people to know Melungeons had children whose coloring was entirely different from each other. . . . [V]ariance in sibling appearance is explained by *atavism*, which is known as *reversion-to-type*. Racial mixing may cause some offspring to bear the impress of one strain of their ancestry and others that of other strains. Judging the degree of mixture by visual appearance is impossible to predict because of atavism, notwithstanding the possibility of infidelity.[84]

Stuart's novel details the food the Melungeons of Sanctuary Mountain eat, which to Dave seems exotic and tasty. In Oak Hill, near the courthouse where the Melungeons gather, there are food stalls. They sell wine and lemonade, turtle-steak sandwiches, rabbit sandwiches, fish sandwiches, and home-cured-ham sandwiches. Early on Dave wonders why they don't buy their lunches at Little Tavern and notes "these were different sandwiches and drinks from the ones sold in Little Tavern."[85] The first meal Dave eats with the Huntoons hints of their customs, with a menu of wild game, fish, mountain blackberries, wild honey, and wine. The Christmas dinner at the Huntoons is even more bountiful and impressive in the creativity with naturally available ingredients it shows.

---

[82]Stuart, *Daughter of the Legend*, 63.
[83]Stuart, *Daughter of the Legend*, 122.
[84]Elder, *Melungeons*, 109.
[85]Stuart, *Daughter of the Legend*, 7.

Everybody was helping himself to two kinds of wild meat
and fish, heaping his plate, taking something from each dish on
the table. And there were many dishes on the table. There were
sweet potatoes and Irish potatoes—boiled, baked, and fried—
turnips and turnip-top greens. And we had cabbage too. We had
dried fish, dried beans, shelled soup beans, dried pumpkin, and
dried apples. We had wild honey and maple syrup. We had
sassafras tea and real coffee [one of Dave's Christmas gifts]. No
one was drinking the tea but everybody, even to little Cress, was
drinking coffee. And we had corn bread baked in a pone and
biscuits cut with the top of a flask and baked brown in the oven.
What a dinner we had before us! . . .

After we finished, we had our choice of strawberry, apple,
peach, pumpkin, or huckleberry pie.[86]

After the violence of Deutsia's death the novel ends on a peaceful
note and the tie to the natural world of the mountains is emphasized
once again. "Each brother-in-law and sister-in-law handed me a bouquet
of wild spring flowers. It was an old Melungeon custom to give flowers
to a departing guest."[87] Stuart's choice of a word to designate Dave,
"guest," is particularly telling. Dave for all his good intentions and even
for his enduring of some ridicule and prejudice has not really become
one of them. He is an interloper, an outsider, who looks in and makes
some categorical judgments, but finally turns his back.

As I have already hinted, I think Dave (and probably Stuart himself)
is somewhat deprecating and somewhat dogmatic in both his thinking
and his actions. This book is a good read for someone looking for an
unreal world where true love paints all with a rosy hue. The tragedy of
Deutsia's death is part of the genre. Dave's melodramatic statement in the
last chapter about how it has been thirty-six years since his year on
Sanctuary Mountain and how he has not remarried is ratification of the
romantic ideal of one true love for each person in this life. I cringe at
some of the platitudes and assumptions that Stuart puts on his characters.
(Examples: "Education will fix everything." "The religion of the snake
handlers is patently crazy." "Confronting the judge or the physician with
rhetoric will change the situation." "Giving a person a bathtub will
automatically convince that person to bathe more frequently.")

---

[86]Stuart, *Daughter of the Legend*, 164–65.
[87]Stuart, *Daughter of the Legend*, 226.

It is interesting that Brent Kennedy—undeniably Melungeon and
definitely an insider—praises the book so highly and does not seem to
feel that Melungeons in the story are treated as inferior or talked down
to in any way. Kennedy says:

> *Daughter of the Legend* is a beautiful book, which captures the
> essence of what it was like to be Melungeon in the early 1900s.
> The characters come to life as people that really did exist. . . .
> [T]he beautiful Deutsia could be any human being, and it is this
> possibility that lends the story its universal appeal. There is
> something of each of us—white, black, yellow, red, or Melun-
> geon—in Deutsia Huntoon, a young girl secure in herself but
> vulnerable in her status, and in love with a boy she should never
> have known. As is true of most people, Deutsia wanted a home
> and a family, but she lost it all just as she touched her dreams;
> who couldn't identify with such human tragedy? Jesse Stuart
> understood the power of these archetypal circumstances and
> wove them into a rich and spellbinding tale.[88]

Wilma Dykeman, in her introduction to the novel, claims that Stuart
was "an explorer not an exploiter of his Appalachian people's lives."[89] I
disagree. I think Stuart comes very close to exploiting the Melungeons he
portrays in *Daughter of the Legend*. I have more genuine sympathy for and
empathy with Sabrina Harkryder, caught between a rock and a hard
place (*She Walks These Hills*) or R. C. Bailey, the Melungeon man who
cannot find a home (*The Devil's Dream*).

---

[88]Brent Kennedy, "Afterword" to *Daughter of the Legend*, 240-41.
[89]Dykeman, "Introduction" to *Daughter of the Legend*, xiii.

8

Mountain Folks
and the "Guvermint":
Four Melungeon Tales Collected
by the Tennessee Writers' Project

There are four stories under the rubric of "Melungeon Tales" in the small
volume called *God Bless the Devil!*, published at Chapel Hill by the Tennessee Writers' Project in 1940. The Tennessee Writers' Project was a part
of the larger Works Progress Administration (WPA) Federal Writers'
Project that produced the books in the *American Guide* Series (critically
acclaimed guidebooks for each state) as well as items that the project and
its designers called folklore.

> The Folklore Project [a subcategory of the Writers' Project] filed
> its material under the general headings "traditional" and "life
> histories."
>   The Writers' Project staff variously described the life histories
> as *life sketches, living lore, industrial lore,* and *occupational lore.* The
> narratives were meant to reflect the ordinary person's struggle
> with the vicissitudes of daily living. . . .
>   [T]he collected lore and narratives were to be used as the
> basis for anthologies which would form a composite and compre-
> hensive portrait of various groups of people in America. The
> entire body of material provides the raw content of a broad docu-
> mentary of both rural and urban life, interspersed with accounts
> and traditions of ethnic group traditions, customs regarding
> planting, cooking, marriage, death, celebrations, recreation, and
> a wide variety of narratives.[1]

New Dealers in the Roosevelt Administration created the Federal
Writers' Project to provide appropriate work situations for unemployed
writers, lawyers, teachers, and librarians. Instead of blue-collar jobs on

---

[1]From "About the Folklore Project and the Life Histories," a page on the
"American Memory – Library of Congress" website, accessed 16 June 2000, at
<http://lcweb2.loc.gov/ammem/wpaintro/wpalife.html>.

construction projects, Writers' Project participants went into the "field" and collected first-person narratives, expressions, songs, essays, and stories. The Library of Congress collection chronicling this undertaking includes correspondence, memoranda, field reports, notes, graphs, charts, preliminary and corrected drafts of essays, oral testimony, studies of social customs of various ethnic groups, narratives of ex-slaves. Unfortunately there are no original documents in the collection from Tennessee, so it is impossible to know anything beyond what is contained in the volume itself about the sort of process James Aswell and his fellow collectors used to compile the stories in *God Bless the Devil!* The American Memory web site notes that "The quality of collecting and writing lore varies from state to state, reflecting the skills of the interviewer-writers and the supervision they received."[2] For us in Melungeon studies this is a lamentable fact.

According to the "Introduction to the New Edition" of *God Bless the Devil*,[3] James Aswell became a part of the project staff in May 1938 during a time of real tension between the then director of the Tennessee Project and the Washington office over exactly what "folklore" was and how it should be collected and written up. According to Charles K. Wolfe, Aswell had a keen interest in folklore. This interest is confirmed in a letter Aswell wrote to his brother:

> Tennessee writers have largely ignored the rich lode of it here. Why? I can't understand, unless it's due to the same back-worldliness which has made for the state's vigorous survival of folk-stuff. The Writers' Project has scratched around at it but it has relied too much on the scant fragments that have been printed. The present director of the state set-up is singularly blind to this sort of thing. . . . I remember when Washington was fairly screaming for color of this sort, he would invariably cut it out of the copy.[4]

Living in Nashville and working on a novel called *Wayfaring Stranger* and sometimes publishing stories in Martha Foley's *Story* magazine at the time he got involved with the Tennessee Project, Aswell was named project superintendent on 10 October 1938.

---

[2]From "About the Folklore Project and the Life Histories."
[3]Charles K. Wolfe, "Introduction to the New Edition," in *God Bless the Devil! Liars' Bench Tales* (1940; repr.: Knoxville: University of Tennessee Press, 1985) xvii.
[4]James R. Aswell, letter to his brother, May 1938.

At the time the Tennessee writers were working on their folklore volume that eventually became *God Bless the Devil!* the folklore editor at the federal level was B. A. Botkin. Botkin is credited with identifying one of the key characteristics of the liars' bench tale: "a strain of elaborate hoaxing and jesting that belongs to the humor of exaggeration and deception but more often borders on pure nonsense or fantasy."[5] Botkin sent conflicting messages to his state office underlings: he said one thing and did another. He told his writers/collectors to record material verbatim from informants in the field, but then he would send submitted manuscripts back to the state offices for changes and improvements. Wolfe notes:

> Presumably he had one set of standards for the archival material, another for stories submitted for publication, but it is doubtful if his writers really understood that. As *God Bless the Devil!* progressed, writers began creating a hybrid genre, in which they rewrote and recast traditional tales. . . . Of the five contributors to *God Bless the Devil!*, four (Aswell, Miller, Lipscomb, and Edwards) are on record as having done substantial firsthand field collecting on their own, but it is unclear whether they rewrote only their own material or also redid material from the project files.[6]

Wolfe in his introduction to the 1985 reprint of the Tennessee volume admits that the methods used by Aswell and his cohorts do not conform to the folklore standards set and endorsed by scholars in that discipline. Wolfe's remarks respond to allegations in Saundra Keyes Ivey's doctoral dissertation that *God Bless the Devil!* is "fakelore." To explain "fakelore," Ivey quotes coiner of the term Richard Dorson, saying it refers to

> the presentation of spurious and synthetic writings under the claim that they are genuine folklore. These productions are not collected in the field but are rewritten from earlier literary and journalistic sources in an endless chain of regurgitation, or they may even be made out of whole cloth.[7]

---

[5]Wolfe, "Introduction," *God Bless the Devil!*, xxvii.
[6]Wolfe, "Introduction," *God Bless the Devil!*, xxviii.
[7]Saundra Keyes Ivey, "Oral, Printed, and Popular Culture Traditions Related to the Melungeons of Hancock County, Tennessee" (Ph.D. diss., Indiana University, 1976) citing Richard Dorson, "Fakelore," in *American Folklore and the Historian* (Chicago: University of Chicago Press, 1971) 9.

Wolfe admits that the Tennessee Writers' Project encouraged writers to "improve" texts and laments that "lack of original sources makes it difficult to tell just how much tampering was done."[8] Wolfe refers to evidence (although he does not state what sort of evidence or how he knows it) that the writers were aware of the importance of field transcriptions; however, he also acknowledges that the writers were too casual in documenting their sources. His final paragraph admonishes the reader:

> *God Bless the Devil!* should be seen as a project of its time. It was a time when traditional culture for public consumption was routinely mixed with journalism, local color fiction, "fakelore," and regional writing. The book was a product of a particular WPA philosophy that de-emphasized the role of the original informant or writer, encouraged a collectivist approach to literature, and championed the art of the everyday working class citizen.[9]

Both Ivey's dissertation, which explores the relationships between oral, printed, and popular culture traditons of the Melungeons of Hancock County, Tennessee, and Melanie Sovine's dissertation titled "The Mysterious Melungeons: A Critique of the Mythical Image" raise issues relevant to Aswell and Miller's "Melungeon Tales." In layman's terms, both Ivey and Sovine want to know if the stories that have been passed down, particularly in Hancock County, are authentic parts of an oral tradition. The alternative would be that the stories come from what Sovine calls "the literature," articles mostly in the popular press about Melungeons that were written as early as 1849. My assessment is that Ivey wishes that the narratives were authentic folklore, but doubts they are because of both ideas and phrases that crop up in her informants' versions of the events and stories that can be traced back to particular written accounts of life on Newman's Ridge. Ivey also notes that

> [t]he difficulty of discerning the nature of the relationship between esoteric belief versus exoteric speculation is complicated by a resentment of many outside writers who have, in focusing attention on traditions related to the Melungeons, seriously misrepresented the county's image, often in extremely stereotypic forms.[10]

---

[8]Wolfe, "Introduction," *God Bless the Devil!*, xxxii.
[9]Wolfe, "Introduction," *God Bless the Devil!*, xxxiii.
[10]Ivey, "Oral, Printed, and Popular Culture Traditions," 205.

Sovine, I judge, goes one step farther than Ivey. She says the articles in the popular media are essentially false (her term is "ideologically biased"), and she attacks three commonly held assumptions about Melungeons: (1) Melungeons are of indeterminate origin; (2) there is such a thing as a collective Melungeon identity; and (3) Melungeon population is centered on Newman's Ridge in Hancock County. In Sovine's assessment, none of these assumptions—all of which are prevalent in books and articles about Melungeons—is true. She asserts that "the literature offers a mythical image that is rarely congruent with the empirical reality corresponding to the people who are labeled 'Melungeon.' "[11] She further asserts in her 1982 dissertation that the integrity of this media-created model's explanatory power is never questioned, that academic research has failed to influence the mainstream of "Melungeon writing."[12] Her complaint is that popular writers tend to reference other popular writers, and thus perpetuate what she calls "the myth."[13] I wonder what she would say today in light of the many new scholarly books and articles (Kennedy, Gallegos, Mira, Everett, Elder, and others) that not only speak to scholars but also enjoy wide readership among Melungeons and other lay readers in Appalachia who are not otherwise involved in academic pursuits.

The Tennessee Writers' Project, which had definite although simpler objectives than either Ivey or Sovine, collected stories, particularly stories of frontier and pioneer life with an emphasis on ethnic group traditions, and documented them in writing. The "Melungeon Tales" meet all these self-imposed criteria. Lack of records for Tennessee does make it impossible to know for certain who was interviewed by whom, what questions were asked, and what answers were given. All we have are the published stories themselves. Aswell makes some comments in an introductory essay to *God Bless the Devil!* titled "On the Courthouse Steps":

> Though most Liar's Bench tales probably sprout from some kernel of fact, each teller garnishes them with fancies of his own, interpolates bits of personal experience, and borrows heavily from accounts of other events and personages about which he has a fuller stock of hearsay. . . . In its passage through space and time the story is bound to shed numerous by-versions. These, in

---

[11]Melanie L. Sovine, "The Mysterious Melungeons: A Critique of the Mythical Image" (Ph.D. diss., University of Kentucky, 1982) 2.

[12]Sovine, "Mysterious Melungeons," 50.

[13]Sovine, "Mysterious Melungeons," 55.

turn, branch and re-branch and are edited and expanded by
many tellers until at length dozens of stories, completely unlike
in detail, have evolved from one original source.[14]

It is tempting here to read between the lines. Is Aswell both defining and
defending the Writers' Project methods? Is he justifying the adding and
editing that later scholars accuse him of? He goes on to tell what he
thinks really happens when those old men who gather on the shady
courthouse lawn in the heat of summer tell their stories.

> At the Liars' Bench a man is relaxed; he gives his mind the reins
> and lets it wander where it will. Because his words will not be
> weighed, judged, and held against his morals or character, his
> stories are most apt to reveal what he really thinks about life and
> death, religion, and his fellow men than does his public attitude
> toward these things.[15]

It is difficult to categorize the stories exactly. Are they folk tales? Are
they legends? Are they myths? In my introductory chapter I defined
folklore as the traditional beliefs, practices, legends, sayings, songs, and
tales of a group of people that are passed down orally. I said that a *legend*
is a story that has a basis in fact, and a *myth* a story about origins that
helps people understand about beginnings. To be consistent with my
terminology, I must use all of these terms to talk about these four
Melungeon tales.

Before I begin my analysis of the stories, however, I want to comment
on the language. These stories are written in dialect. While the forms
used are not as difficult to read and understand as those found in Mary
Murfree's nineteenth-century Appalachian stories, neither does the language flow as effortlessly as that spoken and "written" by Lee Smith's
mountain characters in their own distinctive voices. Aswell himself in his
introductory essay talks about the language.

> Much of the effectiveness and distinctive flavor of Liars' Bench
> stories lies in the vernacular of the teller. It is a vigorous idio-
> matic speech, deep-rooted in the past but still possessing the
> youthful flexibility that characterized Elizabethan English.
> Because the parts of speech have not become frozen and inviola-
> ble, a man freely uses verbs as nouns, nouns as verbs, adverbs

---

[14]James R. Aswell, "On the Courthouse Steps," in *God Bless the Devil!*, xlii.
[15]Aswell, "On the Courthouse Steps," xliii.

and adjectives as nouns, or puts them to any other unorthodox task he chooses. Often he does so with striking effect and genuine creative power.

However, this speech is not the hodgepodge of mispronounced words and bald crippled phrasing that lettered persons with poor ears and, unfortunately, facile pens, are prone to pass on. A good listener is soon aware of a flowing speech pattern that may be as lyrical as an Irish fairy tale or have the measured solemnity of Ecclesiastes—the metrical echo in everyday speech of the ballads, hymns, and scriptural quotations which the small town Tennessean hears from childhood on.[16]

Aswell, here, is certainly defending the way he, who indeed considered himself to be a lettered person with exemplary ears, heard and recorded the speech of his informants. In my judgment he is saying, "I listened carefully, and I wrote the words down the best way I could so that you, my reader, could 'hear' the story I am telling you in as authentic a voice as possible." Yet, Aswell's attempts for me are not good enough. I feel uncomfortable and strangely embarrassed when I read these tales. I am too conscious of the trappings of "story" and the words themselves that feel artificial and overdone, and I find myself having to reread portions because I sometimes have trouble following the thread of the particular tale because I am so put off by the unsuccessful effort to reproduce an informant's language. In his introduction, Charles Wolfe comments on the language and syntax of the stories:

> [A]ttempts to produce dialect strike us today as mawkish, and in the case of black or Melungeon dialect, offensive; . . . in fact, there is a good deal of racist language throughout the stories. . . . Yet the language also contains a wealth of folk idiom and more than a few unusual phrases.[17]

I certainly agree with Wolfe about the mawkish tendency of the expression. Furthermore, it does not alarm me to find racist language in the "Melungeon Tales." The people who told the stories, Aswell and Miller's informants, were products of their environments. Those environments were certainly racist. Racial prejudice is one of the most easily documentable facts about the Melungeon experience; Melungeons have suffered at the hands of the dominant white power brokers in Appala-

---

[16]Aswell, "On the Courthouse Steps," xlii-xliii.
[17]Wolfe, "Introduction," *God Bless the Devil!*, xxxiii.

chian society. Aswell and his colleagues in the Writers' Project would have had to do much more than tinker with language and content to take out the racist content and overtones: they would have in fact had to perform major surgery on the tales.

"Old Horny's Own"

The first story, "Old Horny's Own" is concerned mainly with Melungeon origins. Since it makes mention of a supernatural origin, one could conceivably label it a *myth*. References to the devil as a possible Melungeon ancestor occur in published stories only after the Aswell volume, so his story may well be the first documentation.[18] In any case, the tale makes interesting reading. In this story, credited to the "grannies" (who would be the midwives and herb doctors), the devil, Old Horny, is identified as the progenitor of the Melungeons. The devil has long been depicted as an anthropomorphic being with horns, therefore "horned or horny." Yet, in popular parlance, the word "horny" also means lecherous. The incarnation of the devil here is likely both—having horns as an animal and eager for sexual activity. The play on the word "horny" could easily have been underscored with a grin or a wink. But, then, judge for yourself.

> [O]ne time Old Horny got mad at his old shrew-wife and left Hell and wandered all over the earth till he reached Tennessee. He set on a high bald and looked around him.
>
> "I declare to Creation!" he says. "This place is so much like home I just believe I'll stay awhile."
>
> So Old Horny found him an Injun gal and started in housekeeping. Time came and time went. Everybody knows the Devil's always busy, and soon the house was full of children. And mean? Law! They was every one as mean as the Devil—which is natural, seeing as he was their pappy—and as dark and treacherous as their mammy. They beat and hammered at Old Horny day and night. They tricked and mortified him till it was pitiful. Finally he just couldn't stand it no longer at all.
>
> "I might as well be in Hell with my old crabby wedlock wife," says he. So he packed his traps and sneaked out of the house and went a-skillyhooting back to Hell as fast as ever he

---

[18]There is a reference in Phyllis Cox Barr's M.A. thesis, "The Melungeons of Newman's Ridge" (East Tennessee State University, 1965) and another in Sharyn McCrumb's Lovely in Her Bones.

could. And they do say it was them offsprings of Old Horny that growed up and started the Melungeon kind.[19]

The second origin story is one that is common in many books and articles that discuss possible origins for Melungeons. According to Brent Kennedy and others, there has been a strong oral tradition in Melungeon families that posits Portuguese origin. The obscurity of illiteracy shrouded details that could possibly tie early dark-skinned, fine-featured people in the Appalachian mountains to the sixteenth-century, Pardo's exploratory forays into the interior of the continent or de Soto's expedition. Yet, the people themselves said they were "Portyghee." Whether this was an attempt, as scholar Chris Everett argues, to separate themselves from the stigma of being Negro or an orally transmitted fact, the incidence of the allegation is persistent. Here in this story written down for posterity by Aswell is the assertion fleshed out:

> The Melungeons themselves tell another story. They say they come from Portugal a long time ago and sailed in a big ship across the wild seas till they reached this country. Then some sort of a hardness sprung up betwixt the captain and the sailor-men and they had a bloody scrap and the sailormen won. Soon as they'd hung the captain and his friends, the sailormen set the ship afire and went ashore and hid out in the woods. By and by they found a tribe of Injuns and made off with the women. Then they wandered and they roamed. Where all they went there's no telling. Some time or other they crossed over the high mountains into Tennessee and set down to stay hereabouts and have been here ever since.[20]

This version talks about both the Mediterranean and the Indian connections. It alludes to the notion that these Iberian men took American Indian wives, but they did not assimilate into the Indian tribes. Instead they maintained a separate society. It also postulates movement from the coast to the mountain ridges. The story goes on to explain that those early English-speaking, Christian Melungeons, some of whom were Revolutionary War veterans, first settled in the rich mountain valleys before the white settlers found a way to push them to the ridges.

---

[19]James R. Aswell, "Old Horny's Own," in *God Bless the Devil!*, 207-208.
[20]Aswell, "Old Horny's Own," 208.

[The white settlers] knowed the Melungeons, like the Cherokees, had let runaway slaves hide out amongst them. This with their dark skins was enough to make our grandpappies see pretty plain that the Melungeons was a niggerfied people. The more they looked at them good Melungeon bottom lands, the plainer they saw that nigger blood.

So they passed a law. They fixed it so that nobody with nigger blood could vote, hold office, or bear witness in court. Then they got busy and sued for the bottom lands. Pretty soon the Melungeons lost all their holdings in law suits. They couldn't testify for themselves on account of the new law. . . . There wasn't nothing left for the Melungeons to do but move into the high ridges.[21]

This is, of course, reference to the 1834 law that discriminated against free persons of color in Tennesse. Is this real history in the guise of folklore? The two are mixed in this tale without acknowledgement. Aswell attributes subsequent "trouble"—that is, Melungeons' propensity for violent revenge on their white neighbors—to this law and its immediate result, loss of good farmland.

Yes, it was real murder and bloodshed trouble, not one of your little puny feud fights.

On black nights in the dark of the moon the Melungeons come a-raiding down into the coves and valleys. They done their meanness quick, shooting the farm people—man, woman, and child—and slipping back to the ridges. They left burning barns and houses behind them, they killed the stock, and fired the crops in the fields. Mighty few whites lived to tell of it when them devils had been around.[22]

This propensity for lawless violence attributed to Melungeons came out again during the Civil War, and no doubt was the reason for white mothers' repeated admonitions to their children when they put them to bed at night, "If you don't act purty, the Melungeons will get you!"[23] Aswell's version of Melungeon response to the Civil War follows.

---

[21] Aswell, "Old Horny's Own," 210.
[22] Aswell, "Old Horny's Own," 210.
[23] Aswell, "Old Horny's Own," 207.

Well, first thing anybody knowed the Civil War busted out. Most of the men hereabouts joined up with the Union and started in fighting. But you can bet a pretty the Melungeons didn't burn no shoe leather hotfooting it to the colors—the Stars and Bars nor the Stars and stripes, neither one. They figgered it wasn't their fight. After the war got a-going, a heap of them took up bushwhacking and made a proper good thing out of it. The old folks say for years after the war the Melungeons was still a-trying to get the blue and gray pants and coats they'd taken from supply trains wore out.[24]

Aswell also narrates the traditional story of Melungeon counterfeiting activities. There are many retellings of this story. In some, such as the account of the Swift Silver Mines mentioned by Brent Kennedy,[25] the metal mined is silver, in others gold. "Old Horny's Own" does not mention Brandy Jack Mullins by name, but it talks about the legend of the mining and production of specie or coin money that was prized by back-country merchants and landholders because it contained even more real metal than necessary to meet the U.S. standard.

All at once the whites wanted to plumb bury the hatchet. Yes sir, they decided it the minute the word spread out that the Melungeons had come on some gold back in the ridges. . . .

They must've rigged up some sort of smelter or other and their own mint, because they begun bringing out a kind of rough-cut double eagles. Everywheres in these parts store-keepers took in them double eagles and no questions asked. And for good reason, too! Must have been twenty-five or thirty dollars' worth of fine soft gold in them. So the storekeepers got fat and sassy on Melungeon trade and everything was fine. . . .

Finally the supply of gold must've give out. . . . White folks still tried to find where it come from, but no sir, thank you, them Melungeons kept it their bosom secret.[26]

---

[24]Aswell, "Old Horny's Own," 212-13.
[25]N. Brent Kennedy, *The Melungeons; The Resurrection of a Proud People. An Untold Story of Ethnic Cleansing in America* (Macon GA: Mercer University Press, 1994) 149-50.
[26]Aswell, "Old Horny's Own," 211-12.

Aswell's tale mentions two other characteristics attributed to Melungeons. One is the fact that they know about and harvest herbs both for their own use and for sale.

> After the gold stopped a-coming, the Melungeons was as poor as gully dirt again. Oh, they still done some trading down into the valleys but it wasn't much, just mostly herbs and ginseng and such.[27]

Some would say that Melungeons needed to be savvy about herb lore because no regular doctor would treat them. Amelanchier in McCrumb's *Lovely in Her Bones* gives this slant. In Naylor's *Sang Spell*, the Melungeons know herbs and use them because there is no doctor that even knows they exist who might deny them treatment if he did. In *Sang Spell*, ginseng, sold to the Oriental trader for tea, for its healing qualities, for its aphrodisiac propensities, is the only cash crop.

The story continues to expand the description of the Melungeons and their circumstances.

> Whites left them alone because they were so wild and devil-fired and queer and witchy. If a man was fool enough to go into Melungeon country and it he come back without being shot, he was just sure to wizzen and perish away with some ailment nobody could name. Folks said terrible things went on back yonder, blood drinking and devil worship and carryings-on that would freeze a good Christian's spine-bone.[28]

This passage is interesting in both what it says and what it implies. It clearly comments on the fact that Melungeons kept to themselves and did not invite outsiders to join them. It also shows that the unknown invites speculation. Southern Ohio native Virginia Hamilton in her novel *M. C. Higgins, the Great* explores the mysteriousness of a group of people who may well be Melungeon. Although she never uses the word "Melungeon" to describe the Killburn family, they carry many Melungeon markers. The word "witchy" is used repeatedly to describe them and also how they make M. C., the main character, feel in their presence. Hamilton uses "witchy" to mean mysterious and supernaturally powerful. The passage quoted above implies that Melungeons can hex people so that they die and cites on good authority ("Folks") the awful religious

---

[27] Aswell, "Old Horny's Own," 212.
[28] Aswell, "Old Horny's Own," 212.

rites that Melungeons allegedly practice. Blood drinking and devil worship have long been associated with witches; sons and daughters of the devil might conceivably do such things.

In addition to being found in Aswell's version, the connection between the Melungeons and Satan is reported by Phyllis Barr as one of her collected stories in her 1965 master's thesis for the English Department at East Tennessee State University. Since Barr's work antedates Aswell, and Barr protects the identities of her informants, it is impossible to know whether the story is indigenous or whether someone read Aswell and then told the story to Barr. Jean Bible emphasizes the fact that Aswell's *Nashville Banner Magazine* article notes that East Tennessee mountaineers call Melungeons "Sons of Perdition." I cannot help but wonder where this allegation of kinship to the devil comes from. It is true that violence is a scary thing, possibly something that Satan would like to perpetuate, but violence alone does not indicate a blood relationship to the devil. Melungeons were known to be Christians, in fact they were often Baptists or members of Holiness churches where Satan was scorned and exorcised by tongue-speaking preachers. Believing in the reality of Satan is very different from being descended from Satan.

One final explanatory paragraph in "Old Horny's Own" may be the origin of the terms "Blackwaters" and "Ridgemanites." According to Aswell's tale,

> The whites always claimed the Melungeons was a nigger breed and nobody can deny some of them really was. Some of them mixed and mingled with niggers and got the name of Blackwaters. The pure-breed Melungeons wouldn't have nothing to do with the Blackwaters. They called themselves Ridgemanites or Hill Portughee, and today there's not any difference much betwixt them Ridgemanite Melungeons and the rest of us.[29]

This appears to be a variation on the distinction between "Nigger Melungeon" and "Indian Melungeon" made in 1849 in *Littell's Living Age*. It is also in line with what we can read in Jean Patterson Bible's book about the beginnings of the Newman's Ridge settlement by Vardy Collins, Buck Gibson, and a runaway slave named Goins. The delineation of these three groups goes back in print at least as far as the Dromgoole articles in the 1890s.

---

[29] Aswell, "Old Horny's Own," 213.

This particular tale, "Old Horny's Own," seems to be more of a recitation of lore and history than a fictional short story. There are neither real characters nor an ongoing plot. The tale gives much information—a little that could be called folklore like the section about the devil as progenitor or the statement that Melungeons could cause people who invaded their territory to "wizzen and perish away" and a lot that could more accurately be dubbed embroidered history.

"Six Hundred Honest Pounds"

Both James R. Aswell and Elva E. Miller have their names inscribed at the end of "Six Hundred Honest Pounds," a story that probably could be accurately classified as a *legend* because it features Mahala Collins Mullins, a real person who was born circa 1824 to Solomon Collins and Gincie Goins. "Big Haley," as she sometimes was called, suffered from elephantiasis and weighed at least 300 pounds. She did manufacture moonshine whiskey. Most versions of her story celebrate the testimony of one solemn Hancock County deputy, who reported on Mahala to a judge by saying, "She's ketchable, but not fetchable," for, when officers were sent to her cabin on Newman's Ridge to arrest her, they found that although she was willing to be transported to Sneedville to be tried for distilling corn whiskey and not paying the appropriate tax, she was too big to get through her cabin's door. When she died, the bed she was lying on was boarded over to make a coffin. How that huge coffin made it out of the house is unclear. Some say that the chimney was dismantled to allow for the coffin's removal. However, one of Mahala's descendants in Hancock County gave Saundra Keyes Ivey a more plausible account.

> The house had a chimney built here on this end [draws diagram] which has partly fallen down now. You saw that, didn't you? And at the other end of the house, when she died, the chimney had not been built. It wasn't built. But an opening was left for the chimney. And this opening was boarded over to prevent weather exposure. Then when they moved her body out, they did take the opening out, but the chimney was not built when she died [emphatically]. So the chimney was not torn down.[30]

---

[30]Informant P, interview, August 1973, in Ivey, "Oral, Printed, and Popular Culture Traditions," 216.

Brent Kennedy calls Mahala Mullins "the most famous of all Melungeons."[31] Versions of her story can be found in many books and articles, and she appears prominently in Jesse Stuart's *Daughter of the Legend* as Sylvania. Saundra Ivey devotes a long section of her dissertation's third chapter to a discussion of the problems associated with the truth and the fiction of the story of this famous Hancock County moonshiner. Ivey introduces her discussion by saying that

> stereotypic distortion of the county's oral tradition by outside writers is found in the written accounts of a Melungeon woman who is the subject of a still existing oral tradition in Hancock County as well as a long history of mention in printed sources.[32]

Ivey begins her recitation of the situation and its problems by quoting from a book titled *The Moonshiners* by Henry M. Wiltse. It appears that the mixing of oral and written traditions was already occurring by the late 1930s when Aswell collected the version of the story that he published because the phrase "six hundred honest pounds avoirdupois" is directly attributable to Wiltse's 1895 book.[33] Whether Aswell heard the phrase and recorded it as he heard it, or read the book for himself and appropriated the phrase to be his title cannot be determined.

According to Ivey, Mahala Mullins is well known in Hancock County and the anecdotes about her turn on two points: the excellent quality of her moonshine and her weight. County residents, many of whom Ivey interviewed to gather information for her dissertation, acknowledged that there is more than one version of the story. They were even tolerant of the differences in various accounts. What they did object to was misrepresentations of the truth that might lead to "stereotypic generalizations about an entire community"[34] such as "Hancock County is a moonshiner's haven" or "Bigamy is an accepted state of affairs in Hancock County" or "Inhabitants of the county are slovenly and violent." Ivey reports that county residents wanted both "to correct erroneously published information and to add to the record the information of 'eye witnesses' and/or relatives of Aunt Mahala."[35] When Ivey asked questions about Mahala

---

[31]Kennedy, *The Melungeons*, 17.

[32]Ivey, "Oral, Printed, and Popular Culture Traditions," chap. 3.

[33]Henry M. Wiltse, *The Moonshiners* (Chattanooga: Times Printing Co., 1895) 65.

[34]Ivey, "Oral, Printed, and Popular Culture Traditions," 218.

[35]Ivey, "Oral, Printed, and Popular Culture Traditions," 219.

Collins Mullins, her informants, although they did not always agree with each other in their reports of particular details, would often include phrases like "That's first-hand information" or "My mother knew Aunt Mahala."[36]

"Six Hundred Honest Pounds" is certainly a variation on an oft-rehearsed Hancock County theme. There are things in this version that are both discrepancies from the facts about the real person as they are known in Hancock County and embellishments in a sort of "folk" tradition that is familiar to those of us who have grown up with heroes like Pecos Bill, Paul Bunyan, and John Henry.

The first notable difference between fact and the story is the name of the main character. Wiltse's *The Moonshiner* refers to the main character of the story as Betsy; Aswell calls her Big Betsy. Ivey notes that William P. Grohse, the acknowledged historian for Hancock County, shared information with her that could explain this discrepancy. Mahala's husband Johnnie had a sister Betsey who married Alford Collins; she was Betsey Mullins who became Betsey Collins. Mahala was, of course, a Collins who became a Mullins. Since county residents never confused the two women or their names, Ivey infers that it must have been an outsider who did the initial switch that was then perpetuated in print. Whatever the reason, the character in Aswell's account is called Big Betsy Mullins.

A second point of difference is this woman's supposed stable full of husbands.

> [T]hat Melungeon woman just held her hands to her mouth, taken a long breath, and sung out, "Hoooo *peeg, peeg, peeg, peeg!*" And it rung out through that beech grove like the reaching blast of a good brassy bugle horn, "*Peeg! Peeg! Peeg!*" she bellered. . . .
>
> And mighty soon all the gathered-round folks there did see what she was a-waiting for. They did see seven dark and barefoot Melungeon bucks come a-trotting out of the cane-brake. And each of them toted seven big stoppered gourds slung from a yoke round his neck.[37]

This is the first mention of Big Betsy's many husbands. When the judge to whom she is speaking accuses her of bigamy, she replies, "I thought it was pretty big of me, too, your Judgeship, when I taken them

---

[36]Ivey, "Oral, Printed, and Popular Culture Traditions," 209.

[37]James R. Aswell and Elva E. Miller, "Six Hundred Honest Pounds," in *God Bless the Devil!*, 232.

seven men on last year. I warn't but only sixteen then. But now I'm
turned seventeen and got my full growth I'm a-looking for a few more
good husbands."[38] The husbands are her partners in the moonshining
venture, and the number of them increases as Aswell's story goes on.

> Betsy had got so she didn't even leave her cabin. She didn't
> have no need to. She was taking on one or two new husbands
> every year and sometimes more if one happened to die off on
> her. So her husbands made the likker and sold it and waited on
> Betsy hand and foot and she didn't have a frazzling thing to do
> but set in her special big rocking cheer, that was carved from a
> solid oak stump, and rock and chaw her eating baccy. When the
> Revenuers would ask where her still was she would truthfully
> say she didn't know. Her husbands moved it about from one
> thicket briar-hell to another.[39]

The husbands also rebuild the mash tub that the revenuers destroy on
each visit.

In the narration that leads up to the final attempt to arrest Betsy, she
calls on her husbands to extend hospitality to the revenue officers and the
deputies. "In no time at all a whole pack of Melungeon bucks come a-
trotting up from somewhere on the ridge. One of them was a plumb
young unbeardless boy, but most of them was fairly along in years."[40]
And the one that got there first was "old and white-whiskered and
bent."[41] She directs this old man to "fetch Mister agent here a gourdful
of our best likker to sup while he tells me about what he's a-doing."[42]
Betsy is definitely in charge of the entire operation. The mention here of
a beardless boy being among the husbands seems like an unusual
inclusion and could be perceived as an intended slight.

The final mention of the husbands and an enumeration comes at the
time of Big Betsy's death. "They [her kinfolks] busted out a wall of her
cabin then and wrapped her in quilts and blankets and her husbands and
kinfolks lowered her down. She had thirty-three husbands."[43] This inser-
tion of numerous husbands into the story seems unnecessary. It is verifiable fact that Mahala Mullins had many children, some sources say as

---

[38]Aswell, "Six Hundred Honest Pounds," 233.
[39]Aswell, "Six Hundred Honest Pounds," 237-38.
[40]Aswell, "Six Hundred Honest Pounds," 240.
[41]Aswell, "Six Hundred Honest Pounds," 240.
[42]Aswell, "Six Hundred Honest Pounds," 240.
[43]Aswell, "Six Hundred Honest Pounds," 242-43.

many as twenty, several of whom died as infants. Aswell's many husbands could be an attempted translation of that fact—that is, many children must mean many sexual encounters, and many sexual encounters suggests more than one husband. This is pure speculation on my part to try to figure out where these thirty-three husbands might have come from. However, it is observably true that Aswell's one-dimensional caricatured husbands in the plural present a cumbersome and ineffective contrast to Stuart's depiction of Skinny, the devoted mate to Sanctuary Mountain's Sylvania.

A third point on which Aswell's "Six Hundred Honest Pounds" differs from both fact and Hancock County folklore is his casting of Betsy Mullins as a "wrastler." Not only is she a "wrastler," but a Hulk Hogan of a *woman wrastler*. In spite of her mouthful of chewing tobacco, she announces to the assembled citizens at a political rally and barbecue:

> "I'm Betsy Mullins—they call me Big Betsy—and I do hail from Newman's Ridge. I'm a woman with all the womanly trimmings, but don't let hit bother none of you. For I'm a better man than any of you rounders here!"[44]

She proceeds to take out Black Joe Bascom ("easy the biggest man there . . . fair blaze-snorting for trouble"[45]) and the four men who take her on after his defeat.

> There set Betsy Mullins on a stack of four men, piled up like cordwood. Seemed like the seams of her jumper was sprung a little more, but warn't no other signs on her. She warn't even a-blowing from it.[46]

Winning the match provides Betsy and her husbands with an ideal promotional and marketing opportunity. Betsy refuses the prize of a fat shoat in exchange for a dispensation from the judge.

> Big Betsy says, "Just give me your leave to sell a few little old gourds here, if anybody'll buy. That's all I ask, your Judgeship."

---

[44] Aswell, "Six Hundred Honest Pounds," 229.
[45] Aswell, "Six Hundred Honest Pounds," 229.
[46] Aswell, "Six Hundred Honest Pounds," 230.

So the head judge—and he was a real lawcourt judge as well as a barbecue wrastling judge—he said he didn't see no harm in it, he reckoned. She might as well go on and sell her gourds.[47]

Betsy knows and the reader suspects that the judge is outsmarted. As soon as he realizes that the gourds contain corn likker, he asks whether the whiskey is government stamped. When she says no, he says she can't sell it after all. However, when Betsy reminds him that he just gave his word and that he would certainly not want the world to call him a "barefaced liar, a two-double Injun-giver on [his] own sweared word, . . . the judge studied about it an' did see how slick he'd been sold[;] he just laughed and told her to go ahead and sell her likker."[48]

Another addition is the description of the exaggerated difficulty of the ascent to her cabin on the ridge. Aswell describes a trail that goes straight up for eighty or ninety feet and then an over-hanging section of thirty feet more. There are fifteen years, give or take a few, during which the lawmen scramble up to Betsy's cabin, meaning every time they go to destroy her means of manufacture and to haul her off to court. During these years a pattern develops. Betsy, always laid up with a foot problem—a sprained ankle or rheumatism—and thereby unable to *walk* with them back to Sneedville, welcomes her guests and refreshes them with her best likker. When word of the repeated failures to bring her to justice reaches Washington D.C., there is a final assault on Betsy by the revenue agents and the deputies. A crew of rock drillers and blasters clear away the overhang and set a great big post on the ridge backbone to anchor a block and a tackle. Their intention is to put the huge woman in a sling and lower her down to a waiting wagon. All this builds up to the line that everyone is waiting for: "Mr. Agent, I ain't able to leave this cabin a-tall. I ain't noways able to fit through that door frame now."[49]

This sequence about the foiled arrest sets up the final anecdote, which is also the last piece of "fakelore." Here Aswell gives his version of the death and burial of "the Melungeon she devil moonshine queen."[50]

But her kinfolks did finally use that big iron post and the other fearsome work them agents and debities and rock-workers done. That was after Big Betsy died, must've been eighteen or twenty years after. They busted out a wall of her cabin then and

---

[47] Aswell, "Six Hundred Honest Pounds," 231.
[48] Aswell, "Six Hundred Honest Pounds," 232-33.
[49] Aswell, "Six Hundred Honest Pounds," 242.
[50] Aswell, "Old Horny's Own," 214.

wrapped her in quilts and blankets and her husbands and kinfolks lowered her down. She had thirty-three husbands and fourteen cousins, and they all agreed that Betsy weighed six hundred honest pounds and maybe then some.[51]

As has already been noted, this does not agree with what people in Hancock County know and tell about Mahala Mullins's death and burial. The same informant of Saundra Ivey's quoted earlier went on to say in regard to the erroneous statement that is frequently seen in media accounts about how this woman's body was wrapped in quilts and rolled down the hill for burial.

> No, they carried her out. . . . They did not have a coffin. She was on a four poster bed. . . . They sawed the posts off and boarded up the top of it, and that was her casket. In other words, they just made a box out of the bed, the top part of the bed.[52]

In 1937, James Aswell wrote an article for the *Nashville Banner Magazine* titled "Lost Tribes of Tennessee's Mountains." This article contains a different version of the Mahala Mullins story. It is interesting to compare this earlier telling with "Six Hundred Honest Pounds."

> At the beginning of her career, Betsy is said to have tipped the scales to a neat 600 pounds. Some versions of the story state, in addition, that she towered seven and a half feet into the thin mountain air and that she could "heft" a yearling bull over her head with all ease. When she sat to a light meal, she commonly downed a whole pig, hide, hoofs, and all. She could tear a firm-rooted pine from the earth with one hand and could splinter a two-inch oaken plank with her bare fist. Around her arm, she could bend a forged iron crowbar as an ordinary woman might wrap a length of silk ribbon. In a word, Betsy Mullins would have been a fitting match for that Heracles of the American lumber camps, Paul Bunyan.[53]

As Ivey notes, this paragraph sounds much more like a folktale than it does like history or fiction. How much the heroine eats, how strong she

---

[51]Aswell, "Six Hundred Honest Pounds," 242-43.

[52]Informant P, interview, August 1973, in Ivey, "Oral, Printed, and Popular Culture Traditions," 217.

[53]James Aswell, "Lost Tribes of Tennessee's Mountains," *Nashville Banner Magazine* (22 August 1937): 5.

is, and what she can do with her bare hands gives her the stylized persona we associate with a legendary figure. Ivey contends that "real" folktales gathered in the field rarely sound this phony. It seems to me that in "Six Hundred Honest Pounds" Aswell is exaggerating for effect. The effect he achieves, however, is negative.

Two Preacher Stories:
"Fool-Killing Shep Goins"
and "A Stroke for the Kingdom"

When Saundra Keyes Ivey spent two summers in Hancock County collecting material for her doctoral dissertation in folklore, she interviewed many county residents. Some of these folk were Melungeon; some were not. She did observe that Hancock County was a community which took Christianity seriously, and noted, "As might be expected, . . . preacher stories are a popular genre."[54] Ivey observed that the anecdotes were "related humorously but without malice or a desire to degrade either the preachers of the religious practices involved."[55] Such stories, often about endurance in prayer, preaching styles, or techniques used by preachers to work their parishioners up to a frenzy, were sometimes told to her by preachers themselves. The exclusion of such stories from the souvenir program for the Melungeon outdoor drama "Walk toward the Sunset" she ascribes both "to respect for religious practices . . . and to the fact that many of the anecdotes would not be funny to persons who were not familiar with the individuals or customs the anecdotes described."[56] The stories Ivey reproduces in her dissertation are short, amusing, and very pointed—each one makes one clear statement. People in Hancock County loved to tell preacher stories, yet they were sensitive enough to each other's beliefs and worship styles that they did not parade the stories before the tourists they were hoping to attract by means of the drama who would in turn read the souvenir program. This fact stood out for Ivey, and it also seems important to me.

James Aswell and his colleagues on the Writers' Project had no such scruples. Aswell includes four stories about Melungeons and two of them are preacher stories. Furthermore, the tales themselves show neither respect nor sensitivity to Melungeons or any persons of faith.

---

[54] Ivey, "Oral, Printed, and Popular Culture Traditions," 424.
[55] Ivey, "Oral, Printed, and Popular Culture Traditions," 430.
[56] Ivey, "Oral, Printed, and Popular Culture Traditions," 430.

"Fool-Killing Shep Goins" is one example of the genre that Ivey came to recognize in Hancock County as the preacher story. In this tale, the main character, Shep Goins (note his common Melungeon surname) is duped by an unscrupulous redheaded preacher called Brother Puddefoot. Interestingly, Goins, not the preacher, is the story's protagonist. Shep gets religion at a brush-arbor revival hosted by none other than Puddefoot. After his baptism in a nearby river Shep has a visitation from Old Master, God himself. God appeals to Shep's vanity about how good a marksman he is and commissions Shep to kill any Melungeons who are fools. This fool-eradication program is necessary because Old Master allows that since the Hebrews have let him down (just how they have disappointed him is not clear) he will make the "hill Portughee" his chosen people. Shep goes at his task with gusto, eliminating many foolish Melungeons and causing those remaining to consider their actions carefully lest "Shep Goins'd mark them up for a fool-killing."[57]

After a time, Shep marries a girl named Vandy May, "a likely looking little baggage, as cute as a bug."[58] The preacher suggests that Shep go hunt Melungeon fools farther afield and offers to pray with him to seek God's leading in the matter. After a long and fervent prayer, Shep agrees to go. Old Master visits Shep again in the guise of a "big forky-legged cloud of fire"[59] and confirms Puddefoot's claim that all Melungeons are meant to be God's chosen people. Naively, Shep charges Puddefoot with the responsibility of Vandy May. Shep returns thirteen months later to find Vandy May pregnant and near time of delivery. Shep infers that he has been cuckolded and that Puddefoot is the father, but the preacher assures him that the child is Shep's own alleging that gestation has been miraculously lengthened by the Lord. Puddefoot is suddenly called away; the baby arrives one week later. "Shep he taken one look at that baby's red fuzz and went out and shot his self spank betwixt the eyes! Because Shep was fool-proud of his reputation for fool-killing."[60]

Unlike the two previously discussed tales that focus totally on Melungeon history, lore, and legend, this one is a story that only happens to have a Melungeon in it. While it uses some Melungeon traditions and lore to advantage as the narrative plays out, it puts the main Melungeon character, Shep, in a very unflattering light. If Melungeons wanted to take umbrage at any of the fiction in print that features Melungeon characters,

---

[57]James R. Aswell, "Fool-Killing Shep Goins," in *God Bless the Devil!*, 219.
[58]Aswell, "Fool-Killing Shep Goins," 219.
[59]Aswell, "Fool-Killing Shep Goins," 221.
[60]Aswell, "Fool-Killing Shep Goins," 225.

I would think this tale about fool-killing Shep Goins would be the one to eschew.

It is interesting to see in Charles Wolfe's "Introduction to the New Edition" of *God Bless the Devil!* that there was a rather long prologue to the story that didn't make it past the Folklore Project editors. This introductory section includes information that would have, to my way of thinking, given "Fool-Killing Shep Goins" more substance and credibility.

Well sir, you take Shep Goins now. Even a Melungeon oughtn't to be as queer as that Shep was.

How's that? Never heard tell of the Melungeons? Lord today! Why, they's the orneriest generation of mankind Old Master ever made on this earth. They's mean, they's hateful, they's treacherous. They live back in the coves and on the ridges, mostly over in East Tennessee, in Rhea county and Hancock County. They don't have much to do with nobody else when they can help it. I used to know two or three Melungeon families before I come to Nashville. They was the most uncomeateable folks I've saw anywhere ever.

No, it ain't that at all. Melungeon don't mean what church are they, like Baptist and Methodist and Campbellite. Melungeon means Melungeon just like white folks means white folks and nigger means nigger. Now I'll tell you what they say. The claim they come down from some Portugee sailormen that took and cut the threat of their captain and all over on the oceanwater edge of South Carolina away back yonder a couple of hundred years ago.

That's *their* story. Me, I don't take a dust of stock in it. If you ask me, I say them Melungeons is just a godawful mess of Cherokee Indian and white scoundrels that run off back in the hills to cheat the hanging rope. And I reckon they's right smart lick a nigger comes in there somehow. Anyways, them Melungeons been living pretty close to themselves all this time. White folks won't have no truck with them. Just so long as they don't give white folks no trouble, the Law leaves them alone to settle their troubles amongst theirselves.

White folks not paying no mind to what them Melungeons does up in their hills is how come it that Shep Goins got away with all he done. If he'd been a white man, Law would have took and hung him a dozen times. It was a long time back, and just whereabouts I don't know.[61]

Botkin, the folklore director of the Federal Writers' Project, criticized this prefatory material saying, "The opening is somewhat artificial in its attempt to give the monologue pattern and background of Melungeons, and also needs toning down from the social point of view, particularly more that of race relations and class attitudes."[62] I personally like this opening. I think it describes almost eloquently the situation that Melungeons endured. It *was* a racial thing. They were marked by the stigma of their dark skin, their associations, and their heritage. They could not walk away. Aswell's words may be truly representative of narratives he got from his informants. I think in many cases the lived experiences of prejudice were reasons for touchiness and sometimes bizarre behavior. Aswell's original opening appears to me to be an honest recitation of the situation that existed not only in Hancock County but in other Melungeon areas as well.

This tale includes details and literary conventions that could apply to any group. One familiar archetype in the story is that of the corrupt preacher-evangelist. From Sinclair Lewis's Elmer Gantry to real-life incarnations like James Baker and Jimmy Swaggart, we recognize this figure. Aswell's preacher is true to form.

> Preacher Puddefoot wasn't no Melungeon to begin with. He come from somewheres way over to West Tennessee. Like as not he had to hotfoot it to the hills to keep out of the jailhouse. And he didn't belong to no special church, neither. Just preached for his self. They say when he first showed up amongst the Melungeons he was a sorry sight. Looked like the buzzards picked him, he was so all in rags and jags and hungry-lank. But he hadn't been preaching and taking up collection hardly no time before he had a big fine belly on him and as slick a rig of clothes as you'll see anywheres. Them Melungeons somehow just naturally taken to him."[63]

Puddefoot's charisma joined with the Melungeons' vulnerability and Shep's inside information about how God is going to make the Melungeons His chosen people render this preacher irresistible. The good

---

[61]Wolfe, "Introduction," *God Bless the Devil!*, xxii-xxiii.
[62]Wolfe, "Introduction," *God Bless the Devil!*, xxii.
[63]Aswell, "Fool-Killing Shep Goins," 219.

brother is on hand to perform the marriage for Shep and the lovely young Vandy May, and Shep does not smell a rat when Puddefoot suggests that there are fool Melungeons in Kentucky and North Carolina that need tending to.

Puddefoot's long and fervent prayer to find God's will for Shep is a characteristic of many of the preacher stories that Ivey collected in Hancock County—praying long and fervently is one thing preachers are expected to do. Aswell explains to the reader, "Brother Puddefoot he kept at his praying for most an hour until Shep he was so all-fired sleepy he couldn't hardly see straight. You know how it is when a preacher gits a-praying around like that. You'll get buzzy and foolish in the head spite of all you can do."[64]

The Melungeon character of Shep alternates between wisdom and foolishness. One wise thing he does is take note of Puddefoot's praying. Chased, beaten up, and jailed a time or two, Shep realizes from his persistence and survival through all the trials that there is something supernatural about the protection he enjoys during his odyssey, and he thus begins to use prayer in good faith for both comfort and direction. On his return from Kentucky and North Carolina Shep tells Puddefoot:

"So after a while I got to praying. Just like you showed me,
Preacher. Yes, I prayed unto the Lord. I asked him to tell me if
I could come back to Vandy May. And the Lord he did answer
my prayer. He told me to go back home, and here I am."[65]

This was surely not an expected development for Puddefoot.

The dramatic irony in this tale is well executed. Everybody but Shep can see that Shep is a fool, that God would not sanction wholesale killings for foolishness, and that Vandy May's baby cannot be her husband's. However, Shep's ignorance of these facts provokes us not to pity and fear as they would in a tragedy, but instead to mild disgust. The abrupt and violent conclusion is characteristic of Shep's black-or-white approach to reality and his understanding of his mandate: "God told me all fools should be shot, so I shoot a fool whenever I find one." When Shep realizes that he himself is a fool, suicide presents what he perceives to be his only choice.

At the very heart of this story lies a pivotal question: What is the definition of a fool? The title is an important clue, and the term "fool-

---

[64]Aswell, "Fool-Killing Shep Goins," 221.
[65]Aswell, "Fool-Killing Shep Goins," 222.

killing" has a significant double meaning. First it means that wise folk, God included, want the world to be fool-free. One would assume that this could mean that people should be taught the difference between wisdom and foolishness and then encouraged to practice wisdom in every situation. Foolishness should be killed—eliminated. But in this story that logical understanding is ignored. Instead fools, when identified, must be killed—murdered—immediately. Shep is designated as God's fool killer; Shep kills fools.

The second meaning turns on an understanding of the way the grammar of the English language works. One can make "fool" the subject of the sentence and say that (a) fool kills, or that foolishness "kills" (is destructive). Only an unwise person would use murder as a way to make sure that people choose wise courses of action. The reader/listener knows, too, that only a fool would believe that God would designate him to be the wisdom police, only a fool would be taken in by the conniving of an obviously phony preacher as Shep was. The double meaning of the phrase "fool-killing" operates throughout the story, and the reader is in on the charade from the outset. So, then, here is an answer to the earlier question, "What is a fool?" A fool is a person easily duped, someone who acts unwisely.

One disturbing corollary that emerges from this story is the idea that God is somehow involved in the foolishness of the story. Aswell's tale reports, "That red-headed Preacher Puddefoot must've been one powerful exhorter to get them Melungeons afeared about their souls."[66] Isn't one implication of this statement that only a fool would give in to such concern, that there is no reason to fear for the final disposition of one's soul? I read it to say "Melungeons are wild and fear no one. They don't even worry about real things in this life that should concern them. Yet, this charlatan got them fired up about what could happen to their souls in the afterlife, . . . if there is an afterlife."

Furthermore, Old Master tells Shep that "the hills is full to hard-down busting with fools."[67] God then, using a somewhat under-handed tactic, appeals to Shep's vanity about what a crackerjack shot he is and tells him to get busy—"Take your rifle, Shep. Take it and practice up. Because you got to be a thundering good shot, . . . I don't want no fools amongst my chosen people. I'm leaving it in your hands to weed out the fools, Shep Goins."[68] It seems to me that both history and Scripture prove

---

[66] Aswell, "Fool-Killing Shep Goins."
[67] Aswell, "Fool-Killing Shep Goins," 216.
[68] Aswell, "Fool-Killing Shep Goins," 217.

that foolishness is at the heart of the human condition. Shep certainly is a fool for believing otherwise. Yet, the storyteller's attitude here seems to reinforce the notion that no one can determine true wisdom, for, since God is party to the foolishness, there is no hope. Our "hero" Shep returns chastened from his experiences in Kentucky and North Carolina, where it "[s]eems like the Melungeons . . . didn't know Shep from Adam's Off Ox and didn't fancy him nosing in and shooting their fools up."[69]

I have hope for him at this point, but he soon succumbs again to Puddefoot's facile wordplay and takes in one more lie. Puddefoot tells him, "I been watching that gal [Vandy May] like a hawk. I been taking care of her mighty careful, Brother Shep."[70] The double entendre about just what sort of "care" Puddefoot has been administering is again lost on our gullible hero, and he backs right into his final predicament. The story's final line says it all, "Shep was fool-proud."[71] Shep, the ultimate fool, proud of an absurd reputation for murder that he should have been ashamed of, blew his brains out rather than do the wise thing and admit he had been taken in. Perhaps I protest too much, but if this is a joke, it seems to me to be not only coarse but also irreverent and in very poor taste. This story does not show the consideration and delicacy that Ivey observed among her informants in Hancock County.

Several other details in the story are worth noting. One is the fact that the Melungeons are said to be "Portughee."[72] Another is a bias against education revealed in the statement that "[s]chools is fool factories."[73] A third is the reference to the fact that "[t]he sheriff of whatever county it was didn't bother them Melungeons just so long as they didn't aggravate the white folks."[74] This frees Shep to murder at will with no reprisal. This last implies that the Melungeons were definitely outside the parameters of the mountain communities where they lived and were ignored as long as they don't bother the whites.

"Fool-Killing Shep Goins" then is a preacher story with a bite. In this story nobody wins. The preacher is despicable. The Melungeon protagonist/hero is stupid. And, the reader is left wondering "What's the point?"

The second preacher story in the Aswell volume is "A Stroke for the Kingdom," signed by Elva E. Miller, not by Aswell. Unlike "Fool-killing

---

[69] Aswell, "Fool-Killing Shep Goins," 222.
[70] Aswell, "Fool-Killing Shep Goins," 224.
[71] Aswell, "Fool-Killing Shep Goins," 225.
[72] Aswell, "Fool-Killing Shep Goins," 217.
[73] Aswell, "Fool-Killing Shep Goins," 218.
[74] Aswell, "Fool-Killing Shep Goins," 218.

Shep Goins," this story features the preacher, Brother Billy Stuart, as the main character. A second character that is almost equally important is the story's Melungeon, Shad Bolton. The story turns on two main ideas, the preacher's determination to save Shad from hell forever, and Shad's disgust with what he perceives as Brother Billy's ability and intention to arouse the community's women, Shad's wife Leola included. It is hard to determine how self-aware Billy Stuart is. Does he purpose to get the women to adore him and use talk about heaven to accomplish that, or is he really so sincere and on fire for the Lord that the women's response is merely a by-product? Shad Bolton believes the former, and "Shad Bolton wasn't nobody's fool."[75]

As the story opens, Stuart sets out determined to preach in Hancock County. He knows that the way to a successful revival is to identify the most influential man in the community and work to get him to the mourner's bench. Once that is accomplished, the rest of the people will fall in line. Stuart identifies Shad Bolton as that key person. Shad, implored by his wife to attend the revival and be saved so they can be together in heaven, agrees to go when he realizes that his wife is most surely attracted to the handsome young evangelist. Stuart attributes Shad's presence to the prayers he has offered and decides to do all he can to bring Shad to repentance. Brother Billy says to himself, "Now if I just get Shad Bolton to come through, the rest of the crowd will follow. It will be the biggest stroke for the Lord ever struck in these mountains."[76]

Shad, for his part, observes that Billy has the women in the crowd wrapped around his proverbial little finger, and is moved to real anger. However, he is able to control his temper. Shad says to himself that once the preacher has had his say, then, and only then will he light into Brother Billy. Unfortunately, Shad is not counting on the fact that the preaching could be effective. "Long about the end of the fourth day, Shad was beginning to find out what Brother Billy had. And he found it plenty hot, too."[77] Shad feels the flames of hell, and in spite of his former resolve, he confesses to having been a sinner and shouts out his need to be baptized. "Oh yes! I confess! I repent! Oh lead me down to the river, that sweet, wet, watery river!"[78]

The cold river water brings Shad to his senses, but it may be too late, for the wily preacher souses Shad two more times until the man is "limp

---

[75]E. E. Miller, "A Stroke for the Kingdom," in *God Bless the Devil!*, 247.
[76]Miller, "A Stroke for the Kingdom," 247.
[77]Miller, "A Stroke for the Kingdom," 248.
[78]Miller, "A Stroke for the Kingdom," 250.

as a greasy dishrag,"[79] and in need of a different kind of revival. As the story ends, we are not sure whether Shad is alive or dead from his watery ordeal.

Whatever the outcome, this appears to be a win-win situation. If Shad lives, his actions will more than likely bear witness to two truths: he cannot deny that he has been moved to salvation, and he will take Stuart to task for using his position as preacher to take advantage of the Melungeon women. Shad's life will be "restored," and a scoundrel will be brought to justice. On the other hand, if Shad has died, Stuart will have his most desired convert, and Shad could be the ultimate winner by ending up in heaven himself.

Miller's tale is lavish in its description of both the physical attributes and the preaching skills of Brother Billy Stuart. Of course, two famous Billys, Billy Sunday and Billy Graham (whose preaching came after the publication), come quickly to mind.

> Brother Billy was a young and a mighty man. He preached the glory of God and the sinful Power of the Devil. When he stood before a congregation, six-foot-two-inches tall, his wavy brown hair falling down to his shoulders and gray-green eyes blazing as he told the torments of the damned, people just cowed down before him. The biggest and meanest man in the house would feel like a whipped cur dog.
>
> "Yes!" Brother Billy would shout. "The stink of that blazing pitch and brimstone will be in your nostrils forever! And the horrible stink of your own burning flesh, all rotten with slime and corruption! And the fiery flames leap up from the coals, the white-hot coals that make up the whole floor of Hell! And the fire rains down from the flaming sky forever and ever and ever!"
>
> One mighty arm would shoot out in front of him.
>
> "You!" he'd shout, pointing right at the biggest and meanest man. "You! Yes I mean you, my brother, my friend and brother in Jesus! Give up your sinful ways and come to the mourners' bench! Come and be washed in the blood of the Lamb and be whiter and purer than snow!"
>
> I tell you, it made a man feel low. Even the best of them.[80]

Billy's technique to charm the women was different but no less effective.

---

[79]Miller, "A Stroke for the Kingdom," 253.
[80]Miller, "A Stroke for the Kingdom," 244-45.

Then Brother Billy would tell about Heaven, his eyes all soft and dreamy. Dreamy and faraway they'd look now, near about lost behind his long dark lashes. The very air in the church would be soft and mild and sleepy; . . . the women looked and listened.[81]

This is no ordinary preacher, nor is he a scoundrel like Puddefoot. Stuart is more complex and therefore more real. It is not so easy to dismiss this preacher man. "Yes, Brother Billy was a mighty man. The women all sighed and the menfolks feared him. He made a sight of converts."[82]

Shad Bolton, possibly named after a fish and as short-tempered and ready to bolt as his name implies, "was as ugly and onery looking a slab-sided, hammer-jawed hunk of a man as ever grew to be six foot tall. . . . Shad Bolton wasn't nobody's fool, even if he did have a face like a stubby bear's tail."[83] Even though Shad senses that Billy is dangerous business because of what his wife has told him, he is not prepared for the physical attractiveness of the young preacher. When he sees the handsome Billy, "Shad felt like a holly-tree bush inside him. Red and green all mixed up together, and little stickers all over. 'I'll get that honey-jawed jabber-box,' says Shad, 'if I never do nothing again. . . . I'd just like to see what he's got that's so hot.' "[84]

The word "hot" is layered here, for Billy Stuart is as hot as they come both as a hunk of a man and as a fire-and-brimstone evangelist. Shad is not prepared for the power of the man's preaching that can make the breath of hell blow with fiery heat over the sweltering congregants. So poor Shad burns with the conviction of his sin that might propel him straight to hell if he refuses to attend to it, and he also burns with jealousy and anger as the slick stranger threatens to steal his wife away. "Shad steamed and sweated in fear and steamed and sweated in hate."[85] The preacher's description of a sinner in hell bears some similarity to a depiction of a lover in the throes of passion. Neither image soothes Shad's fevered mind.

It's difficult to decide exactly who Billy is. Perhaps the confusion is no more or no less than a comment on the ambivalence of the human

---

[81]Miller, "A Stroke for the Kingdom," 245.
[82]Miller, "A Stroke for the Kingdom," 245.
[83]Miller, "A Stroke for the Kingdom," 246–47.
[84]Miller, "A Stroke for the Kingdom," 248.
[85]Miller, "A Stroke for the Kingdom," 249.

situation especially when it comes to the power of sexual desire and/or the subtlety of the workings of the Holy Spirit. Stuart prays about converting Shad with apparent sincerity at the beginning of his big Hancock County revival, "Oh God, help me make him sweat! Help me put the fear of Hell in his heart, and bring him through safe to be saved."[86] More than once Shad almost repents in response to the sermons. It is Stuart's shifts to preaching about heaven that rekindle Shad's righteous indignation. We as readers never know whether Shad's perceptions of Billy's designs on the women are real or imagined. However, even Shad has to acknowledge that Billy can tap into an incredible power source.

> Brother Billy got up from his knees and came down off of the platform. He put his hand on Shad's shoulder and looked right into his eyes. Shad felt calmed down a heap and the least little bit afeared. He hadn't never seen eyes like that before.[87]

It's only when the cold water gives Shad a "real turn" that he remembers his anger. This resistance, expressed in blasphemy—"Damn you to hell! . . . I aim to kill you dead, you honey-tongued, jabber-jawed gospel mill, you!"—provokes Stuart to push Shad under the water again and again. It appears that Stuart succumbs here to pride; afraid he will lose all of his converts to Shad's bellowing, he suddenly doesn't care whether Shad dies at his hand or not.

Scary . . . to contemplate that the supposed man of God can be an instrument of evil. This story raises more questions than it answers.

The Melungeon markers in this story are very few and are definitely less important than the interplay of good and evil described above. The first and only neutral marker in the story is that Hancock County is identified as Melungeon territory.

> [W]hen Brother Billy said he was going up into Hancock County to preach, other folks told him to sky clear of it.
> "Only Melungeons and such-like trash lives there," they said, "and it won't do no good to preach to them, they're such an ungodly lot. Some says they worship the Devil. They really ain't worth saving. Why, it's downright dangerous to be among them."[88]

---

[86]Miller, "A Stroke for the Kingdom," 248.
[87]Miller, "A Stroke for the Kingdom," 251.
[88]Miller, "A Stroke for the Kingdom," 245.

These few lines play on many presuppositions that readers might already bring to this story. Melungeons are like trash. Melungeons live without acknowledging God. Melungeons will not respond to the gospel. Melungeons may even be Devil worshipers. Melungeons are not worth saving. Melungeons are dangerous. These clearly stated assumptions are certainly enough to make any Melungeon angry. However offensive these stated slurs are, the story does not really bear them out. Both Billy Stuart and Shad Bolton are characters with some depth. Billy, aware of his personal magnetism or not, may have ulterior motives when it comes to the women. And, Shad Bolton, the stereotypical "good old boy," does have a heart capable of feeling fear and remorse. Because of these more believable characters and the very real problems they struggle with, I find the story much more satisfying than "Fool-Killing Shep Goins."

There are two unstated assumptions—more "mountain" than Melungeon—that also color the story. One, women are weak and either need or are more susceptible to religion than men. Two, men are stronger and hold out longer; however, they have more influence in the disposition of the entire community toward the faith.

The word "stroke" also deserves mention in passing. Its many meanings make it a logical choice for the title of this story. As a verb, "stroke" can mean to fondle or to stir up. As a noun it can be a blow with a weapon, one of a series of repeated actions like arm movements in swimming, a vigorous or energetic effort, the act of caressing. Each one of these casts a slightly different meaning to the title by extension the theme of this story.

I have a great respect for the oral tradition. Ivey's dissertation with its many transcribed anecdotes convinces me that there is a rich oral tradition among Melungeons on Newman's Ridge (and presumably elsewhere). However, stories told orally by just plain folks are rarely as complex as this story. This story is too carefully nuanced to be strictly a transcription of a "folk" tale. I'm not saying it is a bad story. On the contrary, it is a very interesting one—much more artfully composed than the other three tales from the Tennessee Writers' Project volume. This story seems to be more like a true piece of fiction and less like an attempt to write up what the project people saw as folklore. What I am saying is that "A Stroke for the Kingdom" probably does not come to us out of a Melungeon oral tradition.

Saundra Keyes Ivey complains about Aswell saying that he could be forgiven even for misinformation and that discrepancies could be chalked up to "variations in time and space"[89] if his *tone* were different. *Tone* is usually defined as the writer's attitude toward his material and his audience. I think it is clear from the three tales analyzed here bearing Aswell's name, that he has little respect for the subjects of his tales (he often ridicules them), and that he seems almost to look down his nose at his audience. One possible scenario is that he took on the Writers' Project tasks out of necessity and never really accepted the project's aims or its methods. Another possibility is that persons above him in the bureaucracy like Botkin, excised the best parts and left only story skeletons.

Comparing the stories in *God Bless the Devil!* with the stories in *The Hawk's Done Gone* make Aswell's tone, which feels disparaging and disrespectful, all too apparent. Haun worked with the same raw materials that Aswell had at hand. Mary Dorthula White and her extended family live in Cocke County some miles south of Hancock in the mountains of East Tennessee. Yet, their story-telling results are very different. Haun produced prose ballads that weave the folklore seamlessly into the natural speech of her witch-doctor midwife narrator, and I, the reader, believe every word. Reading Haun is much like reading Offutt.[90] As a reader, I am immediately lost in the narratives of both of these writers identifying with one or more characters in every story in various ways. When I finish one of Haun's palpably real stories I draw in my breath, swallow hard, and push down feelings of nausea. She engages me on a very intimate level and even takes me places within my own psyche that I fear to go, for she understands the ways of men and women with each other and with the world in a totally authentic manner that is paradoxically both simple and profound. I relate to Haun even more powerfully than I relate to Offutt because the voices in her stories are women's voices. Offutt's men are no less evocative, but they are, being male, removed from my experience. I compare Offutt to Haun because their stories make me feel the same way. I choose to compare Haun to Aswell because they wrote in the same decade. It is clear—apparently to everyone, as Charles Wolfe's plea to readers to judge Aswell's stories as products of a particular time and philosophy—that Aswell is dated. Haun is not, and is not likely ever to be so.

Immediately after I first read Aswell and Miller's "Melungeon Tales," I wrote my initial reaction:

---

[89]Ivey, "Oral, Printed, and Popular Culture Traditions," 212.
[90]Two short stories by Chris Offutt are presented in chapter 10.

These stories seem to me to be condescending and put the Melungeons in a bad light. In each, the Melungeon characters are seen as stupid or ridiculous. . . . "Six Hundred Honest Pounds" is a boring, embellished version of the Mahala Mullins story.

After more research and hours of honest examination, I still feel the same way.

9

Sneedville Revisited: "Walk Toward the Sunset," the Melungeon Outdoor Drama, by Kermit Hunter

Born and raised in Welch, West Virginia, Kermit Hunter attended Emory and Henry College in Southwest Virginia for a year before going on to Ohio State where he completed his undergraduate work. He went on for graduate study at the University of California and earned a Ph.D. from the University of North Carolina at Chapel Hill. He taught at Hollins College in Virginia in the 1950s and finished out his academic career as dean of Arts at Southern Methodist University in Dallas, Texas. He received a Guggenheim Fellowship during his tenure at SMU. Hunter retired from SMU in 1976 but continued to teach courses there as well as at Texas Christian University and the University of Texas at Arlington.

Hunter wrote more than forty scripts for outdoor dramas. Together with Paul Green, author of the "The Lost Colony" (a drama about the Roanoke Colony performed in Manteo, North Carolina), Hunter founded the Institute of Outdoor Drama at the University of North Carolina in 1963 with funds granted by both the university and the state of North Carolina. This organization has capitalized on the fact that the very first outdoor dramas in the country were staged in North Carolina and provides "national leadership in fostering artistic and managerial excellence and expansion of the outdoor drama movement through training, research, and advisory programs, and serves as a national clearinghouse for its more than one hundred constituent theatre companies across the nation."[1]

Outdoor dramas, original plays often including music and dance, are a uniquely American art form that trace their roots to the tradition of epic theater of the ancient Greeks. Most of the dramas being produced in the United States have been cooperative efforts of local citizens, foundations, and government. The plays themselves focus on the people who shaped

---

[1]Scott J. Parker, "Outdoor Dramas Expand across the Country," accessed 12 April 2000, at <http://www.unc.edu/dept/outdoor/scottarticle.html>.

the heritage of the country, and they make these historical figures and their times come alive for contemporary audiences. As Scott Parker, current director of the Institute of Outdoor Drama notes, "These dramas have been produced out of community desire to commemorate the past and rededicate the future through theatre. . . . Their real success is not monetary. It rests with their ability to emotionally touch the audiences."[2]

Hunter, already well known by the late 1960s for "Unto These Hills" in Cherokee, North Carolina, got involved with the Melungeon drama called "Walk toward the Sunset" as the result of a letter from a woman in Sneedville whose name he could not recall.[3] When I interviewed him on the telephone, he said that she sent him a sheaf of articles from newspapers (chiefly Knoxville papers) and a book to give him the background information he needed to write the script.[4] He recalled being at a meeting one day to discuss the project with a drama teacher and several people from Sneedville.[5]

Community residents were aware of the impressive economic growth in Cherokee and Maggie Valley, North Carolina, as a result of "Unto These Hills." Some people hoped that similar things could occur in Hancock County, Tennessee, as the area needed improved roads and better services for residents as well as the tourists they hoped the drama would attract. It was implied that an influx of tourists could really change the economic climate in the area. There was not agreement, but there was enough consensus to garner funds for the beginning of the project. It is interesting to note that no Melungeons were involved in this effort, nor were any among those who donated time, materials, and labor to build the amphitheater or to undertake all the other tasks necessary to launch the production. Nashville journalist Louise Davis was guardedly optimistic in her articles which stated the benefits for all county residents and also acknowledged that the drama was "an enormous undertaking for a town of less than 1,000, and a county of around 7,000—all at the end of a dead-end road that dips from spectacular and lofty vistas to a picture-pretty valley."[6]

---

[2]Parker, "Outdoor Dramas."

[3]Kermit Hunter, telephone interview with the author, 11 April 2000.

[4]The only book about Melungeons written before Hunter wrote his drama was *The Melungeons* by Bonnie Ball, 8th ed. (Big Stone Gap VA: privately printed, 1991). Hunter probably used an early edition of this book as one of his sources.

[5]Hunter, telephone interview, 11 April 2000.

[6]Louise Davis, "Pushing for a Happy Ending," *Nashville Tennessean Magazine* (30 August 1970): 13.

Ivey discovered in her dissertation research that even after several seasons of production people were still divided about the drama. Most agreed it had increased tourism, but some said they were against industrial development, that they preferred the county to remain rural and unspoiled. One fact that most of Ivey's informants agreed on, "it was that production of 'Walk toward the Sunset' had made the name *Melungeon* respected; all who told [her] this were sincerely proud of that accomplishment."[7] This very real benefit was seconded by John Lee Welton, director of the drama in its early years.

> When we first started the show, nobody would admit they were Melungeons. . . . the men who were working here on the theatre site itself kidded each other in a derogatory way. They'd say, "Hey, you dirty Melungeon, come help me pick this up." That sort of thing. But no one would ever admit they were Melungeons. But by the end of that first season some of these same men would sidle up and sort of nudge me and say "Hey, did you know I'm half Melungeon?" This I think is an indication, perhaps a somewhat covert indication, but at least an indication of acceptance. . . . I'm not Pollyannish enough to say that the whole community is going to immediately accept the Melungeon, because it's *not*; the prejudice has been there too long.[8]

Hunter's script for "Walk toward the Sunset," that was produced in Sneedville first in the summer of 1969 by Vista volunteers and local residents in conjunction with the drama department at Carson-Newman College, contains interesting information about Melungeon history and culture. Hunter himself, in a letter, wrote about the situation he has dramatized in the script.

> The story of the Melungeons is typical of some of the darker impulses in the American dream: those moments when the American dream gets crowded by white supremacy, the arrogance of wealth and position and power. The Melungeons happened to have dark skin, and for this reason they were buffeted and shunted by the white society moving across the mountains toward the west. It is significant that they were cared

---

[7]Saundra Keyes Ivey, "Oral, Printed, and Popular Culture Traditions Related to the Melungeons of Hancock County, Tennessee" (Ph.D. diss., Indiana University, 1976) 344.

[8]Interview with John Lee Welton by Saundra Keyes Ivey, June 1973.

for and aided by the Red Man, who himself had felt the injustices of white supremacy.[9]

There is little character development in the play, but many facts about Melungeons are conveyed with precision and economy. Viewing "Walk toward the Sunset" would make a person aware of many of the issues both historical and practical that set Melungeons apart from the mainstream of Appalachian society.

This play is symmetrical, having two acts each set right after a war, each complete with a love story, and each detailing an important event in the history of Melungeon people in Hancock County, Tennessee. Hunter understands the outdoor drama format well: the vignettes he chooses are set against the backdrop of pivotally significant situations. Within the macrocosm of a historical turning point for the Melungeon people he shows how that event as well as prevailing attitudes would have affected selected individuals. Even though the characters are not well developed, it is easy to identify with them—Pat Gibson and Allisee Bowlin in act 1 and Vance Johnson and Cora Sylvester in act 2.

Act 1 takes place in 1780 just as a group of Melungeons are returning to the Tennessee River Valley after the battle of King's Mountain in North Carolina. This act also introduces John Sevier and Daniel Boone, the men whose vision and energy opened up Tennessee and Kentucky to settlement by white "Americans." There are two problems that come up immediately. The Melungeons, who have lived in the valley for many years, have no official titles to the land they farm. Sevier, soon to be organizer of the doomed state of Franklin and later governor of Tennessee, who is known for land speculation deals even among his admirers, values the contribution that the Melungeons have made by fighting at King's Mountain, but he is also zealous to have the money that he can get by selling the land to white settlers from Virginia and North Carolina. These settlers have cash in hand, want new land that will be open to whites only, and are ready to move. The Melungeons have only squatters' rights. The dialog that the character of John Sevier speaks portrays him as being unprejudiced and sympathetic to the Melungeons' position, but he reminds them that they are "persons of color" and that as such they have no right to own land. Daniel Boone warns that if Sevier gives in to the Melungeons' claims to the land, he (Boone) will be only

---

[9]Kermit Hunter, letter written 3 May 1973, as published in Jean Bible, *Melungeons Yesterday and Today* (Rogersville TN: East Tennessee Printing Co., 1975) 114.

too happy to lead the waiting settlers into Kentucky. Cantrell, the representative of the eager settlers, brings up another practical point saying, "if you declare it to be a mixed society, where every man is equal, then you got to give back this land to the Indians, or else make a treaty with 'em and pay 'em fer their land."[10] In the end, Sevier, by condoning the Melungeons' final decision to clear out of the bottom land that they have farmed for more than a century, indicates that his words are empty, belied by his actions.

Hunter's use of Daniel Boone and John Sevier is worth noting. Daniel Boone's name is familiar to most Americans who would see him in their mind's eye wearing a coonskin cap and carrying a long rifle as he opened up Kentucky by creating the Wilderness Road through the Cumberland Gap. Many could recall the story about Boone killing a bear at the foot of a huge oak tree. Boone is part of American folklore. By putting him in the story at the center of the land controversy involving the Melungeons right after the Revolutionary War, Hunter ties his story to something with which the audience would be familiar. If people are expected to remember new information, it helps to have a "peg" to hang the new information on. Daniel Boone—the westward pioneer movement that Boone represents—is just such a peg for most Americans.

John Sevier is also a well-known figure in Tennessee. If his bid to create the state of Franklin had been successful, he might have been more of a nationally famous figure. A story reported by Brent Kennedy and others references an article by Louise Davis that appeared in the *Nashville Tennessean* in 1963. This newspaper story reported that in August 1784 Sevier encountered a colony of Melungeon people. Sevier reportedly thought the people he found were of Moorish descent and that they had fine European facial features and that they claimed to be Portuguese.[11] Eloy Gallegos in his book demonstrates that Sevier himself (whose name in Spanish would have been Juan Javier) was of Iberian origin: that would connect him to the Melungeons by a more significant tie than chance meeting. According to Gallegos, Sevier's father, a Spanish Huguenot named Valentino Xavier or Javier from Navarre, was forced to leave Spain for France and then finally France for England in the late 1600s because of religious persecution.[12] If Tennessean John Sevier knew his

---

[10]Kermit Hunter, "Walk toward the Sunset" (unpublished script for an outdoor drama performed 1969–1976) 12.

[11]Phyllis C. Barr, "The Melungeons of Newman's Ridge" (M.A. thesis, East Tennessee State University, 1965) 2.

[12]Eloy J. Gallegos, *The Melungeons: The Pioneers of the Interior Southeastern*

family history, his tie to and sympathy for the Melungeons' plight might have been based on more than "doing the right thing." Is it possible he had genuine empathy for the dark-skinned people who had fought beside him at King's Mountain but lacked the military force necessary to protect their interests? Sevier, frontiersman that he was, appears to have been nothing if not pragmatic about what he could accomplish. It is not clear how much Hunter intended, but it is interesting to speculate about Melungeon ties to the high-profile figure of John Sevier.

The issue of origins is also addressed in act 1 as the following dialog demonstrates.

> PAT
> Part of my ancestors, and part of Alisee's, are Scottish. The other part, we can't be sure.
> My father said he could remember his grandfather talking about a village near the ocean: southeast . . . perhaps South Carolina, Florida. . . .
> SEVIER
> That would have been . . . when?
> PAT
> Sixteen fifty, I suppose. They were driven away from the coast by new settlers, so they came out here into this valley. They've been here at least a hundred years.
> SEVIER
> But I mean before that: where did they come from? Why the dark skin?
> PREACHER
> John, I've seen people from North Africa, and they are darker than any of these. Besides, these people have straight noses, thin lips, straight hair, like you an' me. I reckon they could be North African, mixed with white, but I don't think so. Also I figger each new generation is a little lighter in color than the one before.
> CANTRELL
> I still say they are "persons of color," and the laws of North Carolina and Virginia say they can't own property![13]

United States 1526–1997, vol. 2 of *The Spanish Pioneers in United States History* (Knoxville: Villagra Press, 1997) 154-55.

[13]Hunter, "Walk toward the Sunset," 8-9.

The last line reveals another piece of information—the fact of discriminatory laws even in 1780. According to Pat Elder's research, Virginia and North Carolina had laws restricting the rights of Negroes, mulattos, and Indians. Tennessee, or the land that later became Tennessee had fewer such laws, and the ones that existed (depending on what governmental judicatory one believed him/herself to be in) were not enforced.[14] Therefore, the western lands beyond the Appalachians felt safer for persons of color until the push to settle farther west occurred after the Revolutionary War.

Alisee offers thoughts about where the dark skin came from that are supposedly part of the oral tradition in her Melungeon family, "We're darker than the Spanish or Portuguese. My mother has told me many times about papers with strange writing, parchment . . . her great-grandmother said even he could not read it . . . handed down by their ancestors . . . hundreds of years. . . . "[15] A few lines down from this Alisee further alleges that the Melungeons have been in "America" for at least 300 years, lip service to yet another theory of origin—perhaps the Carthaginian theory or a reference to the "Lost Tribe of Israel." "Our people came here long before Columbus," she says, "Whoever had ships and could sail. Somebody sailed west and landed here . . . maybe a thousand years ago."[16]

Later in act 1, Pat Gibson, the hero and veteran of the Battle of King's Mountain, goes to meet with Cherokee Chief Atakullakulla. Atakullakulla offers military support if the Melungeons want to hold their ground. The tradition that the Melungeons and the Cherokees had long been friends is underscored by this offer and by reference to the way the Melungeons regularly supplied the "Indians" with food. The script demonstrates Hunter's familiarity and sympathy for the Cherokees, which he undoubtedly gained by researching and writing "Unto These Hills." Gibson thanks Atakullakulla and Chief Dragging Canoe but declines their help and tells them that neither the Melungeons nor the Cherokees should fight the encroaching whites because the whites are so numerous that they will win in the long run.

It seems that Pat has decided that the Melungeons should move to a place that Atakullakulla tells him about:

---

[14]Patricia Spurlock Elder, *Melungeons: Examining an Appalachian Legend* (Blountville TN: Continuity Press, 1999) 55, 60-61.

[15]Hunter, "Walk toward the Sunset," 9.

[16]Hunter, "Walk toward the Sunset," 10.

> To the north, across three valleys and three mountains, there
> is a great range of high hills, cut off from the rest of the world,
> so far that not even the Red Man travels there. Wild game is
> plentiful, forests are green and rich, the land is good for grow-
> ing.[17]

The description of the land the Melungeons are heading for sounds like
the area just north of Sneedville near Newman's Ridge and Powell Mountain. According to Pat Elder's research, Indians had used the area as
hunting grounds, but no tribe had built a town in this valley—it was a
sort of no-man's land used for hunting by different tribes.[18] The
Melungeons' move is already a sure thing when the drama's hero Pat
Gibson accidentally murders the settlers' scout, Cantrell, in a scuffle. The
murder accelerates the action, and act 1 ends with the move imminent.
The Cherokees will set the whole valley on fire as the Melungeons leave
in order to spite the incoming whites. Pat and Alisee will marry—a
happy event in the tradition of comedy (where marriages often occur at
the end of a drama to signify resolution of the issues raised in the play)
in the midst of much sadness.

Most of the characters that are supposed to be Melungeon in the
drama are designated as dark-skinned in the stage directions; however,
Alissee, like Deutsia Huntoon in Stuart's *Daughter of the Legend*, is blond
and blue-eyed, a fact Daniel Boone states in the dialog. "Well, look at this
girl! Whoever saw a slave or an Indian with yellow hair and blue eyes?"[19]

Act 2 opens in Sneedville at a Fourth of July celebration. There is a
new set of characters. Vance Johnson is a Civil War veteran, studying law
and very much in love with Cora Sylvester, a Melungeon girl whose
grandfather was killed at King's Mountain. These lovers face prejudice
against their plan to marry from both whites and Melungeons.[20] Another
important event—probably the reason act 2 is set in 1868—is the repeal
of the 1834 Tennessee law that had denied rights to "persons of color."

---

[17]Hunter, "Walk toward the Sunset," 15.

[18]Elder, *Melungeons*, 58.

[19]Hunter, "Walk toward the Sunset," 8.

[20]Marriages across racial lines did meet with much disapproval from both
sides. However, the beauty of Melungeon girls was legendary. There was less
stigma associated with a white man marrying a Melungeon woman than with the
reverse situation. Melungeon men who chose to marry white girls could expect
to be chased down by either legitimate lawmen or vigilantes. Either way
punishment could be extreme.

Hero Vance is able to tell the Melungeons about this important change. Vance also acts as an advocate for the Melungeons in negotiations with the Slab Fork Lumber Company that wants to log Newman's Ridge. The company tries to get the lumber they want at very low and unfair prices; Vance insists that the Melungeons will do the logging themselves and be paid fairly for the timber or else there will be no deal.

The issue of origins comes up again in the second act. In one scene, Cora and her father are with Vance in Nashville talking to John Netherland, an East Tennessee politician, and Tennessee governor, Senter. This scene underscores the importance of the new law granting Melungeons rights to legal property ownership, suffrage, and education. Netherland explains to Senter just who Melungeons are:

> Dark-skinned people living on the high ridges in Hancock County . . . scattered all through that Clinch and Powell country . . . not Indian, not black. But . . . there's been a lot of intermarriages by now, even with whites. The pure Melungeon of fifty years ago was exactly like you and me, except with a dark skin.[21]

Hunter has a character in act 1 mention that Melungeons are and have long been Christian—"good, decent, God-fearin' people."[22] In act 2, Christianity comes up again. Mr. Netherland questions John Sylvester about religion and in the answer gets a little history as well.

> JOHN
> The old folks used to tell about living close to the ocean. I always assumed it was Charleston, or Wilmington, or somewhere like that.
> NETHERLAND
> What church before the Baptist and Holiness?
> JOHN
> A lot of families still have Church of England prayer-books, Mr. Netherland, published in Seventeen Forty-Five.[23]

The discussion continues with Netherland asserting that education is extremely important in order for the Melungeons not to "drift back to the primitive."[24]

---

[21]Hunter, "Walk toward the Sunset," 30-31.
[22]Hunter, "Walk toward the Sunset," 9.
[23]Hunter, "Walk toward the Sunset," 34.
[24]Hunter, "Walk toward the Sunset," 34.

The residents of Sneedville and the Melungeons are on the road to living happily ever after only after Cora organizes a group of Melungeon men and women, immune to smallpox from an earlier epidemic, to nurse the valley folk through an outbreak of the dreaded fever. Driven by her love for Vance and her sense of what is right, winsome Cora is able to persuade the Melungeon women to go to town. By means of tender loving care and herb remedies passed to the Melungeons from the Cherokees, the smallpox epidemic is conquered. Cora's future mother-in-law is one of those who recovers, renewed in body and transformed in mind. Cora's father, John, promises to be the foreman on the logging crew and to provide "enough Hancock County corn liquor to make everybody forget about the smallpox and everything else."[25] This line lets the audience know about the tradition that Melungeons make the best moonshine whiskey in the mountains.

One other particular detail worth noting is Hunter's use of typical Melungeon surnames. Gibson, Bowlin, and Sylvester are names given to characters in the play. Hunter intersperses these with common English names like Robinson and Givins.

Hunter packs a great deal of information into a relatively short piece of writing. He mentions many facts of Melungeon history and reveals with accuracy the prejudicial attitudes in East Tennessee that in addition to the discriminatory laws made life difficult for the Melungeon people. However, in spite of factual accuracy, the play seems shallow. The characters are like one-dimensional icons instead of real people. One could argue that the form, that of outdoor theater, is a constraint; however, the ancient Greeks worked in the same sort of physical setting and added masks to the characters' costumes so that even the tool of facial expressions was lost. No one can accuse Antigone or Oedipus of being a one-dimensional character.

Furthermore, someone writing such a drama today might focus on the same issues—racial prejudice and local history—but in different ways. Racial equality was a 1960s crusade, and while still a problem in our society, the focus is different. The laws of the land now mandate equal opportunities for all; the problems are the more subtle ones of attitude. Certainly the Indians would also be treated differently as well. In his play, Hunter buys into the sterotype of Native Americans as violent warriors. The fact that the Cherokees invite the Melungeons to settle in their hunting ground seems unrealistic as well.

---

[25]Hunter, "Walk toward the Sunset," 47.

The play is didactic, but that characteristic cannot accurately be labeled a fault, especially in light of the Institute of Outdoor Drama's definition—"original plays, often with music and dance, based on significant events and performed in amphitheatres located where the events actually occurred; . . . they focus on the people who shaped the heritage of the country."[26]

"Walk toward the Sunset," the Sneedville drama that is our focus here, did come out of a sincere desire of the Hancock County community in the late 1960s to document and commemorate the history of the Melungeons. However, according to Hunter, the drama failed to persist for several reasons: the remoteness of the location where it was produced, the poor quality of the production, and small audiences.[27] It did, nonetheless, have the effect of changing attitudes of many local people. Wayne Winkler notes in his NPR documentary that the drama made being a Melungeon something to be proud of—a situation that had neither existed nor been documented before. Never formally published, the copy of the script that I used for this analysis was in a folder on a shelf in the drama department at Carson Newman College complete with pencil marks and notations that the director made for a production in the summer of 1976. Hunter graciously consented to the E. W. King Library's request to copy the document and add it to the library's collection. "Walk toward the Sunset" is a unique piece of writing in the canon of fiction that includes Melungeon characters. There is interest from time to time on the Melungeon e-mail list to produce it once again. Perhaps that will happen soon in Wise, Virginia, at a Melungeon gathering like Fourth Union, or in Sneedville at some future Fall Festival.

---

[26]Institute of Outdoor Drama homepage accessed 12 April 2000, at <http://www.unc.edu/depts/outdoor/newindex.html>.

[27]Hunter, telephone interview, 11 April 2000.

10

Watch Your Chimney: Kentucky Melungeons in Two Stories by Chris Offutt

Award-winning writer Chris Offutt was born on 24 August 1958 in Haldeman, a clay-mining town that no longer officially exists, in Rowan County, Kentucky. He graduated from Morehead State University with a degree in theater and a minor in art and later attended the famous Writer's Workshop at the University of Iowa, earning an MFA in 1990. His plaudits include the Michener Grant while he was at Iowa; recognitions from the Guggenheim Foundation, the American Academy of Arts and Letters, and the Whiting Foundation; and a position on Granta's "20 Best Young American Fiction Writers" list. His works include magazine articles, two volumes of short stories, *Kentucky Straight* (1992) and *Out of the Woods* (1999), a novel called *The Good Brother* (1997), and a memoir titled *The Same River Twice* (1993).

Son of a prolific science fiction writer, Offutt left Kentucky when he was nineteen to wander the country and in the process worked a series of odd jobs from freelance writing to housepainting to circus performing and dabbled in petty crime,[1] but he could never shake the spell nor the pull of the hills. Offutt journaled during his years away from his native land and once while he was in New York City wrote:

> The journal was my combat arena, the final refuge of privacy in a city of eight million. Each day I saw perhaps two thousand different faces, an enjoyable fact until I realized that my face was one of the two thousand each of them saw too. My math collapsed from the exponential strain. Jahi wasn't in my journal. Those pages were filled with me. Some of the pages held my full name and place of birth on every line to remind me that I lived.[2]

---

[1]See "Chris Offut," in *Contemporary Authors*, vol. 154.

[2]Chris Offutt, "Journals of the Author," quoted by Brett Ralph in "Chris Offutt" at <http://www.raintaxi.com/offutt.htm>, accessed 6 October 1999.

Fellow Kentuckian Brett Ralph comments, "Filling page after page
with his name and place of birth reveals the two things Offutt took with
him on his journey, the only two things any of us can carry long: who we
are and where we're from."[3] Offutt's own sense of identity that may well
be rooted in his sense of place is a prototype for many of his characters.

Offutt treats the wandering/homecoming topic in many of his stories.
He has written about his current coming back to Eastern Kentucky in an
essay that appeared in the *New York Times Magazine*:

> No matter how you leave the hills—army, prison, marriage,
> job, college—when you move back after 20 years the whole
> county is watching carefully. They want to see the changes the
> outside world put on you. . . . Put their mind at ease. . . . Make
> sure and drive a rusty pickup that runs like a sewing machine.
> Hang dice from the mirror and a gun rack in the back window.
> A rifle isn't necessary, but something needs to be there: a pool
> cue, a carpenter's level, an ax handle. . . . Tell them it's a big
> world out there. . . . Don't talk about the beautiful people in
> stylish clothes. Never mention museums, opera, theater, or ethnic
> restaurants. . . . Be prepared at all times to say it's better here.
> You spent 20 years trying to leave this land and 20 more trying
> to get back.[4]

Offutt may be tongue-in-cheek here. Does the sentence offhandedly
describing the second twenty years of his life go with the deprecation, or
does it express his own deep longing for the land of his raising? In truth,
both this author and his readers must face the fact that he did come back.
I have heard Brent Kennedy make an identical statement.[5] For sons of

---

[3]Ralph, "Chris Offutt."

[4]Chris Offutt, "Home to the Hills," *New York Times Magazine* (25 October 1998).

[5]Brent Kennedy, talk at East Tennessee State University, 29 September 1997.

Appalachia, and maybe even for daughters,[6] the love/hate, leaving/re-turning behavior is a common theme.

Offutt is now teaching writing, with somewhat mixed emotions, at Morehead State University. In an interview with Rhonda Reeves for a cover story in *Ace Magazine,* he admits he finds teaching exhausting and then adds that it should be so if one would do a creditable job.[7] Offutt in-dicates in the same interview that he deplores the author's conundrum— "the irony of a successful writer is to get a teaching gig—and no writers I know want to do that." He goes on to state this paradox: "as soon as you develop your craft, there's pressure to give up the time [devoted to] writing."[8]

Offutt is above all a consummate stylist: not one word is wasted. His stories are tightly woven, stretched, and the prose is memorable. According to *Newsday's* Dan Cryer, "The hills and hollers of Chris Offutt's fiction sing a mournful siren song. . . . This is beautiful prose—as clear and pure and flowing as a mountain stream."[9] His use of dialect is sure and natural. "He . . . writes of simple people who find themselves face-to-face with that moment when luck runs out or fate deals its dire hand. . . . [H]e is so Kentucky-to-the-bone that his voice and people are unmistakably his own."[10]

Offutt has written two short stories that focus on Melungeon charac-ters. The main character in each story has a moment of mesmerizing self-realization. Both of the narratives feature Melungeon men who have left the hills and returned. In "Smokehouse" from *Kentucky Straight,* Duke,

---

[6]On the other hand, maybe many of the daughters truly love and value the land from the beginning. Gertie Nevels in *The Dollmaker,* Millie Ballew in *Hunter's Horn,* Mary Dorthula White in *The Hawk's Done Gone* and Alpha Baldridge in *River of Earth* are examples of strong mountain women who are very clear about their love for the land and the growing things it produces. They share none of their men's desire to make money and have the technological gadgets that money can buy. The only female character I can think of who leaves the hills and then spends many of her adult years trying to return is Katie Cocker in *The Devil's Dream.*

[7]Rhonda Reeves, "Back to the Woods," accessed 9 October 1999, at <http://www.acemagazine.com/backissues/981125/coverstory_981125.html>.

[8]Reeves, "Back to the Woods."

[9]Dan Cryer, "Kentucky Bluegrass Runs in Their Veins," *Newsday,* accessed online on 14 June 1999, at <http://www.elibrary.com/s/edumark/ . . . 836498 @library_I&dtype+0~0&dinst+0>.

[10]Cryer, "Kentucky Bluegrass Runs in Their Veins."

the character who provokes the story's conflict has been gone from the community where he grew up for twenty-five years.

> Many years ago there'd been trouble in the coalfields and Duke was arrested for defending his brother. The law gave Duke a choice: join the army or go to jail. He spent twenty-five years in the military, and returned with a Vietnamese wife and no children.[11]

In "Melungeons," from *Out of the Woods*, two characters have gone and returned: Haze Gipson left to find work up north and Ephraim Goins volunteered to serve in Korea (where he was decorated as a hero) to avoid the pressure of a violent mountain feud. In both of these stories, the identities of the characters are tied not only to the Kentucky ground from which they have sprung, but also to being Melungeon and understanding all the nuances of what being Melungeon means. The question of identity, of wanting to know and then finally knowing who they are, is an important theme.

In "Melungeons," Goins says to Gipson, "We're somebody, ain't we."[12] This declaration, which not incidentally has the syntactical word order of a question, is, according to reviewer Brian Alexander, the cry of the Everyman that Offutt's characters portray.[13]

> Offutt's stories of these people are especially welcome now, as we sprint headlong into the mass global village of the information age, another form of going. What will happen to us all, he seems to ask in his short, clipped sentences. Will we have a home? Will we be with people who know us, know who we are, know our families and our traditions as we know theirs? Will we chafe? Or will we be cut loose?[14]

Both of Offutt's Melungeon-focused stories raise important questions and offer brutally violent and honest answers.

"Smokehouse" tells what happens to five mountain men who have known each other all their lives during and after a poker game in

---

[11]Chris Offutt, "Smokehouse," in *Kentucky Straight* (New York: Vintage, 1992) 96.

[12]Chris Offutt, "Melungeons," in *Out of the Woods* (New York: Simon & Schuster, 1999) 48.

[13]Brian Alexander, "Lost in America," *San Diego Union-Tribune*, 17 January 1999.

[14]Alexander, "Lost in America."

Catfish's smokehouse on a snowy winter night. The story is tense with foreboding because of the extreme weather and the presence of coyotes, who have come back to the hills "after the mines shut down and people left."[15] The men trade insults as well as money. The main character, Fenton, by winning the last hand, breaks even for the night. Just after he leaves the smokehouse to walk home, he slips and falls hitting his head on a rock. When he comes to under the questioning stare of a coyote, he realizes he cannot make it home and goes back to the smokehouse. He hears two pistol shots—Connor's ambush of Duke in order to avenge the felt insults of Duke's bluff during the game and Duke's maddening attitude of superiority. Fenton doesn't know the outcome; his more pressing problem is needing to rekindle the fire. He has to use the paper money, his winnings, for kindling. Injured and frost-bitten ("Twice he had to warm his hands against the fading heat of the stove. His fingers were black and smoking but didn't hurt."[16]), Fenton has his epiphany.

> He felt very old and realized that being forty-four meant knowing what not to do. Twenty years before he'd have waited with Connor [to participate vicariously in the excitement of the ambush on the ridge in the snow and the dark]. Maybe in another twenty, he'd warn Duke straight out.[17]

This story, as so many other pieces of fiction about Melungeons, turns on a bit of Melungeon lore. Early in the story, the limited omniscient narrator[18] explains why the men have to go outside for a drink.

> Three years ago Catfish had banned liquor after a scuffle that left a man shot in the forearm. . . . A day later someone shot the shooter's chimney off his roof, following the old Melungeon code of warning. Vengeance escalated until a man was killed and then another in retaliation.[19]

---

[15]Offutt, "Smokehouse," 93.

[16]Offutt, "Smokehouse," 111.

[17]Offutt, "Smokehouse," 111-12.

[18]The term "limited omniscient narrator" means that the person telling the story can see into at least one character's mind in addition to having the voice that describes the events. In this story the narrator knows a lot of background information and also knows what Fenton is thinking. The narrator does not see into the minds of any of the other characters.

[19]Offutt, "Smokehouse," 99.

This custom of shooting the chimney off an offender's roof as a warning, of course, becomes important as the plot unfolds. Fenton's actions in the story and his thoughts show that he is changing, moving away from the impulsiveness of youth.

The last poker hand, seven-card stud, is described in detail. Catfish deals and dramatically names each card as he puts it down. We as readers know only Fenton's two hole cards. He has two pair, Queens and sixes, early. Hoping for a full house, he stays in the game against Connor who has four cards in a straight showing and Duke who has four diamonds up. If Duke actually has a straight and Fenton a full house, Connor knows that he would hold the least valuable cards. Poker, of course, in addition to being a game of cards is a game of nerves. Duke is the real gambler, bluffing against the other two. He never looks at his last card; pushing it under the money piled on the table, he claims he doesn't need it—implying that at least one of his two early down cards is a diamond. Connor actually does have a straight, but he lacks enough cash to ante up and he doesn't want to risk betting his truck. Fenton, with two pair does some quick figuring.

> Fenton's last card was worthless, leaving him with the two pair. He began counting diamonds. He'd seen seven and Duke was showing four more, which left two for the flush. Duke hadn't bet early. He'd been fishing then, and Fenton realized it was a bluff. Duke had nothing. If Fenton won, he'd be even for the night.[20]

So, Fenton calls Duke and raises the bet. The tension snaps as the hand ends with Duke never even showing his cards. Fenton has correctly seen through his bluff.

> [Duke] turned his cards face down and pushed the money across the table. Connor stood, clattering his chair to the floor. His pupils were barely rimmed by iris. He swayed for a moment, trying to speak.
> "The house?" he finally said. "you got a full house?'
> "You don't want to know," Fenton said.
> Connor flipped Fenton's cards to show his hand.
> "Two pair," Connor said. His upper lip rose, showing teeth the size of soup beans. "That's my pot," he said.

---

[20]Offutt, "Smokehouse," 104.

Duke's voice came hard and mean.
"Stay off that money."[21]

Duke's audacity and his attitude are salt in the wound in Connor's pride. Connor leaves the game mad. When his old truck won't start, he refuses to try Duke's jumper cables because they are Duke's, and indicates to Fenton, who goes out in the storm to help him kindle a small fire to thaw the truck's block, that the pistol on the truck's seat will not stay there.

This last hand of poker is not the only incident between Duke and Connor. Earlier in the story Duke makes a categorical statement about how fire burns that makes the men uneasy. This duel with words escalates into a showdown between Connor and Duke.

"It's not wood that burns. . . . "Oxygen burns, not wood,"
Duke said. . . .
His voice held a tone of finality that silenced the men. Fenton didn't know if Duke was joking or presenting fact. Maybe he'd learned something in his years away, or maybe his sights were a little off.[22]

This discussion precipitates a more physical confrontation between Duke and Connor. Connor asserts that his penis is the biggest in the house.

"I'll bet twenty dollars against five I got the stoutest here."
The men grinned shaking their heads. . . .
"Maybe I got what you're after," Duke said. His head was tipped forward, mouth tight, eyes hard. He snapped a five-dollar bill between his hands. "I'll take your bet." . . .
Connor scooted his chair away from the table, slowly stood and turned around. The back of his belt loosened and his jeans went slack. His right arm pumped twice. . . . Connor was cheating with a couple of strikes. Suddenly he spun back, his genitals swinging at the dusky edge of the lantern's light.
Duke's hands lay across his eyes.
"You win," he said. "I fold."

---

[21]Offutt, "Smokehouse," 105.
[22]Offutt, "Smokehouse," 100.

"You never looked." Connor's face turned red as he quickly stuffed and zipped his pants. "I don't know what to say about a man who makes a bet and don't look at the cards."[23]

This incident, of course, establishes the pattern that is played out again in the last hand of poker. If we missed the point, Duke makes it plain to Fenton and the others after Connor has exited, when he says with a tight-lipped smile, " 'All I lost was money.' He poured whiskey into the flask lid and drank it, staring at Fenton [Fenton had wagered his gold inlaid bridgework in the final hand when his cash ran low]. 'I got all my teeth and nobody saw my wiener. I won what counted.' "[24] Duke has perhaps been gone from the community long enough to be oblivious to the threat he is under by virtue of Connor's wrath. Yet, I as a far-removed reader am reminded once again of Old Man Harkryder's warning about Melungeons: "ain't no telling what them folk will do."[25] And Fenton is nervous enough to warn Duke as he leaves the smoke-house, "Watch your chimney."[26]

Fenton's wife is Melungeon, and both Duke and W. (one of the characters is called "W.") have Melungeon blood, but Connor is the story's true Melungeon character. He's the one the others give a wider berth. Offutt spends time detailing Connor's looks and personality.

> Once a month Connor went to Rocksalt with the purpose of going to jail. He'd been married and divorced three times, and now slept with other men's wives. Connor's features marked him pure Melungeon: high cheekbones, black hair, brown skin, and pale blue eyes. He was rat-tail skinny from eating diet pills.[27]

As the story progresses, Connor is shown to be fidgety, touchy, and slightly reckless. His betting is transparent; he is ill equipped against the more calculating Duke. He has what some might term the Melungeon chip on his shoulder—imagining slights where none are intended, enlarging small barbs into major insults, spoiling for a fight. However, Offutt is too careful a writer to rely on the stereotype alone. He builds his story meticulously, making Duke, the outsider by virtue of his years away, a real villain who must prove his superiority.

---

[23]Offutt, "Smokehouse," 101-102.
[24]Offutt, "Smokehouse," 109.
[25]Sharyn McCrumb, *She Walks These Hills* (New York: Signet, 1994) 119.
[26]Offutt, "Smokehouse," 109.
[27]Offutt, "Smokehouse," 95-96.

We never learn what actually happens between the two. Like both Fenton in the smokehouse trying to get a fire going against the cold of a frigid night to fend off both the frostbite that could mean his death and the predatory coyote that has watched as Fenton came to out in the snow, we only hear two unanswered shots. As the story closes, Fenton like the character in Jack London's "To Build a Fire" curls up. He curls up in a smokehouse, a place where dead meat is cured by smoking wood chips. I don't think, as he does, that he will live for Catfish to find him in the morning.

This story does address the issue of where the Melungeons came from originally and some of the commonly held beliefs about them. "Melungeons lived deepest in the hills, were the finest trackers and hunters. They were already there when the European settlers arrived. Melungeons weren't black, white, or Indian, and they didn't know where they'd come from."[28] The county judge, who only gets one line in the story, is said to be prejudiced: "Connor had already served thirty days for assault and the county judge didn't like him. He'd made it clear that Melungeons should stay where they belonged."[29] Fenton has married a Melungeon woman apparently without initial ostracism, but even Catfish, his best friend, must be wheedled out of a prejudicial stance after the shooting incident that precipitated a double killing of vengeance before the events in this story take place. As a result of that incident,

> Catfish shut down the game for six months. When he reopened, he barred guns and whiskey, and considered banning Melungeons. Fenton argued that Connor and W. claimed Melungeon blood and would take it the wrong way. Since Fenton's wife was Melungeon, he'd have to follow the ban as well. Catfish relented. He understood that loyalty to his friend meant preventing Fenton from having to choose a side.[30]

Like Dave Stoneking in *Daughter of the Legend*, Fenton is Melungeon by marriage and therefore must bear the consequences, being treated like a Melungeon in all respects.

Offutt surely knows his territory—Eastern Kentucky—and understands those who inhabit it, including Melungeons. He shows that even those inside the "family" are not above playing on the stereotypes and

---

[28]Offutt, "Smokehouse," 94.
[29]Offutt, "Smokehouse," 108.
[30]Offutt, "Smokehouse," 99.

prejudices that outsiders use against them. This is even clearer in the story "Melungeons" from *Out of the Woods*. In addition to the themes of allegiance to place and articulation of identity, this very compact narrative that has only three characters (all Melungeons) adds another dimension, a blood feud. And from the story it is not difficult to deduce that one of the cruelest results of marginalization of people for generations results in a heightened sense of the primacy of the honor due a family's name and the lengths some will go to preserve both honor and name.

The first character we meet in the story is Deputy Ephraim Goins. At sixty-three, he is the longtime deputy and jailer in the town of Rocksalt. We learn that he left Kentucky for an interesting reason.

> Goins wasn't born when the trouble started between the Gipson and Mullins clans, but he'd felt the strain of its tension all his life. Members of his family had married both sides. To avoid the pressure of laying claim to either, Goins had volunteered to serve in Korea. Uniforms rather than blood would clarify the enemy. . . .
>
> On a routine patrol Goins became separated from the rest, and was not missed until the sound of gunfire. American soldiers found him bleeding from two bullet holes and a bayonet wound. Five enemy lay dead around him. Goins was decorated with honor and returned to Kentucky, but stayed in town. He didn't want to live near killing. Out of respect for its only hero, the town overlooked which hill he was from. Now the town had forgotten.[31]

Goins thinks he has come to terms with his past. He has stuffed his problems with his Melungeonness by ignoring and/or avoiding it. He admits that he has missed all of his family's special events like weddings and funerals, and he never goes up on the ridge. "He didn't hunt or fish anymore, had stopped gathering mushrooms and ginseng. Being in the woods was too painful when he didn't live there. The last few times he'd felt awkward and foreign, as if the land was mocking him."[32] Yet there are stirrings in him. After a sleepless night,

> [a]t dawn he rose and looked at the hills. He missed living with the land most in autumn, when the trees seemed suddenly splashed in color, and rutting deer snorted in the hollows. There

---

[31]Offutt, "Melungeons" (see n. 12 above), 39-40.
[32]Offutt, "Melungeons," 41.

were walnuts to gather, bees to rob. Turkeys big as dogs jumped from ridgelines to extend their flight.

He rubbed his face and turned from the window, reminding himself of why he'd stayed in Rocksalt. Town was warm. It had cable TV and water. He was treated as everyone's equal, but his years in town had taught him to hide his directness, the Melungeon way of point-blank living.[33]

Goins, even though he has renounced his raising, needs to belong in some way even if that way is only in his head. He flirts with the Melungeon origin theories by clipping and saving until it is brittle an article from a Lexington paper.

It was a feature story suggesting that Melungeons were descendants of Madoc, a Welsh explorer in the twelfth century. Alternate theories labeled them as shipwrecked Portuguese, Phoenicians, Turks, or one of Israel's lost tribes. It was the only information Goins had ever seen about Melungeons. The article called them a vanishing race.[34]

Goins's drive to belong shows in his explanation of his views on Melungeon origins to his prisoner, Haze Gipson:

"I kindly favor that lost tribe of Israel idea," [he says] . . . "I've give thought to it. Them people then moved around more than a cat. Your name's off Hezekiah and mine's Ephraim. I knowed a Nimrod once. Got a cousin Zephaniah married a Ruth."[35]

When Gipson is unconvinced, Goins continues his train of thought after he goes back to his desk. "A preacher had donated a Bible for the prisoners and Goins hunted through Genesis for his namesake, the leader of a lost tribe who never made it to the land of milk and honey. He hoped it was hilly."[36]

Goins is definitely the main character of "Melungeons." His epiphany comes after violence, when the feud begun sixty years before between the Gipsons and the Mullinses resumes inside the jail as the old mountain woman kills Haze Gipson with a sawed off shotgun. Goins is faced not

---

[33]Offutt, "Melungeons," 46–47.
[34]Offutt, "Melungeons," 47.
[35]Offutt, "Melungeons," 48.
[36]Offutt, "Melungeons," 48–49.

only with a bloody mess to clean up, but also with all that he has run away from since adolescence.

> The sound bounced off the stone walls and up the hall to his office, echoing back and forth, until it faded. Goins jerked upright in the chair. His legs began to shiver. He held his thighs tightly and the shivering traveled up his arms until his entire body shook. He pressed his forehead against the desk.[37]

Deputy Goins does only the most necessary tasks. He locks up Beulah Mullins, the murderer. He goes back to his desk.

> He put the Bible away and found the prisoner's log and wrote Mullins. Under yesterday's date he wrote Gipson. Goins rubbed his eyes. He didn't write Haze because the man was down to a body now, and the body was a Melungeon. Goins covered his face with his hands. It was true for him as well.[38]

At this moment in the story, Goins realizes that he is Melungeon now and forever and that he must do something radical to ratify this new knowledge. It is not an accident that he steps outside the jail into the morning light; for Goins it is a new day at the beginning of a new era in his life. It is interesting that the citizens of Rocksalt, among whom he has lived and worked ever since he got back from Korea, do not immediately know him. Perhaps his epiphany has really altered even his looks, or perhaps as a Melungeon out of the usual Melungeon mold he has been invisible.

> He opened the door and stepped into the sun. People ducked for cover until they recognized him. He looked at them, men and women he'd known for thirty years, but never really knew. Beyond them stood the hills that hemmed the town. He began walking east, toward the nearest slope. There was nothing he needed to take. The sun was warm against his face.[39]

His peace with nature and satisfaction with what the mountain offers is reminiscent of Mildred Haun's stories where the resolution of the action is just as brutal and the contentment with the beauty and rightness of the mountain habitat is just as strong.

---

[37]Offutt, "Melungeons," 51.
[38]Offutt, "Melungeons," 52-53.
[39]Offutt, "Melungeons," 53.

Haze Gipson, who met his demise at the hand of Beulah Mullins inside the supposed safety of the Rocksalt jail, is the second Melungeon character in this story. Haze was seventy-six. That would have made him an adolescent when the feud began.

> Sixty years before, five Mullins men were logging a hillside at the southern edge of their property when a white oak slipped sideways from its notch. The beveled point dug into the earth. Instead of falling parallel with the creek, the oak dropped onto their neighbor's land and splintered a hollow log. Dislodged tree leaves floated in the breeze. When the men crossed the creek, they found a black bear crushed to death inside the hollow log. They built a fire for the night and ate the liver, tongue, and six pounds of greasy fat.
>
> In the morning, a hunting party of Gipsons discovered the camp. The land was theirs and they demanded the meat. Since the Mullins men had already butchered the bear, they offered half. The Gipsons refused. Three men died in a quick gunfight. The rest crept through the woods, leaking blood from bullet wounds. Over the next two decades, twenty-eight more people were killed, a few per year.[40]

Gipson does not say why he left Kentucky, but he implies that finding work may not have been the only reason.

> "You don't know who I am, do you?" [he says to Goins]. . . .
> 'I'm the one that left and went north."[41]

When Goins asks him why he has come back, he replies,

> "I've got give out on it. . . . I'm seventy-six years old. Missed every wedding and funeral my family had. . . . Some of my grandkids have got kids," Gipson said. "You don't know what it's like to see them all at once. And them not to know you."[42]

Goins probes a little more asking about the feud.

> "You were up to the mountain?" Goins said.
> The man nodded.

---

[40]Offutt, "Melungeons," 43–44.
[41]Offutt, "Melungeons," 41.
[42]Offutt, "Melungeons," 41–42.

"Bad as ever?"

"Not so much as it was. They're married in now and don't bother with it no more. The kids have got a game of it, play-acting. I look for it to stop when the next bunch gets born. Still ain't full safe for me. I'm the last of the old Gipsons left alive."

He moved to face the wall again.[43]

This exchange has dark implications in it, underscored by the fact that Gipson has deliberately gotten himself incarcerated by urinating on the front steps of the jail in Goins's presence.

Goins hopes that Gipson will be gone in the morning of his own accord, but he must secretly doubt because he takes from its keeping place the clipping from the Lexington paper to show to Gipson. Gipson is neither impressed nor interested really. When Goins pleads,

"We're somebody, ain't we," [Gipson expostulates,] "We damn sure ain't Phoenicians or Welshes. We ain't even Melungeons except in the paper. It don't matter where we upped from. It's who we are now that matters."[44]

Ironically, Gipson at the end is reduced to a body, a Melungeon body. He becomes some-body in death, the status he denied in life.

Goins's quest for a history, an origin, is strong. He would like to ask the old woman as she stands before him with the blackened pot that exudes the musk of fresh game, but "he knew from looking at her that she wouldn't know or care."[45] And finally, he must accept the here-and-now definition that Haze Gipson and Beulah Mullins thrust upon him. He must acknowledge the pull of the ridges of his childhood, the reality of the feud, the realization that no one in town knows or cares about him after all, and that he needs nothing he has gathered in his sixty-three years of living—not his TV, not the comforts of modern life, not an intellectual conception of who he is—to thrive on the mountain where he was raised.

The third Melungeon in the story is Beulah Mullins. She is eighty-six years old, plagued with arthritis in her hands and pain in her legs, but hampered by neither, Beulah is a dark and menacing figure from the first mention of her. She has for many years nursed the anger that demands revenge. She would have been twenty-six when the feud began. Perhaps

---

[43]Offutt, "Melungeons," 42.
[44]Offutt, "Melungeons," 48.
[45]Offutt, "Melungeons," 50.

she lost a lover or a husband; we are never told. This woman is Melungeon to the very center of her being. She has never left Kentucky, and she has only been to town once in her long life before she goes there to kill Haze Gipson.

> Beulah had never voted or paid taxes. There was no record of her birth. The only time she'd been to town, she'd bought nails for a hogpen. Her family usually burned old buildings for nails, plucking them hot from the debris, but that year a spring flood had washed them away. Beulah had despised Rocksalt and swore never to return. Tonight she had no choice. She left her house within an hour of learning that Haze was on the mountain.[46]

Like the tracker she is, Beulah can read the out-of-doors the way others read the newspaper.

> A flock of vireos lifted from a maple by the creek, a thick cloud of dark specks that narrowed at the end like a tadpole. Beulah watched them knowing that winter would arrive early. She scented town before she saw the buildings. . . .
> Beulah moved downwind of a police car. She couldn't read, but knew that an automobile with writing on its side was like a tied dog. Whoever held the leash controlled it.[47]

She pauses near the railroad to listen to a cardinal and to notice the morning mist in the hollow. She walks out of her way to avoid the neon sign at the diner.

Beulah has planned carefully and never wavers from her determined course of action. She carries a gamebag with an iron pot of stew in it. This item will be her entrée to the cell area of the small jail; the deputy will not question an old woman bringing food to an old man. Under her long coat she conceals the sawed-off shotgun. It makes her walking awkward as if, Offutt says, she were straining with gout. She enters the jail confidently because she knows it is the only place Haze could have gone. She scoops a squirrel leg and a potato onto the plate Goins provides lulling him into thinking her visit is benevolent. He in fact thinks her harmless, "Goins understood that she was following the old code of proving the pot contained no file or pistol. He relaxed some. She

---

[46]Offutt, "Melungeons," 43.
[47]Offutt, "Melungeons," 45.

wasn't here for trouble."[48] He plays her game, tasting the meat and nodding to signify that she can proceed down the hall.

In the split second before the shotgun blast Goins hears something ominous. "Behind him he heard the woman say one word soaked in the fury of half a century."[49] Only after the deed is done is there any uncontrolled response in her. Offutt writes:

> The woman stepped to the next cell and waited while he un-locked the door. Her face seemed softer. She stepped inside. When the door clanked shut, her back stiffened, and she lifted her head to the gridded square of sky visible through the small window.[50]

Only after the revenge is accomplished does she mourn what she has given up forever, her life on the mountain under the open sky.

White folks' lore about Melungeons is also mentioned in this story:

> [Goins] remembered his fourth-grade teacher threatening a child who was always late to school. "If you don't get up on time," the teacher had said, "the Melungeons will get you."
>
> Melungeons weren't white, black, or Indian. They lived deep in the hills, on the most isolated ridges, pushed from the hollows two centuries back by the people following Boone. The Shawnee called them "white Indians," and told the settlers that they'd al-ways lived there. Melungeons continued to live as they always had.[51]

Physical characteristics and their effects are also noted. First, Goins.

> When a dentist noticed that his gums were tinged with blue, the army assigned Goins to an all-black company. Black soldiers treated him with open scorn. The whites refused to acknowledge him at all. Only one man befriended him, a New Yorker named Abe, whom no one liked because he was Jewish.[52]

---

[48]Offutt, "Melungeons," 50.
[49]Offutt, "Melungeons," 51.
[50]Offutt, "Melungeons," 52.
[51]Offutt, "Melungeons," 38-39.
[52]Offutt, "Melungeons," 39.

Next, Gipson. "He lifted his head, showing blue eyes in rough contrast with his black hair and smooth, swarthy skin"[53]—the typical Melungeon phenotype. When Goins, probably trying to relate Gipson's experience with his own, asks, "What'd they take you for up there?" Gipson says, "Went by ever who else was around. Italian mostly. Couple times a Puerto Rican till they heard me talk."[54]

Finally, Beulah, on whom Offutt spends a few more words. "Beulah's face was dark as a ripe paw-paw. Checkered gingham wrapped her head, covering five feet of grey hair."[55] When she arrives at her destination we get a description that plays on many senses.

> The jail's front door slowly creaked open and a woman's form eclipsed the light that flowed around her. She stepped inside. Goins didn't know her, but he knew her. It was as if the mountain itself had entered the tiny room, filling it with earth and rain, the steady wind along the ridge. She gazed at him, one eye dark, the other yellow-flecked. Between the lines of her face ran many smaller lines like rain gulleys running to creeks. She'd been old when he was young.[56]

All three of these characters, in addition to their Melungeon looks, have carefully chosen Melungeon surnames—Goins, Gipson, and Mullins. They also have first names that come from the Bible, a common occurrence in Melungeon families. A final quality they share is an emotional toughness that is almost stoic, perhaps even bred in by years of persecution. Goins isolates himself totally among people who merely tolerate him. There is no evidence in the story that he ever married or had children. Gipson spent more than half a century in the industrialized north. Finally, when he senses he has not much longer to live, he cannot resist coming home, even though he knows that to show up in Eastern Kentucky could bring him to a violent end. The toughest of all is Beulah Mullins. She walks into the jail, commits a murder, and then stays to be locked up. She will certainly never be free another day in her life. Her sensitivity to nature as she walks to town on her grizzly errand shows what a huge sacrifice she is making.

---

[53]Offutt, "Melungeons," 38.
[54]Offutt, "Melungeons," 41.
[55]Offutt, "Melungeons," 44.
[56]Offutt, "Melungeons," 49.

In the final analysis, Offutt's two Melungeon stories are disconcerting. The skill with which he portrays it makes the violence particularly horrible. These stories are not bedtime reading. To my mind Offutt uses Melungeon characters and lore, not to put anyone down, but instead to show the rest of the world what it's really like in the Kentucky hills. Critics use words like "solitude," "stark," "laconic," and "deadly." These words describe parts of all Offutt's work. He treats the Melungeons in his native land the same way he treats everyone and everything else—he examines carefully, accurately, and then records what he discovers.

11

Are These People Melungeons? The Killburn Family in Virginia Hamilton's M. C. Higgins, the Great

The term "Melungeon" is never spoken or even breathed in the young-adult novel *M. C. Higgins, the Great,* by award-winning author Virginia Hamilton. Yet, there are hints and intimations that the Killburn family living isolated on Kill Mound just north of the Ohio River, are if not Melungeon then certainly a people set apart. I am less sure about the Killburns than I am about Wilma Dykeman's Bludsoes; however, I cannot ignore the possibility of a Melungeon connection. I invite you to explore this novel with me to determine what Hamilton is communicating both with and about these people.

M. C. Higgins, the Great is an extraordinary novel. It is the only book ever to win the three most prestigious awards for a young-adult book in the same year. In 1974 when it was published it garnered the Newbery, the *Boston Globe-Horn Book* Award, and the National Book Award. And, although critics, teachers, and librarians have praised the book, for me the most compelling recommendation comes from a young adult "published" in the Amazon.com customer reviews section. This young person says:

> I have read McHiggins the Great so many times my copy is falling apart. . . . Each time I read it, I see more. . . . [T]he people are unforgettable. MC's best friend, Ben, has the most unique family you will ever meet in fiction, very strange but very loving with magical connections to nature. They are vegetarians, who live on an Appalachian family commune. The mother is a healer.[1]

This introduction to the Killburns may pique your curiosity, but it only begins to tell about this unusual family. Furthermore, there is something else that is remarkable here. When I hear a young person say he/she has

---

[1] A reader from Pennsylvania, "This is one of the best Newbery books I have read" (26 July 1988) at <http://www.amazon.com/exec/obidos/ASIN/0020434901/qid=985967592/sr=1-3/ref=sc_b_4/107-4846986-8289340>.

read a book over and over, I am impressed. I take notice. I wonder what magic such a book has, to be so loved, so cherished.

Virginia Hamilton, a descendent of an escaped slave herself (like the character M. C. in her novel), lives and writes in Yellow Springs, Ohio, where her maternal grandfather Perry settled after fleeing servitude in the South and where the Perrys eventually purchased land in the middle of the nineteenth century. Hamilton is known for her innovative techniques and for challenging readers with her books. Her characters are mostly African-American, and her books are laced with elements of black history and culture. Many reviewers, teachers, and librarians talk about the sense of mystery that pervades her work. I am convinced that the only way to understand this sense of mystery, as well as the myths and folklore, that flesh out the realistic bones of her stories is to read one of Hamilton's books for yourself.

Certain themes do pervade her work. One of those is time. In an interview with Marilyn Apseloff, Hamilton herself commented:

> The time motif goes through many of my books. I have been trying to find ways to say that we carry our past with us wherever we go even though we are not aware of it. You find yourself doing things that are just like your mother, or your father, or your grandfather. You don't mean to, yet sometimes you just can't help yourself—you do the same things and go through the same mental gyrations that they did long ago.[2]

In *M. C. Higgins, the Great*, M. C. is very much like his father even though he spends much time and energy trying to be different.

In the same interview Hamilton talks about the "American hope-scape" as a concept to describe the manner in which American blacks have traversed history. *M. C. Higgins, the Great* is a novel where the main character, a young black boy, does have a poignant sense of his own heritage of descent from his grandmother Sarah McHigon, who fled slavery in 1854 with a baby on her hip and hope of freedom in her heart. Hamilton goes on to talk about portraying two other elements: "the essence of a race, its essential community, culture, history, and traditions . . . and the connection the American black child has with all children."[3] M. C., short for Mayo Cornelius, and Ben Killburn certainly exemplify as

---

[2]Marilyn Apseloff, "A Conversation with Virginia Hamilton," in *Children's Literature in Education* 14/4 (Winter 1983): 204-13, in *Children's Literature Review* 40:58.

[3]Virginia Hamilton, "On Being a Black Writer in America," in *The Lion and the Unicorn* 10 (1986): 15-17, in *Children's Literature Review* 40:60.

strong a connection as I've seen in literature of children from two different races. Appalachia's Melungeons have much in common with American blacks—they, too, could benefit from buying into their own American hopescape.

Although Hamilton uses realistic elements and characters in her stories, her novels illustrate—according to David Russell—that she is "one of those rare writers who insist on venturing into that precarious ground where fantasy and reality melt away into a surreal mist."[4] This tendency toward fantasy and mystery fits well in the mode of romance.[5] Hamilton's characters do go on quests (M. C. goes to Kill Mound with Lurhetta Outlaw in spite of his father's prohibition against Ben and the whole Killburn family) and they (like M. C.) are changed as a result.

Two other elements are very important in this author's work. One is her perception of herself as a storyteller that is part of her heritage. She says:

> I am a teller of tales, in part because of the informal way I learned from Mother and her relatives of passing the time, which they also utilize for transmitting information, for entertainment, and for putting their own flesh and blood in the proper perspective. The Perrys are interesting talkers. They began as farmers who had been fugitives from injustice. Acquiring land and homes, place and time, was to them the final payment in the cause of freedom. After long days, a long history in the fields, they talked their way into new states of mind. They could appreciate a good story in the companionship of one another, not only as entertainment but as a way to mark their progress. Stories, talking, grew and changed into a kind of folk history of timely incidents. And these developed a certain style. True memory might lapse, and creativity come into play. It was the same creativity and versatility that had helped the first African survive on the American continent.[6]

---

[4]David L. Russell, "Cultural Identity and Individual Triumph in Virginia Hamilton's *M. C. Higgins, the Great,*" in *Children's Literature in Education* 21/4 (December 1990): 253-59; in *Children's Literature Review* 40:63.

[5]"Romance" here does not mean the sort of story one can buy at the grocery store, but instead a novel in the romantic mode, in the Latin manner, which involves a hero who is not perfect but who undertakes a difficult quest in search of something important and who is ultimately successful.

[6]Virginia Hamilton, interview with Marguerite Feitlowitz for *Something about*

The second of these elements is a sense of place. Virginia Hamilton grew up on the land near Yellow Springs in the bosom of her extended family. Some of her books are set in New York City where she lived for a time after college. However, she knows and readily acknowledges her debt to the hilly farm country of southern Ohio:

> After a leave . . . I return to that village. Knowing who and what I am, I can go home. . . . I am only reclaiming what was given to me without comment so long ago—that freedom and dependence which was partly happiness. . . . I settle back with the coming of night to write in earnest. And that's happiness.[7]

M. C. Higgins, the Great, the whole of which takes place in only forty-eight hours, is the story of a young boy from a poor black family that lives on Sarah's High, a mountain just north of the Ohio River. The mother, Banina, is a cleaning woman in a nearby town, and the father, Jones, works as a nonunion day laborer at a steel mill. M. C. watches his two brothers and a sister when his parents go to work. The family is close and loving. The father is a complex character both devoted to and yet unable to resist competing with and bullying his oldest son. The boy's most prized possession is a forty-foot steel pole given to him by his father for the feat of swimming the Ohio River. M. C. sits and sways on top of his pole on a bicycle seat and surveys the landscape. He sees two strangers come into his ken from the outside—the dude, James Lewis, who carries a tape recorder and wants to capture Banina's unusual and amazing voice on tape, and Lurhetta Outlaw, a girl who wanders through the hills and teaches M. C. a great deal about growing up and living his life separate from the family that both shapes and restrains him.

This novel is about some important social issues, too. Strip-mining is causing serious pollution of the soil and water and has produced a huge pile of dirt, rocks, and dead trees that threatens to slide down the mountainside right on top of the Higginses' house. M. C. is convinced that the family must leave their beloved mountain home in order to survive, in order to avoid being buried by the slag pile. He thinks that Banina will become a star vocalist and be on the radio and so the family will follow her to Nashville. Then, too, there is M. C.'s long and faithful relationship with his friend Ben, one of the witchy people from Kill

---

the Author 56:62.
    [7]Virginia Hamilton, in *Something about the Author* 4:99.

Mound. As Hamilton herself says on the book's page at Amazon.com, "It
is not a simple one-idea novel."[8]

The most striking hints that the Killburn family could be Melungeon
are the descriptions of their physical traits that recur often in the course
of the tale. Some of these details are of traits that are common in many
Melungeon families, such as six fingers and six toes and remarkable light-
colored eyes. An example of such a description occurs when we first
meet Ben when he is stalking M. C. early in the morning as M. C. goes
to check his traps. Because Jones Higgins has forbidden any contact
between the two boys, Ben and M. C. communicate by calling each other
like birds and animals and by never walking side by side on one of the
mountain paths.

> Ben's unsmiling face was pale yellow and always looked
> slightly peaked. He had shocking red hair, thick and long. All of
> the Killburn children had the same hair, in varying shades of red.
> As M. C. came nearer, Ben's gray eyes lit up. He grinned,
> showing small, pointed teeth.[9]

M. C. is both fascinated and repulsed by the extra digit that Ben and
all his male family members possess. "He even glanced at Ben's hands.
They were small and appeared almost ordinary, except each hand had six
fingers. Ben had six toes on each foot. Folks said all the Killburn men had
toes and hands the same."[10] When Lurhetta comes to the Higgins house,
M. C. tries to explain to her what it is about the Killburns that is so
different. He wants to see through her eyes, but is in essence blinded by
the words of his father that echo in his head even as he tries to talk to the
girl. *"He, with skin so fair, he is near white. But hair is always thick and tight
so you can tell, and always almost red. Them gray eyes, cold. . . . For he is
merino."*[11] These words flash through M. C.'s mind, as the three Killburn
men arrive at the outcropping to deliver block ice.

> Three of them stood there in front of M. C.'s house. Three
> men with an odd, yellow cast to their skin and with reddish hair.

---

[8]Virginia Hamilton, author comments (21 July 1998) at <http://www.amazon.
com/exec/obidos/tg/stores/detail/-/books/0020434901/reviews/ref=aps-koth
-pa1/107-4846986-8289340>; typographical errors corrected.
[9]Virginia Hamilton, *M. C. Higgins, the Great*, reissue edition (repr.: New York:
Aladdin Paperbacks, 1988; orig., 1974) 9.
[10]Hamilton, *M. C. Higgins, the Great*, 11.
[11]Hamilton, *M. C. Higgins, the Great*, 190-91.

Their faces looked almost alike, with no eyebrows, with broad, flat noses and with lips too perfectly formed. Eyes, silver gray.[12]

As M. C. interprets for his father Jones, the elaborate ritual of the ice delivery and payment transpires. And, M. C. waits for a glimpse of the six-fingered hands of one or any of the Killburn men.

> Mr. Killburn took off his heavy gloves and began to pick a line down the middle of the ice. M. C. had been waiting for one of the men to remove his gloves. Patiently, he always waited for this moment to see those hands. And always he looked at the six fingers as if seeing them for the first time. The same as with Ben's hands, he half expected the sixth finger to wave about wildly and uncontrolled. But now it curled around the pick with the other five, shooting down and then out of the ice again.[13]

Toward the end of the novel, Lurhetta wants to go to Ben's house at Kill Mound, first to get a drink of water and second just to meet the Killburns and see where Ben lives. As Ben introduces Lurhetta to his dad, Mr. Killburn acknowledges the girl and Hamilton once again notes the unusual eyes. " 'Pleased. Sure,' Mr. Killburn said. Not exactly watching Lurhetta, but listening at her, his head cocked to one side and his squinting, metal eyes, just to the right of her face."[14] In the ensuing conversation, Lurhetta seems to almost be kin to the strange people that are Ben's family, and M. C. is outcast, feeling "just as if he had blundered into a space too tight for him."[15] Yet as he watches, he cannot stop himself from observing the unusual phenotypical markers. "Witchy hand. The six fingers were perfectly formed, perfectly natural."[16] And once again in the course of this same conversation between Mr. Killburn and Lurhetta, Hamilton underscores the strange quality of Mr. Killburn's eyes, calling them "a vivid mackerel shade."[17]

Ben gets permission from his dad to show Lurhetta the place where all the vegetables the family grows are stored. M. C., uncomfortable all the while, tags along and suddenly is overcome with a desire to escape. On his way out of the storage barn, the old grandmother gives him a

---

[12]Hamilton, *M. C. Higgins, the Great*, 191.
[13]Hamilton, *M. C. Higgins, the Great*, 193.
[14]Hamilton, *M. C. Higgins, the Great*, 228.
[15]Hamilton, *M. C. Higgins, the Great*, 228.
[16]Hamilton, *M. C. Higgins, the Great*, 229.
[17]Hamilton, *M. C. Higgins, the Great*, 230.

cabbage to take home, and Ben's Uncle Joe moves aside in the doorway giving M. C. just enough room to get by.

> Uncle Joe grinned. Gray eyes the color of a sparrow's rain-soaked underbelly. "Now you put that [the cabbage] in with the rabbit," he said, "and when hit's done, you throw away the rabbit and you got yourself something."[18]

In the novel's final pages, M. C.'s perceptions of the Killburns have changed. His trip to the Mound is a turning point. He senses this transformation in his thinking even as he runs up Sarah's High Mountain toward home.

> What he had seen of them made him ponder a moment. Mrs. Killburn, just as nice. Even Mr. Killburn, not so bad if you didn't look at his hands or watch his eyes as he handled the green-grass [snake]. What he had just seen and what he had known for so long about Killburns mixed in disorder in his mind.[19]

Later, when he realizes that Lurhetta is gone for good in spite of her promises and that only he can do something to save his family from the danger of the slag heap, M. C. notices that his prejudice toward Ben is lessened. Hamilton lets us see this change in the way M. C. sees the physical markers. "Ben's red hair and his pale, freckled skin seemed not so strange. Even his hands looked almost ordinary."[20]

These three outward descriptions that occur over and over throughout this novel are difficult to ignore—the strange "yellow" skin, the piercing pale-gray eyes, and the extra finger on each hand. Hamilton makes sure that the reader knows how unusual the Killburns are. The extra digit and the eyes are common traits in many Melungeon families. The yellowish skin tones and the red hair are less common.

One other word deserves mention. As M. C. remembers what Jones has drummed into his mind about the Killburns, the word "merino" is a part of that description. A merino is a breed of white-wooled sheep originating in Spain and producing a heavy wool of exceptional quality. Jake Toney, Lee Smith's Melungeon, is described similarly to the Killburns in *The Devil's Dream*, "real pale light eyes, and dark skin, and frizzy

---

[18]Hamilton, *M. C. Higgins, the Great*, 238.
[19]Hamilton, *M. C. Higgins, the Great*, 238.
[20]Hamilton, *M. C. Higgins, the Great*, 276.

hair like sheep's wool."[21] I wonder whether calling the Killburns "merino" is more than a description of the thickness of their hair. Could it also be a hint of Spanish ancestry? There is no other mention anywhere of the origin of Ben's family. Ben's grandmother is very old and is described as a root woman skilled in the use of plants and in herb lore,[22] but neither she nor any of the Killburns know where she came from or who her ancestors were. This not knowing could indicate Melungeon descent; after all, this book was published in 1974 before it was easy to claim to be Melungeon. Many Melungeon families did deliberately obfuscate their heritage to try to escape the stigma of difference from those around them.

Another characteristic that could be a Melungeon marker is the constant use of the word "witchy" to describe them. According to my dictionary, "witchy" means "relating to or characteristic of a witch" or "produced by or suggestive of witchcraft." In turn, "witchcraft" means "the use of sorcery of magic," "intercourse with the devil or with a familiar [an embodied spirit]," or "an irresistible influence or fascination." The only other place I have seen the term "witchy" used to define or describe Melungeon people is in Aswell's Melungeon tale called "Old Horny's Own." In this story that was collected by the Tennessee Writers' Project, this description of Melungeons occurs:

> Whites left them alone because they were so wild and devil-fired and queer and *witchy*. If a man was fool enough to go into Melungeon country and if he come back without being shot, he was just sure to wizzen and perish away with some ailment nobody could name. Folks said terrible things went on back yonder, blood drinking and devil worship and carryings on that would freeze a good Christian's spine-bone.[23]

Hamilton's use of the term "witchy" pervades *M. C. Higgins, the Great* from beginning to end. She never really defines it but she builds on all the possible dictionary senses by putting the word in her characters' mouths and minds in many situations. She wants readers to know that there is something decidedly different and marvelously mysterious about the Killburns of Kill Mound. This "witchiness" has spawned fear and animosity in Jones who in turn enforces his prejudices in his wife and

---

[21]Lee Smith, *The Devil's Dream* (repr.: New York: Ballantine Books, 1993) 57.
[22]Hamilton, *M. C. Higgins, the Great*, 221.
[23]James Aswell, "Old Horny's Own," in *God Bless the Devil! Liars' Bench Tales* (1940; repr.: Knoxville: University of Tennessee Press, 1985) 212; italics added.

children. The word "witchy" comes to M. C. over and over when he encounters and thinks about his best friend Ben. It is only the no-nonsense
outsider/outlaw Lurhetta who finally breaks the spell this word has cast.

The first time we meet Ben and see him and M. C. together, Hamilton
lets us know that something unusual is going on.

> Calling like birds and animals wasn't just a game they
> played. It was the way M. C. announced he was there without
> Ben's daddy and his uncles finding out. M. C. wouldn't have
> wanted to run into the Killburn men any more than he would
> want his own father to know he was playing with Ben. Folks
> called the Killburns witchy people. Some said that the Killburn
> women could put themselves in trances and cast out the devil.
> Killburn men and women both could heal a bad wound by
> touching, although M. C. had never seen them do it. Boys
> scattered around the hills never would play with Ben. They said
> it was because he was so little and nervous. But M. C. had
> played with Ben from the time he was a child and didn't know
> better. When he was older, he had been told. Now he guessed
> Ben was like a bad habit he couldn't break and had to keep
> secret.[24]

This long passage provides the chink in the wall of what M. C. is
supposed to think by showing that he is undeniably attached to Ben in
spite of the fact that the other kids shun him, in spite of the fact that
Jones has forbidden contact, in spite of the fact that M. C. has been
"told."

Maybe "witchy" means magic: "Not only were they [the trees]
massive but they were entwined with vines as thick as a man's arm.
Maybe the vines were poison ivy grown monstrous from Killburn magic.
M. C. liked the idea of witchy vines."[25] Maybe "witchy" means a mysterious and magnetic person: "M. C. liked Ben and felt sorry for his being
small and alone when he didn't want to be either. He admired Ben
because Ben was a witchy."[26]

Maybe "witchy" means having special, supernatural powers—like the
Killburn men do. After all, Jones had warned M. C. never to let a
Killburn cross his path.[27] The Killburn men do in fact lay hands on the

[29]Hamilton, *M. C. Higgins, the Great,* 130-31.
[30]Hamilton, *M. C. Higgins, the Great,* 132.
[31]Hamilton, *M. C. Higgins, the Great,* 16-17.

mining cuts trying to find a way to magically restore health to the mountain. " 'Daddy says it didn't work straight off but that maybe it will slow the ruin down. . . . He just can't find a way to heal a mountain is all,' Ben said. Looking at M. C., his eyes were anxious, innocent."[28] Mr. Killburn also keeps snakes in a box. The children see them on the visit to the Mound near the end of the book.

Then there are the Killburn women. According to Banina, they have the power to stop wounds from bleeding. Banina tells M. C. that she has witnessed this power with her own eyes.

> "They have the power," Banina said. . . . "There's no denying. I've seen it. They are different. . . . Seen it, and I haven't been back since."
>
> "Tell," [M. C.] said.
>
> "Well," she began, "it was farmer in the valley behind the plateau. He was using a sickle on a patch of wheat. You know, it with that hooklike blade fitted into a little handle. Anyway, he was working and not seeing the child creeping up on him to surprise him. He thrust back with the sickle. And sweeping it forward, he caught that child in the curve of the blade. Laid his thigh open the way you slice to bare the bone from a piece of ham."
>
> "Oooh!" M. C. said.
>
> "No doctors, only in Harenton, just like it is now. But there was the Mound. I was over there that day with her. We'd just got back here, Jones and I, and she was my neighbor. I liked her. I'd heard the tales of their power, but I paid no attention. Until farmer come running up all covered with blood. The child, so white and blood so much on his leg, you couldn't see it. And she—"
>
> "Who?" M. C. said.
>
> "Viola Killburn," Banina said. "Why, she simply took the child and arranged him on the ground. He appeared death-still. She didn't touch the wound gushing blood all over. But move her hand over it like searching for something above it in the air. All of a sudden, the hand stop and tremble like over a hump and then move slowly the length of the wound curve.
>
> "Vi had her eyes on that wound in the strangest look I never will ever forget. Only her lips move. Secret prayers of the Bible,

---

[28]Hamilton, *M. C. Higgins, the Great,* 12-13.

they say, but I don't know," Banina said. "I know this. The blood gushing away that child's lifetime clotted all in a minute. The wound ceased to flow. It turn gray and darker. It heal."

"Man!" M. C. whispered.

"Vi ran to pick the ginseng and other weeds I don't know the names of," Banina continued, "and she pack the wound with all this messy weed juice and stuff and leaf and dirt right off the Mound. The child was conscious. He have no pain when his father pick him up to carry him home."[29]

Banina cannot deny that healing is a good thing. Yet when M. C. wants to know why she and Jones won't go to the Killburns for help when they need it, she allows one more thing.

"Theirs might be power for bad in some way we don't recognize—isn't the Lord suppose to have the power for good?" She added: "A man, a child will go over there just for a visit. And will end staying and working for who is related to them. He'll become practically a Killburn. Nobody know who is related to who over there. That's what your father and me wonder about."[30]

Maybe "witchy" means the force that drives the special kinship that Ben and M. C. share, the sense they have about proximity to each other.

In less than five minutes, Ben was somewhere off the path, stalking M. C. from behind. The thought that Ben was near but unseen was all right with M. C. Although M. C. was still edgy, he felt his senses become heightened with minute sight and sound. Where he moved and saw, Ben was moving and seeing the same. The fact was a comfort.

He's my spirit, M. C. thought. He can see me and everything around me and the path, too. Good old spirit.[31]

A little later Ben and M. C. communicate with thoughts only, no words. Could this be construed as witchiness?

[M. C.] looked in back of him up to the plateau. He knew Ben had stopped there, and was turning around now, ready to trot home.

---

[29]Hamilton, *M. C. Higgins, the Great*, 130-31.
[30]Hamilton, *M. C. Higgins, the Great*, 132.
[31]Hamilton, *M. C. Higgins, the Great*, 16-17.

> See you, Ben, he said to himself.
> Ben answered in his thoughts, *See you.*[32]

Maybe "witchy" has something to do with touch, a six-fingered touch that leaves an invisible yet deadly imprint. When the Killburn men deliver ice to Sarah's Mountain, Mr. Killburn touches M. C., and the contact is significant.

> [B]efore M. C. could stop him, he had placed the flat of his own hand over M. C.'s. He had curled his six fingers round M. C.'s hand, pulling it off his shoulder.
> Witchy fingers touching his hand were electric. They seemed to snap and sting. M. C. never would forget the feel of them, ice cold, like something dead. He jerked his hand away. . . .
> "Don't you go near my ice," Jones warned M. C. "Wash your hands, you let one of them touch you."
> "I won't touch it," M. C. said. He didn't know why Jones had to make such a fuss. Mr. Killburn hadn't tried to hurt M. C.
> Did he mark me with his hand? Maybe now I'm all witchy, M. C. thought.
> Part of him believed and part disbelieved. Still he couldn't get that cold touch out of his mind.[33]

M. C. understands this phenomenon; he knows that his brothers and sister understand it, too, because they will not touch him for the rest of the day even though he has washed his hands after being touched by the witchy Mr. Killburn. However, he cannot communicate what he understands to Lurhetta and knows that he is powerless against her repeated "Prove-it" injunction. His explanation has the whiny feel of a protest.

> "They each have twelve fingers and twelve toes. And that *witchy* skin and that hair. . . . People here believe the icemen are *witchy*," M. C. said. "And anyhow, you can't change my daddy's ways, ever."
> "Well," she said, "people make up a story and then they believe it." . . .
> Anxiously, M. C. stood there, not sure of what next to say and uncertain of what he felt. Killburns were *witchy*, that was all

---

[32]Hamilton, *M. C. Higgins, the Great*, 21.
[33]Hamilton, *M. C. Higgins, the Great*, 194-95.

there was to it—could he say that without having her say again, "Prove it"?[34]

In this passage, "witchy" is used in at least two different ways. The first time it could have something to do with color, texture, or translucency. The second time it has more to do with the intangible traits of personality and personhood.

Maybe "witchy" an irresistible magnetic force such as the pull M. C. feels from Ben's mother:

> [H]e kept his eye on the woman who was watching him. And slowly he sifted her features out from the general look all of the Killburns had. He recognized her as she seemed to recognize him. Ben's mother, Viola Killburn. A big woman, not fat, but strong and lanky, with gentle movements and an easy smile. She was smiling at M. C. right now. Smiling and nodding.
>
> He felt glad, a relief at seeing her after so long a time. How long had it been? He couldn't remember when he'd seen Mrs. Killburn. But he felt good about finding her again. Leaning there at the side of the shed, he would have liked to skip over the rows of vegetables to sit at her side.
>
> Sit on one side, his memory told him, with Ben on her other side.
>
> The both of them leaning against her, without either one of them saying a word. Never a war between her and them and whatever they wanted given. If she had ever wanted anything, they would have given it. But she never wanted.[35]

Soon M. C. has told Viola all about his mother and the dude's tape recorder. "Instantly M. C. wished he hadn't said that. But it was so easy to tell Viola Killburn things, it had just slipped out."[36]

Maybe "witchy" is the essence of the ancient grandmother, an old crone who brings to mind all the scary old witches of the fairy tales. Ben takes Lurhetta and M. C. to see where all the vegetables are stored:

> In the midst of the stillness—the muted stripes of light, the yawning pits—sat an ancient, shriveled woman on a green folding chair. . . .

[34]Hamilton, *M. C. Higgins, the Great*, 196.
[35]Hamilton, *M. C. Higgins, the Great*, 216.
[36]Hamilton, *M. C. Higgins, the Great*, 225.

Ugly, old witchy, [M. C. thinks to himself].[37]

Maybe "witchy" means all that it has meant through the ages, the burnings at stakes across Europe and the terrifying trials in Salem, Massachusetts. There with Ben, Lurhetta, and Mr. Killburn, M. C. suddenly knows he has to leave and flees terrified at having to pass Ben's Uncle Joe standing against the light in the barn doorway. Thoughts come to him unbidden, "Witchy, kill you. Burn you at the stake."[38] Ben runs away from the Mound, stopping when he is out of breath to make sure no witchy follows and to throw the gift of the cabbage far into the ravine.

Suddenly he begins to doubt his long-held beliefs. Is he outgrowing the sins and misconceptions of his father or is he merely leaving childhood acceptance for adolescent awareness?

[He] scanned the pines above him at the edge of the Mound, but there was no one.

Well, that's that. Nobody with me, not even Ben.

He would have liked to stay awhile up there, where all seemed fresh with growing and sun.

Except for the witchies. Were they witchies?

What he had seen of them made him ponder a moment. Mrs. Killburn, just as nice. Even Mr. Killburn, not so bad if you didn't look at his hands or watch his eyes as he handled the green-grass [snake]. What he had just seen and what he had known for so long about Killburns mixed in disorder in his mind.[39]

As these many examples and excerpts show, the word "witchy" is a touchstone in this novel. The word has almost as many meanings as it has uses. It grows and changes through the story as the character of M. C. Higgins grows and changes.

The question of Melungeon connections is as much raised as answered by Hamilton's descriptions of the Killburns themselves apart from their looks—who they are as people, what they do, what they wear, and where they live. They are as isolated as any Melungeon community in fact or fiction and seem to be fenced onto their mound by an invisible barrier that separates them from the black community for sure. Their solitary existence on Kill's Mound also sets them apart from the rest of the Ohio valley that M. C. surveys from the top of his pole. The Killburn

---

[37]Hamilton, *M. C. Higgins, the Great*, 232.
[38]Hamilton, *M. C. Higgins, the Great*, 237.
[39]Hamilton, *M. C. Higgins, the Great*, 238.

land is between Sarah's Mountain and the Ohio River. It is "a low hill called Kill's Mound. On the Mound lived the Killburn people."[40] M. C. knows it is a flat place full of crops, but the reader must wait until the three—Ben, M. C., and Lurhetta—go there near the end of the novel to get a full description.

There were at the foot of the Mound on a stepped path cut out of rock. . . .

Something about tall white pine trees forming an entrance grove, a semicircle of evergreens on each side of the path. Entering the Mound, the three of them became aware of their place in the mood around them. They were made less self-conscious among trees whose height alone caused them to reach out and upward, away from themselves. It didn't seem odd that Ben reached out to pat a pale pine trunk, sliding his six fingers along its rough bark. Lurhetta patted the tree, not to imitate Ben, but because it seemed natural to do so. Without hesitation, M. C. did the same and with the same result. He felt he'd introduced himself to a being he hadn't the sense to greet before.

They were on the Mound. It was a place unexpected and out of tune with the hills. Lower than the plateau but higher than the ravine, it was a valley reach of land unmarred by a single curve, jagged boulder or coal seam. It was a fifteen-acre Midwestern plain perhaps transported by Killburn magic to the top of the Mound. An unbeatable square saved from being a burning, dull landscape by the straight thread of a wide stream that dissected it, fed it from underground springs and in the past had made its soil rich and black. To come upon such flatland without a single tree on it in the midst of the hills was a surprise in itself. . . .

The houses of the Mound were grouped together to one side, a short distance away. Surrounded by outbuildings, every inch of space between the buildings was planted with crops. No yards, no dried, caked earth swept clean as were the yards of many hill houses. Up to the porches and foundations of piled stones, every foot of ground was taken up by tomatoes or potatoes. Runner beans, beets, lettuce and peas. Even in the hot darkness under the houses grew ghostly spreads of mushrooms. The trouble was none of the vegetables looked healthy. Some had

[40]Hamilton, *M. C. Higgins, the Great*, 4.

a blight of rust eating at the leaves. And others were being
attacked by a black and white mold similar to mildew. . . .

[T]he Killburn houses, sheds and barns were grouped to form
an enclosure. This compound was in no way extraordinary to
look at, at first sight. The sheds and barns were weathered silver,
sagging and almost shapeless. The houses were not the unpaint-
ed crate construction of most hill houses, but on the order of
rambling, frame farmhouses. They had been added onto at the
rear each time a child was born; and they had been painted once,
all the same color. A dark, deep brown trimmed in blue. There
was still a thick covering of paint on the houses, although they
hadn't been retouched in years.

So that what happened right before M. C.'s eyes was that the
enclosure of chocolate and silver sheds and barns took on the
appearance of a fairyland. Carved out of dark soil and bold, blue
sky, it looked unearthly all of a sudden, and slightly sinister.

There were men and women scattered over the land, working
at hoeing and picking, and dropping vegetables into bushel
baskets. At least four were bent to the task within the enclosure
where row upon row of plants took the place of what would
have been one large common yard.[41]

M. C., being out of his usual place on Sarah's Mountain, and now in
a different sort of relationship with Ben, because Ben is in his own home
the leader instead of the follower, is suddenly overcome with feelings
that go back before his conscious memory. "[H]e remembered with sadness, with regret, that the Mound had been the happiest place he'd ever
known."[42] He must have gone there with Banina when she and Viola Killburn were good friends, before the strange healing of the bleeding child,
before Jones's prohibition kept all his family away from Killburn land.
M. C. suddenly notices one important detail, important because it underscores the total isolation of this group of people who are, as Ben tells
Lurhetta, all relatives.

[S]urrounding everything, even the chatter of the children, was
an enormous stillness which the chatter could not penetrate. No
sounds of the town of Harenton, no river boat sounds. But a

---

[41]Hamilton, *M. C. Higgins, the Great*, 210-14.
[42]Hamilton, *M. C. Higgins, the Great*, 217.

silence that swept over the land in every direction, as did the sunlight.[43]

This place, Kill Mound, *feels* much the same as Canara, Phyllis Naylor's Melungeon settlement deep in an Appalachian mountain valley. Both are isolated; both self-sufficient; both have little traffic with the outside world.

There is one strange characteristic of the Mound that is not Melungeon, but it is so interesting that it deserves mention. Since every available inch of soil is used for cultivation, the Killburns construct a magical elevated play space for their many children that is better than any McDonalds' PlayPlace.

> It's the biggest cobweb I ever saw in my life," Lurhetta said. "See, that's just what it looks like."
>
> "I know," M. C. said, "I remember now." He eased himself up on the web next to her and Ben. . . . M. C. must have been very little when he'd last seen it. . . .
>
> What it was the three of them were looking at: Guidelines of thick rope and vine twisted so as to combine. These connected the houses in the area of the common ground. The lines were held to each house just under the roof edge with iron stakes, around which the rope and vine were knotted.
>
> The three of them sat near the top and in between two guidelines where began a loose weave of rope weathered to a softness not unlike old cornshucks. There were at least eight guidelines and in between each was that soft weave. Nearer the ground, the lines came closer together. Their weave grew tighter at dead center of the common, some five to six feet over the ground. Here began a hub connected to the weave. It was some twenty feet across and just as long, made of twisted vines and rope loosely tied into six-inch square shapes.
>
> The effect from guidelines to hub was one of an enormous web or net, or even a green and tan sunburst. In the hub were many children of various sizes and ages. Most had the light sickly complexion of Killburn people. With a color range from orange to reddish-brown hair, they looked like a fresh bunch of bright flowers jumbled and tossed by breezes, their stems dangling through the square shapes of the hub. . . .

---

[43]Hamilton, *M. C. Higgins, the Great*, 224.

"I sure like the way that thing up there looks like a spider web," [Lurhetta] said, as they passed under guidelines.

"No, sir," Killburn said. "Looks like a eye."

"Really" It looks like an eye to you?"

"Is a eye," Killburn said. "Better than any old eye. Bigger. *A eye* of Gawd."[44]

Virginia Hamilton explained this wonderful creation in her interview with Marilyn Apseloff:

> I knew people who were living on communes, perhaps, and the idea sort of stuck in my head. For the webbing, I had to get some way to deal with all those children, yet the web is symbolic: it is the eye of God, as Mr. Killburn says. It's hard now to figure it out. Except—I think that I do have an idea. Those vines that made the bridge—I know where that comes from. I had a lot of green string, tons of green string (I collect things). There was an auction and there was all this old-fashioned green string that you used to tie packages with that I remembered from my childhood, and I bought the string on a big spool. I don't know how to knit, but I put it on my fingers. I began to weave, and I made shawls out of it. They became very interesting, and I used that in two books. . . . I was weaving the shawls with my fingers at that time. When I began to make the structures of the vine bridge in *M. C. Higgins*, I was doing the same thing. The webbing, when I was weaving it on my fingers, looked just like the God's eye that children make, and that's where it came from.[45]

It is apparent from the amount of detail in the description of the Mound that Hamilton deems it important in this novel. No less important to this discussion are the descriptions of the Killburns, the people who inhabit it. Besides the instances already mentioned that tell what they look like, there are many passages that talk about who they are in other ways. Viola Killburn is not only a healer, but also a midwife. Early in the novel Ben tells M. C. that his mother has been gone most of the night.

> "Getting out the devil?" M. C. said, respectfully. He tried to be polite when speaking of Mrs. Killburn's power.

---

[44]Hamilton, *M. C. Higgins, the Great*, 218-30.
[45]Apseloff, "A Conversation with Virginia Hamilton," 57.

"Deliverin' a baby," Ben said.[46]

It appears that Viola is an important part of her community. I have already noted the influence she has on M. C. One word that she utters in the course of her brief conversation with M. C. is perhaps an important clue to the identity of the whole clan.

> Now and then Viola Killburn had a word or two for M. C.
> "Haven't seen you in so long, M. C., where you been? Got just as tall." Her voice gentle and soft-spoken.
> "Yessum, I been all around," M. C. said. "I seen Ben about every day."
> "Well—" Mrs. Killburn saying the word the way hill women did generally. A rising inflection so that it came out with sympathy, comforting.[47]

This clue is so small that it is easy to miss. However, we learn from this one word, "Well—" that Viola is a mountain woman. She is not black, but she is mountain. There is a difference. If she is mountain, she may be Melungeon.

Besides their farming activities on the Mound, the Killburn men are the icemen for the community. They carry fifty-pound blocks of ice on their shoulders and walk to deliver it to isolated families like the Higginses on their mountain outcropping. They sing a song that Hamilton describes as "a weird outlandish yelling."[48]

> *Ah'm hot and ah'm a co-o-old. . . .*
> *Ah'm a snowbody, Ah'm a snowbody.*
> *Freeze-a-water!*
> *Hear-ah. . . . Ice-a-m-a-a-a-n. . . .*[49]

This ditty is interesting on two counts. "Snowbody" is close in sound to "nobody." Are these men intimating that they are nobodies? Secondly, the word "iceman" brings the title of Eugene O'Neill's 1946 play immediately to mind: *The Iceman Cometh* is a play about social outcasts.

The Killburn grandmother, Grandymama, ninety-six years old, is matriarch of the Mound. Ben acknowledges that although she has no idea about where she came from, she knows about many things.

---

[46]Hamilton, *M. C. Higgins, the Great*, 12.
[47]Hamilton, *M. C. Higgins, the Great*, 224-25.
[48]Hamilton, *M. C. Higgins, the Great*, 189.
[49]Hamilton, *M. C. Higgins, the Great*, 190.

"She was always here," Ben said. . . . See, she so old, most times she only talk to herself." Ben grinned. "She can be a young girl and she can talk to the pictures on the walls. Talks like they were talking back to her." He laughed softly. "But when my mother bring her tree bark and moth wing, she will mash them up. She will get out her bottles and she know everything. Everything."[50]

The Killburns are close to nature and espouse a strange philosophy that is foreign to M. C. Mr. Killburn explains the ideas to Lurhetta when she comments on how different it is to see houses without any yards of grass, but gardens instead.

"Grass can't grow nohow with kids tramping," Mr. Killburn told her. "But even the babies can 'preciate some vegetables. They understand that vegetables is part of the human form." He looked around to make sure everyone was listening. "Piece of the body you pull up by the root. Or piece that you cut away when it get the blight. Or heal it, depending on how bad it is." He nodded to himself. Others nodded back. "Or eat it, it's still body," he said, letting loose a strap and raising the hand for emphasis.

Witchy hand.

The six fingers were perfectly formed, perfectly natural. "Just like soil is body. Stream. Mountain is body." Killburn paused significantly. "We don't own nothing of it. We just caretakers, here to be of service."[51]

Mr. Killburn then continues his lecture saying, "If you could think about it every day, you never could own a piece of it. Wouldn't want to."[52] He goes on a bit later to expand the ideas of the obviously vegetarian philosophy a little further to Lurhetta and M. C. "None of my children ever kill an animal, let alone skin it."[53]

Hamilton goes to some trouble to describe the clothing that the Killburn adults wear:

---

[50]Hamilton, *M. C. Higgins, the Great*, 221-22.
[51]Hamilton, *M. C. Higgins, the Great*, 229.
[52]Hamilton, *M. C. Higgins, the Great*, 229.
[53]Hamilton, *M. C. Higgins, the Great*, 234.

The brand new, starched overalls Mr. Killburn wore had not completely wilted from his labor under the sun. The other man wore the same outfit. And the brilliant stitching of pockets and straps was like a cloth sketch of the prosperous farmer. The strange headgear they wore had once been identical old felt hats. But they had cut triangle holes in the felt to let air circulate. The hat brims they had cut away to an inch of their former shape, the shortened brims then cut deep in a jagged design. What was left of the hats was an improvement over the originals, M. C. was sure. Dashing, kingly crowns.[54]

Some of the women and the young men wear faded overalls to work amongst the vegetables.[55] Viola Killburn wears a dress.

She was the only one of the women M. C. had seen who wore anything resembling a dress. It was more in the shape of a tent. Homemade, belted, with just a neck hole and armholes, of a faded, neat flower pattern.[56]

There is one more important fact about the Killburns that cannot be ignored in an analysis of the possibility of Melungeon connections in this novel. The Killburns are feared and scorned by Jones Higgins and his family. There are many stories both factual and fictional that tell about the prejudice of whites against persons with Melungeon ancestry. But, if the Killburns are indeed Melungeon, this is the only instance I have discovered of prejudice against Melungeons by blacks. We discover early on that Jones has issued an interdict: M. C. is not to play with Ben. In typical adolescent fashion, the two boys get around the ban by adhering to the letter of the law but not the spirit. Friends since early childhood, they have worked out an intricate pattern of relating to one another that includes using the animal and bird noises to communicate, walking not together but with M. C. on the path and Ben "stalking" him a few yards away, and agreeing that "Ben was never to touch M. C. with his hands and risk losing his only friend."[57] By adhering to these self-imposed rules the two boys can be together and, as the text puts it, not have any "trouble."

[54]Hamilton, *M. C. Higgins, the Great*, 227.
[55]Hamilton, *M. C. Higgins, the Great*, 220 and 227.
[56]Hamilton, *M. C. Higgins, the Great*, 216.
[57]Hamilton, *M. C. Higgins, the Great*, 10.

On the way to the lake for their early morning swim, Banina talks to her son and explains the reasons she and Jones don't think M. C. and Ben should play together.

> "Never let your father see you playing with Ben. Stay away from over there, you hear? Living all bunched together. Nobody knowing which is real father to what son, and which mother to daughter. The wives never leaving the plateau. Those people aren't right. . . .
> A man, a child will go over there for a visit. And will end staying and working for them. He'll become practically a Killburn. Nobody knows who is related to who over there. That's what your father and me wonder about."[58]

For Jones Higgins the prejudice seems to be rooted in genuine fear. We see Jones react very strangely to the Killburns when the three icemen climb Sarah's Mountain to the outcropping.

> Kindness and light seemed to drain from Jones's face. He grew rigid and slammed the nutmeg tin down on the counter. M. C. felt coldness on his scalp, as though his hair stood straight up as the sound [of the icemen's yelling] grew louder. The children stared wildly. Lennie Pool [M. C.'s brother] slid off his chair; and pulling Macie [M. C.'s sister] down with him, hid under the table. . . .
> Jones rushed from the kitchen, through the parlor and to the front porch. M. C. was right behind him.
> "Daddy,' he said.
> "Don't tell *me!*" Jones said through his teeth. He flew out the door just as the iceman was about to come up the front steps.
> "Back off, damn your hide!" Jones told the man. . . .
> The three icemen were fanned out in front of Jones in a semicircle.
> "Don't' touch that step," Jones said softly, "not no part of my house, you hear?" . . .
> The leader iceman was Ben Killburn's father. The other two were Uncle Lee and Uncle Joe, although M. C. didn't see them often enough to have figured out which was which. The leader came slowly forward toward Jones. Around his waist he wore a

[58]Hamilton, *M. C. Higgins, the Great*, 130-32.

thick rope belt on which were strung several icepicks and burlap sacks.

"Get back! Get on back!" Jones yelled.

"Mr. Killburn grinned. "Afternoon, Mr. Hig-gon," he said, in a voice that was as smooth as oil. . . .

"How much ice do you want, Daddy?" M. C. asked.

Killburn stood still now. He grinned absently as he untied a sack from his belt and spread it on the ground. Easily, his muscles bulging, he heaved the heavy block of ice onto the sack and took up an icepick. In a crouch, he waited. A ripple seemed to eddy over the three men, ending with one of them breaking out in a dance on his toes.

Jones got hold of himself. He closed the door and stood there with his back pressed against it. Lurhetta stared at him, at his fearful eyes.[59]

This is strange behavior indeed, especially for a grown man. Lurhetta is incredulous and M. C., even though he knows and partly understands his father's performance, is disquieted.

M. C. stood there feeling vaguely helpless. The wild and unbelievable imprint they had left behind seemed still suspended on the air. He wondered if Ben was out there and had seen it all, hidden in the trees.

"Don't' you go near my ice," Jones warned M. C. "Wash your hands, you let one of them touch you." . . .

Lurhetta Outlaw stared at Jones in disbelief a moment before gazing off after the icemen. . . .

"Treat other people like that," she said, "like they were dirt." She looked disgustedly at M. C. as though he had done something to hurt her.

But he knew she was talking about Jones. . . .

"You saw them. Not just 'other people,' " M. C. said, defending Jones. He didn't know why he felt he should.[60]

M. C. has a real problem here. He has seen something for the first time. Until this incident—the icemen's visit to his house with Lurhetta watching—he has accepted his father's prohibition as an annoyance, but also simply as a part of his life. However, forced by Lurhetta's presence

[59]Hamilton, *M. C. Higgins, the Great*, 189-92.
[60]Hamilton, *M. C. Higgins, the Great*, 195.

and by his admiration and infatuation for her to acknowledge that something is amiss, he realizes deep inside himself that he will shortly be faced with a decision on this issue of how to treat the Killburns. He makes his decision in part by agreeing to go to the Mound with Ben and Lurhetta. Once there he notices and must admit something to himself. "It was a fact, none of the Killburns had acted strangely, Viola gave no hint of her healing power."[61] M. C. thinks, though, that Lurhetta had better watch out, because Mrs. Killburn has the power to fool anybody, but then immediately he is ashamed. Once he runs away from the Mound, he realized that he is no longer sure what he thinks. He has seen Lurhetta be quickly accepted by the Killburns, he has heard her say, "I've never seen anything like this place. You all must never want to leave it, it's so beautiful."[62]

At the very end of the story, this issue is finally resolved. Lurhetta has moved on, telling neither M. C. nor Ben good-bye and leaving her knife at the lake for M. C. to find. M. C. realizes that his family's tie to Sarah's Mountain is too strong to deny and that they will never leave willingly. If the Spoil is to be stopped, he must do that himself. Once he sees these truths he begins to build a wall of dirt and debris from his yard to protect the house. While he is working, Ben appears in the yard stinking from taking a skunk out of one of M. C.'s traps. Jones is repulsed both by the odor and by Ben himself.

> A shudder of revulsion that he could no more help than he could help picking at the mosquito bite. A moment hung over all of them in silence as Jones, in one great effort, seemed to pull himself together. He cupped his had over the mosquito bite—it must have been hot with fever. He did not scratch it again.
>
> "Should of let M. C. take care of it. Skunk is worse than anything to handle," Jones said evenly.
>
> "Yessir," Ben said. "I take care of the traps for M. C. when he's busy."
>
> "For M. C.—and you didn't mind the smell a-tall," Jones spoke solemnly.
>
> "No, sir, I didn't mind it."
>
> Jones ran his hand over his face once. . . . Without another word, he went inside the house.
>
> M. C. grinned at Ben. Ben grinned back. . . .

---

[61]Hamilton, *M. C. Higgins, the Great,* 226.
[62]Hamilton, *M. C. Higgins, the Great,* 226.

"Do I smell real bad?" Ben asked M. C., looking over at the children.

"Not near as bad as this morning," M. C. said. "Anyway, skunk is most like anything else in the woods. I never minded it."[63]

On the surface this is two boys and and a man having a conversation about a skunk caught in a trap and how bad the skunk smell is. Underneath it is much more. The bad odor represents the "bad" about the Killburns that M. C. has heard all his life from his father Jones. When he says he doesn't mind the smell of skunk and never did mind it, he is affirming the friendship that he and Ben have shared and rejecting the prejudiced view that his father holds. It is a graphic and poignant ending for this powerful story.

One final idea cannot be ignored. Just as there are intimations that the Killburns may be Melungeons, there are also hints that they are fundamentalist Christians. When I read the first description of the Killburns saying that the women can put themselves in trances and cast out the devil and that men and women both can heal bad wounds by touching, when I hear M. C. ask Ben whether his mama has been up all night casting out the devil,[64] when I read about the Killburn men laying hands on the violent strip-mining cuts of the mountains to heal them forever, when I see Viola healing the bleeding child with "secret prayers of the Bible,"[65] when I find that the Killburns have snakes of many kinds, the verses in Mark 16 come immediately to mind.

> And these signs will accompany those who believe: In my name they will drive out demons; they will speak in new tongues; they will pick up snakes with their hands; and when they drink deadly poison, it will not hurt them at all; they will place their hands on sick people, and they will get well. (Mark 16:17-18 NIV)

Suddenly I am at the brush-arbor meeting on Sanctuary Mountain with Dave Stoneking and Deutsia Huntoon: I sense Clem Cloyd close by in the springhouse; and I remember Mattie Ruth Johnson's description of the church meetings of her childhood. Ben's simple acceptance of the powers of the adults in his life is clear witness to the authenticity of the

---

[63]Hamilton, *M. C. Higgins, the Great*, 274-75.
[64]Hamilton, *M. C. Higgins, the Great*, 6.
[65]Hamilton, *M. C. Higgins, the Great*, 131.

practices. The description of the snakes and how both Ben and Mr. Killburn deal with them is worth noting here.

> [A]head of them was the weirdest sight. M. C. had seen it a few times in his life, he couldn't recall where or when. But it was familiar. He turned to Ben. Ben raised his hand, those witchy fingers, motioning M. C. to stay still. Lurhetta was completely absorbed. M. C. knew she'd never seen anything like it before.
>
> A snake rolling away from them down a runner bean row. They must have scared it coming off the path. It had taken its tail in its mouth and run off like a hoop. Grinning, Ben sidled up to it, careful not to step on any runners. He stuck his arm through the circle the snake made and lifted it, a dark wheel, still turning. He held the hoop up for them to see. Then he swirled it around and around his wrist. He let it fly; in midair, it snapped open and straightened like a stick.
>
> Was it a stick by magic?[66]
>
> Falling, hitting the ground, it hooped again and rolled and rolled until it felt safe and hid.
>
> "What in the world—!" Lurhetta said.
>
> "Just a hoop snake," Ben said, coming back to where they stood. "We have hoop snakes and milk snakes, garter snakes, green-grass snakes and some copperheads. Only the copperheads will kill you. Daddy don't mind the copperheads but he's been hating the green-grass snakes for longer than a month. The milk snake will steal the cow's milk, but we don't have a cow.
>
> "You mean your father likes them?" Lurhetta said.
>
> "He feeds them," Ben said. "He sets out milk for the milk snakes just to see them slither. He lets the garters sun and have their babies on the cement of the icehouse step and feed off the gardens. He don't mind any kind of snake, can handle them like they were puppies. Copperheads, he talks to and if they don't listen right, he grinds their heads into the ground."[67]

This is not the usual practice of Holiness snake handling that we see in Stuart's *Daughter of the Legend* or in Alther's *Kinflicks*, but it alerts us to the possibility that the Killburns are some variety of snake handlers.

---

[66]Is this an allusion to Moses before Pharaoh with his staff that turned into a serpent (Exodus 7:8-13)?

[67]Hamilton, *M. C. Higgins, the Great*, 211-12.

The magnetism that Viola Killburn exudes is a perfect picture of someone filled with the love of Christ that draws all to itself. And, finally, one other hint is the Killburns' familiarity with the Bible. The fact that the old grandmother, seeing a figure against the light streaming in the barn doorway, thinks that Gabriel has come to blow his horn. The fact that Ben knows what she is referring to also indicates a more than passing familiarity on his part with Bible stories.

> Grandymama cackled suddenly, sending a chill up his [M. C.'s] spine. "Who's parading?" she said. "I see you. Blow the trumpet!"
> They glanced around. "No Gabriel here, Grandy," Ben said kindly.[68]

So, then, you have the evidence. There are many details that line up. The six fingers and toes of the Killburn men and their striking grey eyes point to Melungeon heritage. Hamilton's emphasis on the word "witchy" to characterize all the Killburns is a clue that ties the novel to at least one other description of Melungeons. The implications of mystery and supernatural power line up with what many believe about Melungeon people. The fact that Mrs. Killburn talks like a hill woman makes me wonder; I know for sure she does not share the Higginses' slave history. The hints about a kind of Christianity that some Melungeon people practice give another clue. The description of the Killburn matriarch who is a Bible-believing woman who does not know her origins starts my mind working and I remember the story about the strange people "discovered" by John Sevier in the trans-Appalachian back country. Both the old grandmother and Viola have skills with herbs, roots, and moth wings to bring healing to those who are suffering. One slander often leveled at Melungeon people is that they have intermarried more than is proper; this criticism is voiced by Banina. The prejudice Jones Higgins harbors and disseminates sounds as bad as what W. A. Plecker perpetrated in Virginia.

However, there are indications on the other side as well. The constant reference to yellow skin and red hair does not line up with the typical Melungeon phenotype: Melungeons are usually said to have copper-colored skin and dark hair, although many Melungeon families have persons with varying phenotypes. The fact that Hamilton herself talked about people she knew who were living in a commune most likely by choice mitigates against the enforced isolation that Melungeon communi-

---

[68]Hamilton, *M. C. Higgins, the Great*, 233.

ties endured. Other common markers are missing. There is no mention of any Portuguese connection. No Killburn in this story makes moonshine. No Killburn talks about any sort of Indian heritage, nor does anyone else imply such.

I did send Virginia Hamilton an e-mail message asking her point blank: "Are the Killburns Melungeons?" She replied:

> I have never heard of Melungeon. I base my characters from my imagination and childhood re-memories. The six-finger children and family were acquaintances when I was a young girl. I know nothing of their ancestry. VH[69]

We must accept her reply, of course; yet I still think the family she remembers from childhood could have had Melungeon connections.[70] While the evidence remains inconclusive, the markers are too many to ignore.

---

[69]E-mail message from Virginia Hamilton to Katherine Vande Brake, 7 July 2000.

[70]The presence of Melungeons in Southern Ohio is the subject of a recent book: John S. Kessler and Donald B. Ball, *North from the Mountains: A Folk History of the Carmel Melungeon Settlement, Highland County, Ohio*, The Melungeons: History, Culture, Ethnicity, and Literature (Macon GA: Mercer University Press, 2001).

12

Big Stone Gap, Virginia: Melungeons in Perspective, from John Fox, Jr. and Adriana Trigiani

[J]ust over the Kentucky line, are the Gap and "The Gap"—the one made by nature and the other by man. One is a ragged gash down through the Cumberland Mountains, from peak to water level; and the other is a new little, queer little town, on a pretty plateau which is girdled by two running streams that loop and come together like the framework of an ancient lute.[1]

The Gap is in the southwestern corner of Old Virginia. . . . [A] swift stream . . . runs through a mountain of limestone and between beds of iron ore and beds of coking coal. That is why some three-score young fellows gathered there from Bluegrass Kentucky and Tidewater Virginia not many years ago, to dig their fortunes out of the earth. Nearly all were college graduates, and all were high-spirited, adventurous, and well-born. They proposed to build a town and, incidentally, to make cheaper and better iron there than was made anywhere else on the discovered earth.

A "boom" came. The labor and capital question was solved instantly, for every man in town was straightway a capitalist. You couldn't get a door hung—every carpenter was a meteoric Napoleon of finance. Every young blood in town rode Bluegrass saddle-horses and ate eight-o'clock dinners—making many dollars each day and having high jinks o' nights at the club, which, if you please, entertained, besides others of distinction, a duke and duchess who had warily eluded the hospitality of New York. The woods were full of aristocrats and plutocrats—American and English. The world itself seemed to be moving that way,

---

[1]John Fox, Jr., "To the Breaks of Sandy," in *Christmas Eve on Lonesome, "Hell-fer-Sartin," and Other Stories* (New York: Scribner's, 1909) 219.

and the Gap stretched its jaws wide with a grin of welcome. Later, you could get a door hung, but here I draw the veil. It was magnificent, but it was not business.

At the high tide, even, the Gap was, however, something of a hell-hole for several reasons; and the clash of contrasts was striking. The Kentucky feudsmen would chase each other there, now and then, from over Black Mountain; and the toughs on the Virginia side would meet there on Saturdays to settle little differences of opinion and sentiment. They would quite take the town sometimes—riding through the streets, yelling and punctuating the sign of our one hotel with pistol-bullet periods to this refrain:

... G.r.a.n.d. C.e.n.t.r.a.l. H.o.t.e.l. ...
Hell!! Hell!! Hell!!

—keeping time meanwhile, like darkies in a hoedown. Or, a single horseman might gallop down one of our wooden side-walks, with his reins between his teeth, and firing into the ground with a revolver in each hand. All that, too, was magnificent, but it was not business. The people who kept store would have to close up and take to the woods.

And thus arose a unique organization—a volunteer police-guard of gentlemen, who carried pistol, billy, and whistle, and did a policeman's work—hewing always strictly to the line of the law.

The result was rather extraordinary. The Gap soon became the only place south of Mason and Dixon's line, perhaps, where a street fight of five minute's duration, or a lynching, was impossible. A yell, a pistol-shot, or the sight of a drunken man became a rare occurrence. Local lawlessness thus subdued, the guard extended its benign influence—creating in time a public sentiment fearless enough to convict a desperado, named Talt Hall; and, guarding him from rescue by his Kentucky clansmen for one month at the county-seat, thus made possible the first hanging that mountain-region had ever known.[2]

So does Big Stone Gap's favorite son, John Fox, Jr., describe the town at the turn of the twentieth century. Fox was born at Stony Point in the Bluegrass region of Kentucky. Educated first at home by his schoolmaster father, then at Transylvania, and finally at Harvard (class of 1883), Fox

---

[2]Fox, "Man-Hunting in the Pound," in *Christmas Eve on Lonesome, "Hell-fer-Sartin," and Other Stories*, 155-58.

worked as a newspaper reporter in New York before returning to Kentucky because of an illness. Shortly after his return, he, his father, and his brother began speculating in mountain land and mining operations at Jellico, Tennessee, and then at Big Stone Gap. The Fox family built a home in the small Virginia mountain town, and John wrote there in a book-lined study (preserved to this day by the faithful ladies' auxiliary of Lonesome Pine Arts and Crafts Association) several novels and many short stories about life in the Southern Appalachians. Although he lived at "The Gap" and was instrumental in the formation of the Home Guard that brought law and order to the Powell Valley, he probably would have lived in New York City had not the collapse of the boom economy of Southwest Virginia mandated that he stay at home. It is reported that he "despised mountain life, considered the Gap to be 'commonplace' (his term), and much preferred to live in New York City when he could afford the high cost of living there."[3]

One of the most, if not the most, famous of his works is *Trail of the Lonesome Pine*, the sentimental and romantic chronicle of Jack Hale and June Tolliver. Jack is a mining engineer from the outside world who falls in love with a beautiful and talented girl of the mountains. Their story is one of striking cultural differences and the effects of a sophisticated education on a mountain girl and of mountain living on an unsuspecting outsider. This theme of the effects of education and the cultural clashes education causes for mountain boys and girls comes up again and again in Appalachian literature: Can a mountain child get an education and go back? Is the educational bridge a one-way street out of the hills? Can an educated mountaineer or mountain lass come home again? Jack and June do finally marry, and thus the romance thread of the novel reaches its mandatory happy ending, yet the novel contains much more.

Fox is termed by many a local-color writer. As such he creates many memorable characters in *Trail* (Devil Judd Tolliver, Bad Rufe Tolliver, and Red Fox, to name three) and gives a vivid account of mountain life:

> mountain entertainments like bean stringings, corn shuckings, and quilting parties; the pipe-smoking women who eat after the men have finished; entire families sleeping in their one-room

---

[3]Darlene Wilson, "Some Reflections on Appalachian and Melungeon History," at <http://www.melungeons.org/dgw-hist.htm>, accessed 21 June 2000, but now (temporarily?) unavailable.

houses; the need for the man of the house to construct a still to get needed money by selling moonshine.[4]

Although this novel by Fox has no identified Melungeon in it, I spend time here talking about it because of the importance it has in the canon of Appalachian fiction and the central place that the outdoor drama, "Trail of the Lonesome Pine," has in Adriana Trigiani's recent novel *Big Stone Gap*. Accurate or not about how things really were at the turn of the twentieth century, the best-selling novel about the beautiful June and dashing Jack Hale by an "adopted" native son is something from which "The Gap" cannot escape.

Darlene Wilson in an article written for *The Coalfield Progress* of Norton, Virginia, alleges that regional history "has been grossly misrepresented by the 'Trail of the Lonesome Pine' [Big Stone Gap's outdoor drama based on the Fox novel]."[5] Fox left behind among his papers several written accounts stating that June Tolliver did not exist, but she has been canonized by the townspeople in an attempt to turn the drama into what they call "documentary history." The truth is so buried in Big Stone that there is a house she supposedly occupied when she came to "The Gap" to attend school. John Fox apparently tried to set the record straight in his final novel, *The Heart of the Hills*, but as the town and now the town's newest favorite daughter, Adriana Trigiani, attest, June Tolliver, Jack Hale, and the unreal world they inhabit are alive and well in Southwest Virginia. Many criticize *Trail* for being romanticized, but no one save Wilson tells in print how life really was in "The Gap" at the turn of the twentieth century. And, romanticized or not romanticized, Fox's description of the Gap and "The Gap," quoted above, paints the picture against which his story "Through the Gap" plays out and also provides the setting for the drama that is central to both the new novel by Trigiani and to the small town's twenty-first-century tourism.

"Through the Gap" is the tale of a nameless mountaineer and his woman. Walking through the Gap, they appear one day in town. A "Malungian" follows them. The mountaineer goes to work on the railroad. The Sunday following, the "Malungian" is seen talking with the girl. Readers can only assume that he is telling her finally with a mocking sneer that her man has been with a woman of questionable reputation.

---

[4]Edward L. Tucker, "John Fox, Jr." at <http://www.galenet.com/servlet/Lit . . . [parameters missing] Fox+Jr&PX=0000033326DT=Biography> accessed 17 May 2000.

[5]Wilson, "Some Reflections."

Soon the Malungian is injured on the job, his head split open by the mountaineer, his coworker. A Home Guard member, the narrator, arrests the mountaineer for assault, but he is not punished because no one shows up in court to accuse him. The girl disappears into the hills only to reappear one day and be seen waiting for her man when he gets home from work. We are not privy to the words that pass between them, but they go to the preacher to be married, after which she follows the man—a respectful distance behind him—back to their shack. Then, as mysteriously as they have come, they walk over the bridge and out of town into the Kentucky hills.

Fox's very short story of perhaps a thousand words is an interesting piece that cannot be properly understood without knowing others of his stories and novels. For example, it is really important to have a picture of the town and its society in mind against which to place this story. Another element that Fox uses in "Through the Gap" is the archetype of the "mountain woman" that he delineates in detail in other places. Here the girl gets few words, but in the story "Down the Kentucky on a Raft" he spends more than half a page describing mountain women.

> I got a last glimpse of the women shading their patient eyes to watch the lessening figures on the raft and the creaking oars flashing white in the sunlight; and I thought of them going back to their lonely little cabins on this creek to await the home-coming of the men. If the mountain-women have any curiosity about that distant land, the Blue-grass "settlemints," they never show it. I have never known a mountain-woman to go down the river on a raft. Perhaps they don't care to go; perhaps it is not proper, for their ideas of propriety are very strict; perhaps the long trip back on foot deterred them so long that the habit of not going is too strong to overcome. And then if they did go, who would tend the ever-present baby in arms, the ever-numerous children; make the garden and weed and hoe the young corn for the absent lord and master. I suppose it was generations of just such lonely women, waiting at their cabins in pioneer days for the men to come home, that gives the mountain-woman the brooding look of pathos that so touches the stranger's heart to-day; and it is the watching to-day that will keep unchanged that look of vacant sadness for generations to come.[6]

---

[6]Fox, "Down the Kentucky on a Raft," in *Christmas Eve on Lonesome, "Hell-fer-Sartin," and Other Stories,* 183-84.

I think Fox assumes his readers understand the mountain culture and play the spare narrative of "Through the Gap" against the backdrop he has described so richly elsewhere. His mountain women are often etched in doorways looking out at men either leaving or coming home. The girl under discussion in our story gets short shrift, but she is part of this canon. When the mountaineer inquires the whereabouts of a preacher, "[t]he girl flushed slightly and turned her head away with a rather unhappy smile."[7] At dusk the following day the narrator sees the man chopping wood outside the shanty and "the girl was cooking supper inside."[8] A few days later on Sunday, after the man has been seen talking with a loose woman, our writer says:

> Passing on by the shanty, I saw the Malungian talking to the girl. She apparently paid no heed to him until, just as he was moving away, he said something mockingly, and with a nod of his head back towards the bridge. She did not look up even then, but her face got hard and white, and looking back from the road, I saw her slipping through he bushes into the dry bed of the creek, to make sure that what the half-breed told her was true.[9]

Next, the assault occurs and the mountaineer goes free to return to his cabin and his job, but the woman has disappeared.

> Every dusk [writes the narrator] I saw him in his doorway, waiting, and I could guess for what. It was easy to believe that the stern purpose in his face would make its way through space and draw her to him again. And she did come back one day. I had just limped down the mountain with a sprained ankle. A crowd of women was gathered at the edge of the woods, looking with all their eyes to the shanty on the river-bank. The girl stood in the door-way. The mountaineer was coming back from work with his face down.

---

[7]Fox, "Through the Gap," in *Christmas Eve on Lonesome, "Hell-fer-Sartin," and Other Stories*, 102.

[8]"Through the Gap," 103.

[9]"Through the Gap."

"He haint' seed her yit," said one. "He's goin; to kill her shore. I tol' her he would. She said she reckoned he would, but she didn't keer."[10]

The narrator then surmises that the man is likely to do the girl serious harm, but he misses the mark. Instead the two come out of the shack together and go to be married by the preacher. We read:

In the doorway just then stood the girl with a bonnet in her hand, and at a nod from him they started up the hill towards the cottage. They came down again after a while, he stalking ahead, and she, after the mountain fashion, behind.[11]

Whatever words may have come from this woman's mouth or from the man to her, there is a strong bond between the two, man (a mountaineer and a devil according to the railroad foreman) and woman. He calls her back from the hills to his side with clairvoyant power, and she, in spite of his consorting with another "hideously rouged" female, convinces him to make the bond permanent. Did she declare her undying love? Did she tell him she was going to bear his child?

The story obviously raises as many questions as it answers. As Darlene Wilson asks on the Melungeon Homepage where this story is printed in its entirety, "[O]f what ethnic background is the woman? What's her relationship to the 'Malungian'?"[12] The woman may be a Melungeon herself even though the only reason we have to think that is her conversation with the half-breed man. I would guess that either the "Malungian" is her brother or a suitor for her hand. Whoever he is, he wants her to know that the man she fancies is a scoundrel. She, on the other hand, must tell her man that the "Malungian," her brother or her suitor, has his number because the crusty mountaineer takes revenge.

There are other assumptions in this story worth noting. Fox uses the terms "Malungian" and "half-breed" interchangeably to refer to the Melungeon character. This is a definite statement about who Melungeons might be: half Indian and half something else. Then, too, there is the aura of class distinctions between the narrator and the story's three main characters. Is this narrator Fox himself? Is he a lawyer? Is he an engineer?

---

[10]"Through the Gap," 104.
[11]"Through the Gap," 105.
[12]Darlene Wilson, "A Melungeon Homepage" accessed at <http://www.melungeons.org/mel_fox.htm> on 20 September 1999, but currently (temporarily?) not on line.

We cannot be sure, but we do certainly know that he is allied with the preacher, and the doctor. He enjoys enough leisure to go onto the mountain for no particular reason, and to come back down with a sprained ankle. This narrator is a member of the Home Guard, and he assumes that the readers understand all that office entails. There is a code operating in the mountain society that the narrator is not a part of. The fact that the "Malungian" does not press charges indicates that he is following rules of mountain justice unlike the law and order of "The Gap," and the crowd of women think they know things about the girl, the mountaineer, and their relationship that we readers can only hope to learn in the future.

The little story is framed by two sets of parentheses: the reference to the light that causes from time to time a rainbow to span the Gap and the coming and going of the mountaineer and the young woman. Note here the beginning and the ending that both utilize the light that makes rainbows, the footbridge over the stream, and the entrance and exit of the characters.

> When thistles go adrift, the sun sets down the valley between the hills; when snow comes, it goes down behind the Cumberland and streams through a great fissure that people call the Gap. Then the last light drenches the parson's cottage under Imboden Hill, and leaves an afterglow of glory on a majestic heap that lies against the east. Sometimes it spans the Gap with a rainbow.
>
> Strange people and strange tales come through this Gap from the Kentucky hills. Through it came these two, late one day—a man and a woman—afoot. I met them at the footbridge over Roaring Fork.[13]

Then similar to this opening frame comes the ending:

> They came down . . . he stalking ahead, and she, after the mountain fashion, behind. And after this fashion I saw them at sunset next day pass over the bridge and into the mouth of the Gap whence they came. Through this Gap come strange people and strange tales from the Kentucky hills. Over it, sometimes, is the span of a rainbow.[14]

---

[13]Fox, "Through the Gap," 102.
[14]"Through the Gap," 105.

John Fox, Jr., wrote many other stories. Several of them mention characters named Mullins (two of whom are moonshiners). However, in no other published story does the term "Malungian" occur.

Big Stone Gap, the new novel by Adriana Trigiani, is a romance called in a recent review "part travelogue, part Bildungsroman, and part 'Cinderella' "[15] with a contrived yet satisfying girl-marries-boy ending. Anyone who has been to "The Gap" and strolled through the Poplar Hill neighborhood can feel the aura of the picturesque mountain town and sense the mists and pines of the mountains on every side. Southwest Virginia is re-created with mostly truthful details like the visit to the Carter Family Fold, a snake-handling preacher, a handsome coal miner, a beautiful Melungeon, Elizabeth Taylor's 1978 senate campaign visit turned disaster, and Big Stone Gap's outdoor drama, "Trail of the Lonesome Pine." Trigiani grew up in Big Stone Gap and has heretofore written TV sitcoms, including "The Cosby Show," and documentaries. *Big Stone Gap* is her first novel.

The novel's main character, town spinster and superwoman Ave Maria Mulligan—pharmacist, rescue squad cocaptain, heiress, drama director, and the Gap's only Italian-American—journeys through the valley of the shadow of the death of her beloved mother and in the process moves from prickly self-sufficiency to vulnerability borne of self-knowledge. The theme of the book—"be sure to tell your children the truth about their heritage"—is played out on two levels: in the life of Ave Maria, the main character, and in the life of Worley Olinger half-hillbilly, half-Melungeon.

Named for Ave Maria Albricci, a woman or perhaps an angel who paid mother Fiametta's passage to America when an unplanned pregnancy mandated leaving her Italian family to save their reputation, Ave Maria Mulligan is thirty-five and because of her knowledge of Chinese face reading, believes the year following her thirty-fifth birthday, her thirty-sixth, will be her most momentous. She thinks she doesn't need or want a man; however, as events unfold she has to admit to herself that one of her life's most poignant longings is to be "chosen." Just weeks after Fiametta's death, Ave Maria reads a letter from her mother that changes her life—she discovers the long-guarded secret of her origin. She ultimately realizes she will never be able to give herself to any man until

[15]Monica Williams, " 'Gap' Is a Portrayal of Peculiarities," book review in *Boston Globe* (16 May 2000) accessed 18 July 2000 online at <http://www.omaha.com/Omaha/OWH/StoryViewer/1,3153,338776,00.html>.

she solves the mystery of her own paternity. Trigiani gives readers glimpses of life in the small mountain town through the eyes of Ave Maria, its favorite outsider who is the book's believable if not always perceptive narrator. College-educated, career-oriented, single, and "eyetalian," Ave Maria must sort through the puzzle of her Appalachian raising (she has an accent) and her gene pool (she looks Italian) to find where she truly belongs.

There are, in fact, two eligible men in Ave Maria's life: her best friend, Theodore Tipton, band director at Powell Valley High School, and her since-childhood admirer, Jack MacChesney, Big Stone Gap's most eligible bachelor. Both of them propose at least once in the course of the narrative. There is Ave Maria's best girlfriend, Iva Lou Wade, the librarian on the Wise County bookmobile whose philosophy of life is remarkable. When Ave Maria proposes a trip to Italy to unravel the mystery of her paternity, Iva Lou gets real:

> "Do you deprive yourself of a ripe strawberry or a spritz of nice perfume because you don't think you deserve them? Hell, no. Sex is no different. It is a delightful gift from God that makes life pleasant. Now, what could be wrong with that? You'll find out a heluva lot more about yourself in bed with a good man than you will traipsing off to some foreign country with a camera and a guidebook. You need to get honest with yourself. You're afraid. But you want sex. You ought to have you some sex."[16]

Another noteworthy character is Fleeta Mullins, chain-smoking fifty-something World Wrestling Federation (WWF) fanatic. With a name like Mullins she is probably at least married to a Melungeon even though such a possibility is never mentioned. Fleeta is Ave Maria's only employee at the pharmacy until she hires Pearl Grimes, a high-school girl Ave Maria recognizes as a clone of her growing-up self. Overweight Pearl has acne and a poor self-image, but blossoms under Ave Maria's tutelage.

The Melungeon character never actually appears in the novel. She exists only in memory. She is the girl that the Gap's handyman Otto Olinger fell in love with at fifteen.

> "I done had me a true love, but it was many, many years ago. Well, it was summer. I was 'bout fifteen. Mama done made me go to town fer jars. She was canning her some chow chow. Walkin' down, I passed a trailer. Lot of kids runnin' around.

---

[16]Adriana Trigiani, *Big Stone Gap* (New York: Random House, 2000) 224.

Their people, I could just tell, was Melungeon. They had that dark color, and that look of them. There was a girl there. She had her some black hair, shiny and straight in braids. I 'member thinkin' that the braids look like them garlands over the bank door. They was that long. And she had her some black eyes like coal. And she was small. Tiny, like a matchbox. Reminded me of that story book about the fairy girl."

"Thumbelina?"

"Yeah. Thumbelina."

"What was your girl's name?"

"Destry." Otto looks away at the mention of her name. "Best name I ever heard." He says quietly.

"So what happened?"

"The summer passed. And pert near every day she walked with me. I grew to like 'at and look forward to it. One day she couldn't go with me, and I missed her bad. I knew then that I loved her. Turned out her pappy moved their trailer over to Stonega. I walked over there about five miles. I done had something to give her. My mama had a little silver ring with a red stone in it. And I loved Destry so much, I stole it and give it to her."

"How do you like 'at!" Worley said, laughing.

"You must have loved her very much to steal for her."

"That I did, ma'am. That I did." . . .

"Where is Destry now?"

"She died." Otto sighs.

"That's the sad part of the story," Worley says. He looks at his brother with great feeling.

"Yes, Ma'am. She died. Melungeons git all sorts of things— they catch just about anything that's out there, and they're weak, so it tends to take 'em. She was sixteen when she died. I wanted to murry her, but she was too sick."

"Why do the Melungeons die like 'at?" Worley asks.

"Well, the theory is that there's a lot of inbreeding there. Up in the mountains, folks didn't mix with the general population. And that hurt them. Because the more of a mix you get, the stronger the blood. Or so the doctors believe."

"Where do they come from?"

"*Melungeon* comes from the French word *melange*. It means 'mixed.' "

"I thought the Melungeons were them folks from the Lost Colony down in North Carolina."

"That's another theory."

"What's the Lost Colony" Worley asks.

"Ye tell him, Miss Ave," Otto says.

"I think the lost Colony was more of a tale told in the hills rather than actual fact. But the story goes that settlers from England landed on the North Carolina coast near Virginia. The ship dropped them off with supplies, and they built a colony. There was a fort, gardens, little houses, a church—things were going well. But when the ships returned from England a year later, the colony was a ghost town. Clothes were hanging in the closets. But no people. The people had vanished. They looked for them but never found them. There was only one clue: the word *Croatan* was carved on a tree. Some believe that a settler carved that before he was kidnapped away by the Indians. It's just a guess, though. So, a Melungeon could be a person who descends from a mix of the settlers and Indians, who hid here in these hills and never left. Your Destry could have been a descendant of those people."

"Well, all I know is I never loved no other." Otto says this with such clarity, I know it is true.

The three of us sit and drink our coffee. We're all thinking about little Destry. Otto had the real thing and lost it.[17]

This passage does more than advance the story; it reveals facts and attitudes about Melungeons. Destry is a beautiful girl with long black hair. Her father is obviously not a landowner. The two young people, Otto and Destry, did not marry. Folks in the Gap, Ave Maria at least, believe certain facts about them: too much inbreeding has made them biologically weak and therefore subject to disease; the name *Melungeon* has a French origin.

Earlier in the novel when Ave Maria is telling about the general population of the Gap she mentions a different origin theory that implies familiarity with Brent Kennedy's book, "The people around here are mainly Scotch-Irish, or Melungeon (folks who are a mix of Turkish, French, African, Indian, and who know that; they live up in the mountain hollers and stick to themselves)."[18]

---

[17]Trigiani, *Big Stone Gap*, 28-30.
[18]Trigiani, *Big Stone Gap*, 6.

The two characters of Otto and Worley Olinger are present through-out the story. They are fixtures in the Gap known as "the Are Y'all Using That? Brothers because that's how they greet you when they want some-thing from your yard."[19] Narrator Ave Maria describes them with some affection:

> Otto appears to be the older of the two. He is short-legged and sturdy, with gray hair and a few teeth left on the bottom. . . . Worley has thick red hair and is tall and lean. His long face matches his long body. Nobody in town is exactly sure how old they are because they did not matriculate through the school system. But they seem to have been around forever.[20]

They repair the roof, repoint the bricks at the pharmacy, put up storm windows, clean the gutters, and scavenge for old furniture. How-ever, their real purpose in the workings of this novel is the way their per-sonal story parallels and underscores Ave Maria's own situation. Because Ave Maria is a member of the rescue squad, she is often on hand at moments of crisis in the lives of Big Stone Gap's citizens. Near the end of the story, as she is preparing to leave town on her trip to Italy, even though she has officially left the squad, Otto has a heart attack and Spec, squad captain, seeks out his former partner to go with him to the hospital.

> Otto asked Worley to take him to Saint Agnes Hospital instead of Lonesome Pine. The Catholic nuns appeal to his super-stitious nature. When Spec and I check in, we're told Otto is in intensive care. The tone of the nurse's voice tells us that the situation is serious. Nurses have many excellent skills, but they are never good actresses.
> Worley kneels next to his brother's bed, holding his left hand, the one without the IV, in both of his hands. . . . Spec goes to the opposite side of the bed, close to Otto's face. I gently place my hands on Worley's shoulders. He has been crying.[21]

Ave Maria convinces Worley to go with Spec for a cup of coffee so she can get information for him from Sister Ann Christina, the head of

---

[19]Trigiani, *Big Stone Gap*, 26.
[20]Trigiani, *Big Stone Gap*, 26.
[21]Trigiani, *Big Stone Gap*, 192.

the intensive care unit. The news is bleak. Ave Maria leans in to talk to Otto.

"Otto, what in the hell are you doing in the hospital?"

He smiles at me weakly. His eyes are lively, though. He motions to the oxygen mask. He wants me to lift it off. I lift it ever so slightly, so he can catch some air to speak.

"I need you to tell Worley something."

"Sure."

Otto and I settle into a breathing-and-speaking routine. I push the mask up and down as he finishes a sentence. He catches his breath and continues.

"I ain't Worley's brother." I look confused. Sometimes folks go out of their minds when their bodies shut down on them, but hallucination isn't usually part of a heart attack, nor is memory loss.

"Who are you, then?"

"I'm his daddy."

I grip the stainless steel bed guard to steady myself. It is cold.

"Remember Destry?" I nod. "Destry was his mama. She died when she had him. The state wanted to take him, but Mama told them Worley was hers so they couldn't."

"He doesn't know?"

Otto shakes his head.

"You have to tell him, Otto. You have to." I say this slowly and deliberately, emphasizing the *you*.

"I can't."

"Yes, you can. You just told me. You can do this. You must."

Otto takes a long breath, and his eyes fill with tears. "I can't."

"Why can't you?" Otto closes his eyes tightly, hoping I will change my mind once he opens them. Then he opens his eyes and looks up at the ceiling. He barely whispers, "He will be ashamed of me."[22]

Suddenly Otto's confession and admission of the reason for his long years of silence make a light go on for Ave Maria. She knows why her mother never could tell the truth about who her father was. "My mother

---

[22]Trigiani, *Big Stone Gap*, 193-94.

could not bear the thought of me ever being ashamed of her," she reasons, "so she lied to me. A lie is better than rejection by your own flesh and blood when they find out that you are not perfect."[23] The realization spurs her to insist that Otto must tell Worley the truth about his Melungeon mother and he must do it immediately.

> "Goddammit, Otto. I'm a bastard. Not because of the circum-stances of my birth, but because I was lied to. The lie made it wrong. You had something most people only dream of: a real and true love. And you were graced with a baby! A baby that came from you and Destry. Haven't you spent your entire life thinking about it? Thinking about her? Wouldn't you have given everything to hold her again? What is wrong with that? You loved her. That is a sacred thing!"
>
> "I was gonna marry her," he whispers.
>
> "Tell him that. Tell him what your plans were. Tell him what Destry wanted for him. Anything you can remember. Tell him everything It's the best thing you will ever do for him."[24]

With this scene an important theme in the novel is poignantly under-scored: teach your children well, and always tell them the truth. When Ave Maria finally meets her father, she thinks,

> I wish my mother could have told me this story herself. I find myself angry with her, not him. . . . My mother and I were so close, practically inseparable. It hurts me that she could not tell me the truth. Even shameful mistakes can be rectified, healed, and forgiven once they are dealt with. How sad for us that Mama could not let go of her shame.[25]

Ave Maria is clear about the need for truth when it is her mother or Otto who need to come clean. It is harder in her own life to admit that she has been living a lie in her determination to be self-sufficient and not to fall in love. It takes a confrontation by Nan MacChesney and nearly killing a mother cat with her jeep for Ave Maria to see what she herself must do. "Eventually [the mother cat] crawls out and tends to the babies. She licks them. They seem to be okay. I start to cry. I realize what a phony I am. I told Otto in no uncertain terms that he had to be honest

---

[23]Trigiani, *Big Stone Gap*, 194.
[24]Trigiani, *Big Stone Gap*, 194.
[25]Trigiani, *Big Stone Gap*, 218.

with Worley about his shame. And yet I cannot be honest about my own."[26] The dam has finally broken and the story careens towards its resolution, the Melungeon story line being a clear restatement of one of its important messages.

There is a postscript. The truth about Otto and Destry, the fact that she died in childbirth, echoes other stories we have looked at in this study. Remember Deutsia in *Daughter of the Legend* and Effena in *The Hawk's Done Gone*? Having babies without much medical support is both a life-giving and a life-threatening endeavor for young mountain girls.

These two stories from the Gap then give us glimpses of Appalachian society. Set a century apart, their commonality is the romantic setting that John Fox, Jr. so adroitly sketches. Both he and Trigiani build on that foundation. Both choose a Melungeon character and there are in each narrative a winsome mountain girl to add a question to the matrix: Why must life so often be such an inexplicable heartbreak?

---

[26]Trigiani, *Big Stone Gap*, 234.

13

Borrowing the Legend: The Process Comes Full Circle in Naylor's Sang Spell

Phyllis Reynolds Naylor has written more than seventy books, most of them for children and young adults. Her many awards over the years are reliable testimony to her skill as a writer, the most prestigious plaudits being the Edgar Allen Poe Award from the Mystery Writers of America in 1985 for *Night Cry* (1984) and the Newbery Award for *Shiloh* (1991). Naylor was born in 1933 in Anderson, Indiana. She moved often during her childhood and adolescence and felt she had no real roots in any particular state or town. Taken with the idea of writing from early childhood on, she would compose and illustrate stories, stapling them together into books of her own making.

Naylor is open about her personal writing process and what she sees as influences on her work. In an interview with the publisher of *Contemporary Authors* she said:

> Two things that Willa Cather once wrote have stayed with me always: "Let your fiction grow out of the land beneath your feet," and "The years from eight to fifteen are the formative period in a writer's life." I first copied these sentences down without having any idea, really, of how they applied to me. It wasn't so much that there was nothing to write about back in the Midwest, as that we never seemed to stay in one place long enough to put down roots. My father was a traveling salesman; as he changed jobs, we changed houses, and by the time I entered high school we had lived in eight different neighborhoods stretching across Indiana, Illinois, and Iowa. The land beneath *my* feet was constantly changing.[1]

I believe the character of Joshua Vardy, the hero of Naylor's Melungeon-focused novel *Sang Spell*, was born out of this childhood.

---

[1]"Phyllis Reynolds Naylor," *Contemporary Authors*, New Revision Series, vol. 24 (Farmington MI: Gale Group, n.d.) loc. cit.; italics in original.

Naylor knows what it is like to be the new kid at school, to have to begin again to make friends and to find her niche in an already connected peer group. Josh's displacement is a strong echo of Naylor's own childhood displacements. Perhaps in her own growing-up years on the first day of school in a new place she wished she could disappear into a mysterious and magic world instead of living out that initially painful period in a new environment.

In an essay she wrote for the Internet Public Library's "Ask the Author" feature, Naylor comments further on how she gets ideas, collects material and actually writes her novels.

> Getting an idea for a book is not hard for me; keeping other ideas away while I am working on one story is what is difficult. My books are based on things that have happened to me, things I have heard or read about, all mixed up with my imaginings. The best part about writing is the moment a character comes alive on paper, or when a place that existed only in my head becomes real. . . .
>
> When I get an idea for a book, I put the name of it on masking tape and place it on the spine of a large 3-ring notebook. On a shelf beside my writing chair are about 10 of these notebooks, each with the name of a book-to-be on it. Every time I get an idea about one of these books, I jot it down in the notebook. There are pockets in each notebook which I fill with photographs, maps, pages from telephone books, newspaper clippings—anything at all that will help me in the writing of the book. When I feel ready—when I start waking early in the mornings and can't wait to get writing—then I know that a particular book is ready.[2]

It is fun to speculate about this process in reference to *Sang Spell*. On the back of the title page before the narrative even begins, Naylor acknowledges her debt to Brent Kennedy. "Parts of this book," she writes, "were based on material found in N. Brent Kennedy's book *The Melungeons: The Resurrection of a Proud People*." She goes on to mention other sources,[3] and gives more information about Melungeons than the story

---

[2] "Phyllis Reynolds Naylor," Internet Public Library (IPL), Youth Division: Ask the Author, accessed 25 August 1999, at <http://www.ipl.org/youth/AskAuthor/Naylor.html>; typographical errors corrected.

[3] Naylor mentions these sources: *The Melungeons: An Untold Story of Ethnic Cleansing in America* (*Islamic Horizons*, November/December 1994) by N. Brent Kennedy; "Melungeon Connection" (*The Coalfield Progress*, 6 June 1995) by Jeff

itself reveals in an afterword.[4] Were the articles she mentions actually tucked into her Melungeon notebook? We wonder. Did she have some pages from a Hancock County, Tennessee, or a Lee County, Virginia, phone book? Were there real photographs from Sneedville, Vardy, and Wise or a picture of Mahala Mullins' cabin on Newman's Ridge in one of her notebook's pockets?

Naylor's articulation of her reasons for writing sound somewhat like Lee Smith on the same topic.

> I'm not happy unless I spend some time every day writing. It's as though pressure builds up inside me, and writing even a little helps to release it. . . .
>
> . . . I'm . . . lucky to have the troop of noisy, chattering characters who travel with me inside my head. As long as they are poking, prodding, demanding a place in a book, I have things to do and stories to tell. . . .
>
> . . . I think the most important thing for writers is to write what really moves them emotionally, what they enjoy writing most, and what they feel most strongly about. . . . It is also important to remember that the story is everything. It if is well done, the message will be so much a part of it that the author doesn't even have to think about it.[5]

It is interesting to see how these things play out in *Sang Spell*, Naylor's 1998 novel with a distinct Melungeon focus. No one since Jesse Stuart has written a story that concerns only the Melungeon experience. Naylor focuses on what it means to be a Melungeon in an unusual way because the novel takes place in a curious wrinkle in time and space. As the story opens, the main character, Joshua Vardy, is hitchhiking from Boston to Dallas. He is trying to make sense of his life gone awry since his mother's recent death in an automobile accident. An athlete of some reputation and promise at his old high school, Josh faces the prospect of being a nobody at his new school. He is too young to face the future on his own, so he must go to Texas to live with his aunt.

It is August as he sets out, and the story opens on a surprisingly cold and rainy night somewhere in the Appalachian mountains. Josh has been

---

Lester; and "Historic Ancestry Explored" (*Tuscaloosa News*, 1 November 1993) by Dana Beyerle.

[4] Phyllis R. Naylor, afterword to *Sang Spell* (New York: Atheneum Books for Young Readers, Simon & Schuster, 1998) 175-76.

[5] "Phyllis Reynolds Naylor," IPL (see n. 2, above).

left off at a remote exit by a trucker and decides to hike up the road he finds himself on to look for shelter. Shivering, soaked, and miserable, Josh is not choosy about a ride. He is mugged and robbed by the driver of an old Buick and left senseless by the side of the road. Soon after he comes to, a woman driving a wagon indicates that he may climb on. It's not long until he reaches a village in the hills that time has truly forgotten—no electricity, no motorized vehicles, no paved streets. Naylor lavishes time and energy on describing this place that she names Canara. Brent Kennedy discusses this name in his book.

> "Canara," unknown among other Anglo-Appalachian families, is especially intriguing.
>   The name "Canara" has been in my family at least since the 1700s. It is nearly identical to "Canaira," the surname of a principal Spanish monk assigned to the southeast during the time of the Santa Elena colony. It is also pronounced virtually the same as "Caneiro," a small Portuguese village not far from Fatima. It could also be a variation of the "Canary Islands," the way station for many Iberian explorers and settlers heading for the New World, as well as a "dumping ground" for Berber exiles. And Canara was a family tradition well before any of our family could have read about the Santa Elena colony or even randomly selected "Canaira" from a map of Portugal (which in and of itself would have been a highly improbable action for my "uneducated" eighteenth-century ancestors).[6]

Canara, or Kanara/Karnataka (formerly Mysore), is in fact a verifiable place in southwestern India where a group of mixed-race people sometimes called Dravidians live. Knowing what scholars now believe about the Indo-European family of languages, it is possible to speculate that this name meant "mixed race" long before anyone came up with the term "Tri-Racial Isolate," or the theory that goes along with it. Naylor more than likely took the name from Kennedy's book, but a ten-second foray into a good dictionary yields an actual meaning for Kanara/Karnataka which adds richness to what Kennedy says by bringing in the idea of a people of mixed-racial background. Whether the reader catches this allu-

---

[6]N. Brent Kennedy, *The Melungeons: The Resurrection of a Proud People. An Untold Story of Ethnic Cleansing in America*, 2nd ed. (Macon GA: Mercer University Press, 1997) 139-40.

sion or not, the name seems as mysterious as the remote and phantasmal village actually is in the story.

Josh Vardy stays in Canara not because he wants to but because he is held there by forces he can neither explain nor understand. Every time he tries to escape, by walking, by swimming, by rowing away in a small boat, he rather quickly circles back to the village. Life is simple in Canara: the days are regulated by the ringing of a bell, the community takes meals in a primitive cookhouse, residents live by subsistence farming and hunting, and they gather wild ginseng as their one cash crop. The government is a direct democracy; transgressions against the community's rules are dealt with immediately by trial, which is followed by swift punishment. Readers and Josh learn about Mavis's father who was stoned for starting a devastating fire that killed four people. When he loses one of the community's two rowboats in one of his escape attempts, Josh himself is sentenced to dig a new privy, by all measures a demeaning task.

Josh has two mentors in the valley, the man called Pardo and a young woman named Mavis. Pardo tells Josh that only Melungeons come to Canara, that he is free to leave, but that no one knows how to show him the way out. Mavis becomes his closest friend, shows him consistent kindness, tells him the history of the Melungeons, and reveals that Canara is a place of healing. She assures him that when he is healed from whatever is hurting him he will be able to go.

One other person overshadows Josh's time in Carana—Kaspar. Kaspar is the second-most-recent "recruit" in the village. In his life on the outside he had been a college student at Penn State. On a rappelling trip, he got trapped in a canyon he couldn't climb out of and was ultimately rescued, as Josh was, by the mute Leone. Kaspar makes no attempt to hide his anger at what he views as imprisonment by the Melungeons or his frustration about not being able to leave. He badgers Josh continuously to side with him and to try to escape. Josh plays along, but when Kaspar plots to kill Leone and Isobel, the ancient village matriarch, Josh takes the two women to a safe place and reveals the details of the plot to the village elders.

The novel ends with Kaspar's trial and punishment and Josh's leave-taking. In the incident with Kaspar, Josh finds important strength and resources inside himself. He knows that walking away will be permanent. Mavis starts to leave with him, but turns back. He walks until dawn when suddenly he reaches the interstate.

This novel is interesting in that it can be billed several ways. One could call it a bildungsroman (a story about the adventure of growing up) with fantastic interruptions—or a fantasy with a realistic main character, or a quest without the classic loss of a body part before the ending, or an adventure/accomplishment romance.[7] However, whatever terms are applied, it is the story of a young man who is separated physically, emotionally, and spiritually from the nurturing love of his mother (by virtue of her death). This young hero, who embodies the noble qualities of adventurousness, bravery, and athletic prowess, undergoes several tests of courage and stamina. There is a happy ending because he succeeds in finding his way back to civilization where we trust he will soon be reunited with his aunt and be able to find friends and security in his new school, especially due to the wisdom he has gained from becoming aware not only of his Melungeon heritage but also his inner resources.

Reading the last page, I find myself wondering whether I should label the novel a "dream vision" story since the whole fantastic narrative may have taken place in a dream that begins on the rainy night when Josh is bludgeoned into oblivion on that lonely byway and ends possibly the very next morning when Josh "wakes up" to find himself hiking back to the busy-ness of the interstate highway.

Sang Spell is a novel formed in large part by its setting. Naylor spends much time describing Canara, interweaving information about Melungeons in the process. The place itself is one of the ways she explores what it means to be Melungeon. The first mention of where Josh might be on that cold, rainy night in August is ominous, coming from the surly driver of the Buick in response to Josh's question about where they are, "Don't know it's got a name. Folks "round here call it Sang Hollow."[8] Twenty miles later, sure that they must by now be somewhere else, Josh asks again,

"Where are we?"
"Told you. Sang Hollow."
"We were in Sang Hollow an hour ago!"
"It's here and about."[9]

The beating at the hands of the disagreeable man, Josh's struggle to deal with his painful injuries, and the ride on the horse-drawn cart take

---

[7]"Romance" is defined as a novel with a happy ending, enough exaggeration to make the story more interesting than real life, a quest in which the protagonist experiences doubts and undergoes severe trials, and success in the end. Paraphrased from Kenneth L. Donelson and Aileen Pace Nielsen, *Literature for Today's Young Adults*, 5th ed. (New York: Longman, 1997) 109.

[8]Naylor, *Sang Spell*, 5.

[9]Naylor, *Sang Spell*, 8.

this young protagonist into another world. In the first few hours that he is in the remote Appalachian village he meets the three people who will shape his time there—Kaspar, Pardo, and Mavis.

> [Kaspar:] "We could always kill him."
> [Pardo:] "I can tape up those ribs for you. . . . Make you feel better."
> [Mavis:] "Stay here. I'll bring you a biscuit."[10]

In these first utterances the relationships are delineated—Kaspar the adversary, Pardo the healer, Mavis the nurturer.

After eating his simple breakfast, Josh takes interest in his surroundings:

> He was in a long building of rough-hewn logs, with stalls along one side, hay at both ends, and enough room to park two wagons. He made his way over to the door of the stable and looked out over the rural landscape. A scent he could not name teased his nostrils, then wafted away again, so subtle he could almost have missed it. It was nothing he had smelled before, and he wasn't entirely sure it was an odor at all. An aura perhaps.
>
> Everything was sealed in fog—a hut, a shed, a wagon, a well. Everything was gray—gray sky, gray trees, gray hut, gray ground. Gray people in gray clothes moving about the clearing, and there was no sound at all now but the drip, drip of water off one corner of the roof, splashing slowly, one drop at a time into a large barrel.[11]

His injuries and the trauma of his displacement induce sleep. When he wakes he begins to explore and in doing so realizes how far away he is from everything he has ever known.

> [He] stood in the doorway waiting for whoever would show. The fog had lifted, and Josh was surprised to see that there were hills, layers of hills, rising high above the trees. He had thought when he left the interstate that he had climbed and climbed to the place he had been robbed. Perhaps the woman in the cart had taken him down again to a valley on the other side, for a valley it seemed to be. Or perhaps the valley where she had taken him was a hollow high in the mountains, and he would have to go

---

[10]Naylor, *Sang Spell*, 13.
[11]Naylor, *Sang Spell*, 18.

through a pass and down the other side before he could get back
to the highway. Up or down? Down or up? He was thoroughly
confused.[12]

The more he learns the more puzzled Josh becomes. Not only is
Carana set in the middle of wilderness, its social order seems backward
to Josh. He learns that the primary task of harvesting the ginseng is
undertaken in common, all able-bodied people in the village who do not
have other assigned tasks participate in it. The single men live in a large
dormitory; the single women stay with their families. Space is at a premi-
um, so cooking is done in the cookhouse, and the small family cabins are
used for sleeping space. Level land is scarce and needed for growing
food crops, so no new cabins can be built. The entire community is contained in one narrow valley; the Melungeons cannot expand their holdings into another valley. When Josh states his intention to leave as soon
as possible, someone tells him in jest yet dead serious, "There's only one
road, and it ends at the barn."[13] Josh verifies this fact for himself the first
time he tries to leave. Shouldering his backpack on the first rest day after
his arrival, he walks on a rutted mountain road *away* from the barn for
an entire morning.

> [T]hings began looking the same to him—the hills, the road,
> the mud. At last he sensed an opening in the trees ahead, and
> could hear the steady sound of a shovel hitting the ground and
> striking rock, someone clearing a field, perhaps. He was certain
> he was close to human habitation, if only a hermit far out in the
> woods. He would offer to work for a meal. A few directions, and
> he'd be off again in an hour or two.
> Hurrying on a little faster and ignoring the rawness of his
> shoulder, Josh went over the last rise and around the bend. He
> stopped, his breath coming fast, his strength giving way. There
> below was Canara, yellow in the morning sun, and Pardo,
> clearing a patch of ground. . . .
> He could understand that he might have taken a wrong turn
> and circled back to Canara, except that he was positive there had
> been no fork in the road, not a single place he'd had to decide,
> *this way or that?*[14]

---

[12]Naylor, *Sang Spell*, 21-22.
[13]Naylor, *Sang Spell*, 30.
[14]Naylor, *Sang Spell*, 56-57.

The customs seem as foreign as the place:

> Outside [after the evening meal], the women moved one
> way, men the other. Josh soon discovered that the women went
> to an outdoor pump off in the trees to wash, and the men
> walked to the river. Heaven knew he needed a bath. He could
> feel blood still encrusted in one nostril, blood in his hair. . . .
> It was a setting that seemed medieval—workers in their
> earth-colored pants and shirts, filing down past the cow barn
> toward the river. That scent again! From one of the cabins off to
> the side came a warm glow from the window—a flickering light
> from a kerosene lamp, perhaps, or a fireplace. Josh wasn't sure.
> As they passed the barn he could hear the soft crunch of cows'
> teeth chewing hay. Here and there a villager went from garden
> to hut, from barn to well—drawing water, emptying pots,
> sweeping a doorstep, wheeling a cart. Had no one heard of the
> Industrial Revolution? He wondered. They could all have
> emerged from an Old World painting. . . .
> [T]his was an isolated community, so far back in the hills that
> there was almost no contact with the outside. They had made
> their living for decades—centuries, perhaps—doing for them-
> selves.[15]

Another oddity is the way time works in the village. As the boy Gil
tells him, " 'Time isn't the same here Josh. . . . Here there is yesterday,
today, and tomorrow. That and the seasons.' "[16] And, time is not the only
weirdness. Canara moves inside the mountain wilderness. Gil says,
" 'You go to bed at night with the hills on your left, and you wake up to
find them on your right.' "[17] When Josh questions Pardo about the location of the settlement, he gets no satisfaction, just a beginning of the
Melungeon saga. " 'Canara was here long before there were states,' Pardo
replied. That alone told Josh that Pardo knew a great deal more than he
let on."[18] Later Mavis, too, talks of this phenomenon: " 'Canara is in its
own little orbit in the place where the Melungeons settled, but it moves

[15]Naylor, *Sang Spell*, 31.
[16]Naylor, *Sang Spell*, 46.
[17]Naylor, *Sang Spell*, 47.
[18]Naylor, *Sang Spell*, 48.

around. We are always somewhere in Appalachia, but just where we are at a given time I don't know for certain.' "[19]

This setting, strange and confining, of course, mirrors Josh's imprisonment inside both his grief over his mother and his fears about the new situation of living with his aunt and going to an unfamiliar school in Dallas. In spite of all the strange things, Josh cannot really complain that he is treated without kindness. When he explains to Pardo that he must have taken the wrong road in his attempt to hike back to the interstate, Pardo does his best to give comfort.

> "No, lad, there is no wrong road. You took the only road we have." . . .
>
> Pardo put out his hand and gently touched Josh's arm as if to calm him. "Joshua, there are no gates, no locks, no walls. We keep no prisoners. You may wander as you will. Truly, if I knew the way out of Canara, I would tell you—Kaspar, too. But I don't. If there is a way, you must find it yourself." . . .
>
> Like a cold wind sweeping in from the pass, a feeling of profound dread crept over Josh's body, causing goose-flesh on his arms.[20]

Another characteristic that the villagers accept without question is the way buildings appear and disappear in the rhythm of the seasons. One of these is "The Stop," a sort of country roadhouse that appears to have been a restaurant/gas station/truck stop sort of place. On the night when The Stop appears, the young people are in charge. They bathe before dinner; the young men put on fresh shirts; and the girls exchange their muslin trousers for dresses. They get lanterns from the stable and start off across the cornfield in the dusk. Mavis tries to explain the phenomenon to Josh by telling him that The Stop comes around "when the time is right."[21] When Josh asks,

> "What would happen if you went and it wasn't the right time?"
>
> "It wouldn't be there!"
>
> "You mean it comes and goes? It disappears?" . . . Josh couldn't help feeling annoyed.

---

[19]Naylor, *Sang Spell*, 122.
[20]Naylor, *Sang Spell*, 58–59.
[21]Naylor, *Sang Spell*, 71.

Mavis looked uncomfortable, as though being asked to explain a physics problem she didn't understand. "I don't *know* any of that, Josh! Can't you just enjoy it, like everyone else?"[22]

Josh's first glimpse of The Stop gives him hope that he has returned to civilization at last. Without thinking, he finds himself reaching in his pocket to get change for a phone call. However, getting closer he discovers

there was no electricity; those who arrived first had set their lanterns in the windows. . . . Going up the cracked sidewalk thatched with weeds, he could see an old green and white sign dangling askew from one corner of the low wood building. THE STOP, it said, with the faded caricature of a steam engine on it. . . .

Josh was startled to hear music, . . . and suddenly the floor in front of him was filled with whirling couples in a strange dance he could not quite recognize. . . . At what had once been a bar, some of the young men were filling mugs with a golden brown liquid from a large cask they had brought along. Josh walked over to taste some and found it to be hard cider. . . .

There was a large blackboard by the doorway to the kitchen, the chalk notations so faded that Josh could scarcely read them. Two of the entrees were legible, however—BISCUITS AND SAUSAGE GRAVY and CORN BREAD AND SOUP. . . .

He went to the jukebox in the corner—dusty, broken, tilting slightly to the left. There must have been electricity once, he thought. Songs he didn't recognize: "High Cotton," She Drives Me Crazy," "Buck Naked," "Cherry Pie," "Paradise City." . . .

Farther on, in a dirty glass case off to one side, Josh saw items that convinced him that although this might have started as a train depot, it had since become a truck stop. . . . There were diesel fuse holders, CB parts, booster cables, power cords.

Within moments, it seemed, he was caught up again by the music of the hammered dulcimer, as rhythmical and haunting a beat as he had ever heard. The girlish faces flashed past him once again as bodies whirled. Men's boots were pounding the floor, women's hands were clapping, dresses spinning, hair flying,

---

[22]Naylor, *Sang Spell*, 71.

arms flinging . . . and then . . . almost as soon as the evening had begun, it was over.[23]

There is a second building that comes around on the autumn equinox:

> "[F]or that one day, we will all go to the schoolhouse," [Mavis tells Josh]. . . .
> "Pardo explained it once, but I'm not much good at science. It's like anything else. . . . What happens to a full moon? What happens to a storm? A sunset? Where do they go?" she shrugged. "They all come back again in their own time."[24]

Josh fantasizes about the schoolhouse before it appears, thinking that if he stays in the building after everyone else has left he might go with it back to civilization. He wonders whether the schoolhouse is the gateway to the world beyond, where Leone meets the Chinese ginseng traders, and he begins to wait impatiently for its arrival.

> The morning of the equinox, Josh followed the others along the path that led to the schoolhouse. . . .
> The school loomed before them, as solid a structure as Josh had ever seen, sitting on ground he knew he had traversed that was mere mud and leaves before.
> Eulaylia was at the desk in front when they went inside, along with Pardo and Daniel. They welcomed the students and everyone sat, smaller children at the front, young men and women at the back.
> "It was the best of times, it was the worst of times," Eulaylia began, reading from Dickens, and while she read Josh's eyes scanned the doors and windows to see how he would get back inside the schoolhouse once it was closed for the night.[25]

The school day progresses not as a school day Josh had known in Boston, but a school day reminiscent in rhythm to the one-room schools of yesteryear. Once lessons are over, the students walk back to the village to prepare for a night of dancing and merrymaking. Josh is engrossed in his own plans to leave along with the schoolhouse and pumps Mavis to get as much information as he can about the disappearance phenomenon.

---

[23]Naylor, *Sang Spell*, 72-77.
[24]Naylor, *Sang Spell*, 121-22.
[25]Naylor, *Sang Spell*, 155-56.

Mavis clutched Josh's arm tightly, as if guessing somehow that he was going to leave.

"Dance with me tonight," she pleaded. "My feet want to fly, I'm so restless."

He joked, "I'll wear out long before you. You'll have to hold me up." And then he inquired, "How long can we stay? If we feel like dancing all night, can we?'

"Not all night, surely."

"Why not?"

"The equinox. It wouldn't do. I mean, the schoolhouse wouldn't *be*."[26]

In appearance much like the earlier night when all the young people went to The Stop, the night at the schoolhouse suddenly looms different when Kaspar reveals his desperate plan. The equinox is the night that Kaspar has slated as the time he and his forcefully enlisted accomplice Josh will murder Leone and Isobel. Kaspar believes that these two women entrap and detain outsiders by some magic spell and that by killing the women the spell will be broken. Josh has been driven all through the novel by his desire to leave Canara, but as the story nears this climax he is conflicted. He has come to see Canara as a true haven, the place of healing. He senses that he himself has changed. By the time of the festivities at the schoolhouse he has difficulty thinking with any degree of clarity about his problems or how to solve them.

He clearly did not want to spend the rest of his life—the rest of the year, even—in Canara, but in some ways it was as though he belonged. As though the world of sports and proms, applause and write-ups, was only one part of him, and the rest—the soul, perhaps—was made for here. Was it really this that kept him back, however, or a lack of courage to begin again? To begin in a new place where no one knew what he could do, who he was, what he had done?[27]

Kaspar's wicked plan does jolt Josh to action. He realizes that being right is more important than leaving Canara. He protects the two women by moving them to a safe house and goes to the elders with the information about the murder plot. When the schoolhouse disappears, it is not

---

[26]Naylor, *Sang Spell*, 158.
[27]Naylor, *Sang Spell*, 157.

Josh who is inside moving toward freedom in the outside world, but
Kaspar incarcerated there as punishment and clearly going to a place of
torment.

> Josh dropped his pack and stood on the edge of the crowd,
> watching, bewildered, as Kaspar was marched up the steps,
> shoved inside, and the door locked after him. Josh was the one
> to whom Isobel and Leone owed their lives, yet it was Kaspar
> who got to leave?
>   Something was amiss, however. From inside the small build-
> ing, Kaspar suddenly began to beat against the walls. The school-
> house was fading, as though caught in a light fog. First the roof
> began to disappear from view, then the rafter window, then the
> top of the door frame, and finally, where the building had once
> stood, there was nothing at all. . . .
>   "It was justice," [Pardo] said. "It had to be done."
>   Josh stared, "It's *not* the way out, then?"
>   "No, lad. Not that." . . .
>   "How do you know he won't get out and come back here
> again?"
>   "Because once, long ago, another left with the schoolhouse.
> And when the autumnal equinox was on us again, we opened
> the door to the building and out fell a heap of bones."[28]

For Josh this is a sobering revelation.
   One more unique trait that Canara has is its pure Melungeon population. Josh entertains several theories about the why of the strange people
as he ponders the situation and his predicament. Kaspar gives the first
hint when Josh asks him, "Why *can't* we get out?" "We're Melungeon,
they tell me," replies the malcontent.[29] This fact is more confusing than
helpful until Mavis finally sets Josh straight, and Pardo later underscores
the reality.

> "You think it's your ending up here that is the problem, but
> I tell you it's not. It's what you make of it that's important, "
> [said Mavis].
>   "Then why won't anyone tell me the truth? How did Leone
> find me, and why can't I leave?"

---

[28]Naylor, *Sang Spell,* 168-70.
[29]Naylor, *Sang Spell,* 76.

"I never said you couldn't. People come to Canara by different ways, and some of the new ones leave again, but none of us
know how." . . .
"How often do you get new people?"
Not often. Everything has to be just right for it to happen,
and only those with Melungeon blood can find their way in."[30]

One day Josh sets out to find The Stop, and is in despair when he
gets to the exact place where it had been on the night of the revelry only
to find the clearing bare with no road or building in sight.

A sound he had never heard before came from his throat—a
rasping croak, so hopeless and distressed that gooseflesh rose on
his arms. . . .
Closing his eyes for a few minutes, he lay still, and when he
opened them again, Pardo was looking down at him. . . .
Finally Pardo said, "You wonder why you are here."
Silence. Why comment on the obvious?
"You are here because you are Melungeon, because we are
every man who has ever lost his way, every race who has ever
lost its compass. That you should have come along at the exact
second you did, in the exact place . . . only the merest chance
there was it could have happened to you, Joshua; yet we were
there at that same moment, and took you in."[31]

Then, too, there is something about the place that almost defies
description—an aura. Josh says it is like a sweet aroma that assails the
senses. He says, "Sometimes when I'm outside I feel this . . . sensation.
I don't know. Other times I think it's a scent. As though the air around
us is charged. Do you feel that, Mavis?"[32] It's as if the village itself casts
a spell over those who dwell there. Mavis denies that she feels anything,
yet every day when the diggers return to the settlement from their excur-
sions to the woods, Mavis sings softly, a paean to the verity of Canara.
While all these characteristics are interesting and worth noting, probably the most important fact about the remote village is revealed to Josh
by Eulaylia, the kind woman who is the teacher of the community's
children: "We are our own doctors in Canara. . . . This is a place of

---

[30]Naylor, *Sang Spell*, 102.
[31]Naylor, *Sang Spell*, 111.
[32]Naylor, *Sang Spell*, 79-80.

healing. For some it just takes longer than for others."[33] This is a hint of the prejudice that Melungeon people have historically faced in their attempts to get good medical care, but it is also one of the main ideas of this novel—the simple life and the single-minded devotion to traditions and self-knowledge that Canara stands for can have a wonderfully salubrious effect. Pardo's first encounter with Josh is his offer to bind up the painful cracked ribs; and Mavis's consistent bringing of food when Josh is hurt or sick, her willingness to spend time with him even when he is out of sorts, show the healing nature of the environment. The longer Josh stays, the more he understands this truth even though he is loath to admit it. Early on, when he thinks about what he has to face in the outside world, he realizes "he felt like an open wound that would never, ever heal."[34] However, as time passes, he perceives changes. He decides he should help the pudgy Gil learn to be a runner and thereby to lose some weight. At the time of the first training session he notices, "That he *wanted* to do this for the boy, and was surprised again, when the session was over, that he had enjoyed it as much as he did, that he took such pleasure in Gil's gratitude. *Some*thing was beginning to heal, he thought."[35]

This intimation that he is getting better, stronger, and more peaceful comes to him again.

> Waiting for the coming equinox, Josh found himself more reflective, calmer, kinder, as though a wound inside himself were healing. He went out each day with the diggers, looking for the elusive ginseng, knowing all the while that there was the largest batch in the world growing on the high rocky island in the river. He assisted Leone with the water barrel at noon when she brought lunch to the diggers, helped Old Sly harness up the horses, and to all appearances, seemed to be "settling in."[36]

Then, in the novel's final pages, when he has truly come of age, his final epiphany occurs, and therefore his healing is complete. "He could only conclude that life renewed itself here in Canara, again and again, that each generation went back to the distant source. A spell unbroken, a village undisturbed, a homeland at last."[37]

---

[33]Naylor, *Sang Spell*, 62.
[34]Naylor, *Sang Spell*, 117.
[35]Naylor, *Sang Spell*, 127.
[36]Naylor, *Sang Spell*, 152.
[37]Naylor, *Sang Spell*, 164-64.

Like almost every piece of fiction that has Melungeon characters, *Sang Spell* has references to how distinctive the characters' physical appearance is. The first description is of Pardo. "Josh studied the coppery face, the ageless eyes, a deep blue. It was impossible to estimate how old the man was. One moment Josh guessed he was ancient, yet at other times he seemed almost young."[38] Another description of Pardo is inserted near the end of the book like a frame, the second half of a set of parentheses, to remind us that Melungeons not only live in a different reality, but that they also look different. Pardo is teaching a history lesson to the children assembled in the ephemeral schoolhouse as the author notes, "Pardo's lined face was the color of sunlit copper, his eyes the deepest blue."[39]

Early in his time in the village Josh notices the way the people look and suddenly realizes that he has many of the same physical traits.

The garments were earth-colored, and so were most of the people, from the olive hue of old leaves to the dusky tones of clay. Their delicate features seemed to have been drawn with a fine-tipped pen, and though many had brown eyes, in keeping with their skin, a surprising number of eyes were blue, like Josh's. Like Pardo's. Josh had always wondered why, with as Boston Irish a mother as one could imagine, he himself looked Italian. His skin turned red-brown when he tanned.[40]

Mavis, whose father was an outsider like Josh, is described as "large-framed,"[41] but the other women look different—"smaller and darker than Mavis, their hands and feet petite and well-shaped, despite the physical work."[42]

Sang Spell also has copious information about the history of the Melungeon people. Both Mavis and Pardo, Josh's mentors during his sojourn give him lessons when there is opportunity. On Josh's first day in Canara, he is left in the barn to rest when the others go out to gather ginseng. He wakes and walks outside to see if he can find something to eat. A copper-skinned, blue-eyed, ageless looking man in a primitive log cabin speaks to Josh in an unfamiliar language; the only word Josh can make out is "Portyghee."[43]

[38]Naylor, *Sang Spell*, 15.
[39]Naylor, *Sang Spell*, 156.
[40]Naylor, *Sang Spell*, 22.
[41]Naylor, *Sang Spell*, 16.
[42]Naylor, *Sang Spell*, 52.
[43]Naylor, *Sang Spell*, 21,

Pardo is a real historian ready to share the important information about the Melungeon heritage as soon as Josh is able to assimilate it. In response to Josh's query about what state Canara is in, there comes the first hint: "Canara was here long before there were states."[44] Later when Josh is devastated in his attempt to find The Stop after it has disappeared, a conversation with Pardo reveals more:

> "You are here because you are Melungeon. . . . We go so far back, Joshua, that everyman's story is our own."
> "Cursed, that's what!" Josh was bitter.
> "Cursed and blessed both, perhaps."
> "How do you figure that?"
> "We have been robbed, ridiculed, converted, murdered— *think* of it! And yet . . . we continue to exist. Destroy us in one place, we pop up in another. Lost, perhaps, but indestructible."
> . . .
> "But *why* couldn't you leave if you wanted to? What keeps you here in Canara? Do you even know?"
> "Only a guess. That there were other groups of Melungeons who fared better than we, I've no doubt. Perhaps they are all assimilated by now, and you couldn't even find them if you tried. But our own little band of people was pushed so far, so deep into the mountains that we were lost to time and space. We have continued to exist in our own little orbit, it would seem, with its own rules and physical properties, its own laws. Were we to leave, we would not exist at all."[45]

This is an exposition filled with fantasy, yet it does illustrate important truths about the experience of living in a community that is outside the dominant culture. If such a group of people does not consciously choose to preserve its heritage, that heritage surely dies. Melungeon families who passed for white in Wise County, Virginia (according to Brent Kennedy), destroyed their written family records like birth certificates, marriage licenses, baptismal records, and death certificates, burned photographs, and even fabricated oral history to pass down. The truth of Melungeon heritage in those families was lost forever. Pardo's sense that the Melungeons of Canara have something worth preserving is noteworthy.

---

[44]Naylor, *Sang Spell*, 48.
[45]Naylor, *Sang Spell*, 111-13.

In the day at the schoolhouse, the autumnal equinox, Pardo tells another story, one that neither Josh nor most of us ever heard in school.

"On the last day of July," he said, looking somewhere above and beyond the heads of his listeners, "the year 1502, off the island of Jamaica, Columbus came upon a strange people on a ship not familiar to those waters. It was forty feet long and eight feet in diameter, with a shaded pavilion in the center, much like a Mayan Indian design. But to Columbus, it looked like the Moorish galleys he had often seen in the Mediterranean Sea. There were some forty men and women on this galley, and unlike the Jamaican Indians, these people wore clothing: sleeveless shirts with bright colors and designs like those Columbus had seen in Granada, so he has written.

"The people carried a cargo of tools—copper, and forges for working the copper," Pardo continued. "But perhaps what interested him most was that the women aboard this ship covered their faces, like the women of Granada. These were not Mayan Indians, I tell you, but Muslims who had reached the New World before Columbus. Even he, my students, considered the possibility. If the historians will not tell the truth, we shall, for we in Canara are making our own history in our new homeland."[46]

Mavis, like Pardo but a little gentler, also gives Josh important insights into Melungeon history.

"I like history best," she added, "but it's only *our* history. . . . Again and again we circle back." . . .

Josh studied the girl. "What do they teach you about your own history?"

"Who we are. Where we came from."

He was interested. "Then you can be *my* teacher. How *did* you get here? I thought you were born here."

"I mean way way back—where the Melungeons came from."

That word again. "The who?"

"Melungeons. That's who we are. You too."

"Not me," Josh told her. "I'm Scotch-Irish."[47]

---

[46]Naylor, *Sang Spell*, 156-57.

[47]Not only does Naylor give the real history of the Melungeon people in this section, she also parades one of the most common misconceptions that is passed down in Melungeon families. Because many in the Appalachians are Scotch-Irish,

Her eyes danced. "Vardy? That's Irish?

He shrugged. "Well, that's what I always thought."

"We were studying names last unit. Many of the Melungeons came from Portugal, and the names changed over time. As soon as I saw you—your dark hair, dusky skin, blue eyes—and heard your name, I knew you were Melungeon."

"How?"

"Vardy is from Navarro. You're as Portuguese as Sylvania and Alonso and Elvas and Helena. I'm half Portuguese, half Celt. That's what my grandfather tells me. And there are still people in Canara who speak only Portuguese, who have passed it down all these hundreds of seasons."

"What does Portugal have to do with anything?"

"It's where the Melungeons started. Some of us, anyway. In truth, I guess, we come from everywhere. The English at James-town were not the first European colony in America—we were. I know that much of history."[48]

Another day when Josh is recovering from a flu brought on by his attempt to swim out of Canara in the frigid river, Mavis tells more.

"Tell me the rest of the story about the Melungeons." Settling back against the hay, Josh took a bite of chicken, pulling the meat off with his teeth.

"It will bore you."

"No, it won't. Go ahead."

"Well, we first came—our ancestors—from the mountains of Portugal, recruited by Captain Juan Pardo."

"Pardo?"

"Our Pardo is a descendant, he tells us. And we settled the first European colony here—Santa Elena, in South Carolina."

"When was all this?"

"In your year of 1566. When the settlement was overrun by the English, our people escaped into the backwoods, making their way to the mountains of Appalachia. Some married the natives—the Indians."

---

and probably because of some exogamy, it was easy to adopt a heritage from those close at hand.

[48]Naylor, *Sang Spell*, 81-82.

"And that's who the people of Canara are descended from? The original settlers of Santa Elena?"

"Oh, it's much more complicated than that." . . .

"Complicated how?' he asked.

"That same year, the English pirate, Sir Francis Drake—and he *was* a pirate, Josh, no matter what else he did—made a raid against the Spanish and Portuguese on the coast of Brazil. He liberated hundreds of prisoners—Moorish and Turkish galley slaves captured in sea battles. There were also South American Indians and West African Muslims." . . . She grinned broadly. "Eulaylia praises me in our history lessons because my memory is good."

"So I see," said Josh, returning her smile.

"Drake planned to release the Turks and Africans on Cuba to defend against the Spanish, but it was stormy, and the ships were blown off course. They were forced up the coast to Roanoke Island. Drake left most of his passengers there, as he was sailing to England, saying he would be back for them. But two weeks later, when Sir Walter Raleigh visited the island, guess what? The people Drake left had vanished."

"What happened to them?" Josh could tell she liked this part. He wanted to keep her going just to see her eyes sparkle. "They made their way to the mainland, and eventually met up with the survivors of Santa Elena. We are Christian, Jew, and Muslim, thousands of miles from our home. We are Portuguese, Spanish, Berber, Arab, Jew, and black, yet we all live together peaceably. . . ."

"But how do you know this is true" I never heard it in school."

"Eulaylia said they don't teach it in schools beyond The Edge. They tell of a place called Jamestown, but the books never mention Santa Elena."

"So when did you start calling yourselves Melungeons?"

"It's the name others called us, and it's not a good one, Josh. To many, a Melungeon is a nobody. Worthless. It's a Turkish word, meaning 'one whose life or soul has been cursed.' "[49]

This recitation, of course, rehearses some of Brent Kennedy's theories espoused in his 1994 book. Not every scholar (myself included) would

---

[49]Naylor, *Sang Spell*, 99-101.

agree with every point, but there are many facts included here that no
one can deny. There were Europeans in the New World long before the
English settled at Jamestown. Santa Elena was a large and prosperous
Spanish colony for twenty years from 1566 to 1587. People did leave
Santa Elena and other Spanish settlements for the interior, never to be
heard from again. This is documented in journals by people who were
part of Pardo's party. There were battles on the high seas and on foreign
shores; galley slaves, many originating in the lands bordering the
Mediterranean, were passed from hand to hand. This century, the sixteenth, is not much discussed in American classrooms. Students know
Columbus and 1492; they know Jamestown and 1607, but the hundred-
plus years between those dates is unexplored territory.

Josh in turn tells Mavis about his world, and she does think about
what life on the outside would be like. Yet, she has deep loyalties to the
people and traditions she has grown up with. In trying to explain them
to Josh she alludes to the laws passed in the 1830s and the discrimination
perpetrated by the likes of Virginia's Dr. Plecker.

> "I'm not sure that I do want anything else. I belong here, I
> guess. For centuries, Eulaylia said, we belonged nowhere. No one
> wanted us. No one believed us. They didn't know what we were.
> Free persons of color, they called us, but we couldn't vote or own
> land. I don't mind being here, really. I *like* being Melungeon, and
> Canara is ours."[50]

Mavis teaches Josh yet another lesson the evening after the young
men of the village have gone out in the forest to castrate a wild boar.

> "You went out after the boar today, I know," she said.
> "Pardo was pleased, but my grandfather calls you a *converso*."
> "What's that?"
> She smiled ruefully. "It is an old, old word from our history,
> the name given to Melungeon Jews and Muslims who were
> forced to convert to Christianity, for not all of them fled the
> Inquisition. No one quite believed them, and with good reason.
> Who truly believes out of fear? Old Sly doesn't know whether
> you are sincere or not."[51]

---

[50]Naylor, *Sang Spell*, 119.
[51]Naylor, *Sang Spell*, 154.

Other "Melungeon" elements in the novel fall into the category of customs—or practices. Some of these are traditional in Melungeon communities. Others I have never encountered in any other source, either fictional or sociological/anthropological. These are things Naylor wishes were true about Melungeons because they fit with her ideas about the way Melungeons ought to be and the effect that years of isolation would cause.

The first true tradition is the practice of naming children so the child's name echos a parent's name. Josh is talking with Gil, a boy just a few years younger than he is.

> "The night I came, someone mentioned Jack. . . . Who was he?"
>
> "Mavis's father, I think. Yes, I'm sure of it. Mavis Jack is her name, so he was her father."
>
> "You take your father's first name for your last?"
>
> "Sometimes. They call me Gil Daniel."[52]

Another tradition is that the stories of Melungeon origins in Portugal and other countries around the Mediterranean have been delivered by means of an oral tradition in some Melungeon families. The narratives that Mavis and Pardo deliver are not from books; instead they have been told over and over by elders in the community to the children. This, of course, makes perfect sense. Soldiers of fortune, such as those with Juan Pardo, most likely, did not carry books in their bundles. Food and weapons would have taken precedence. The later laws that denied persons of color access to public education were also a factor. A person who cannot read must learn by listening and pass knowledge on by telling.

Another tradition that is based in fact—at least in the "fact" of early printed accounts—is that of early Melungeon communities being regulated by the ringing of a bell in the center of the settlement, just as time was measured in Iberian communities by the ringing of the church bell. According to Samuel C. Williams, deceased former president of the East Tennessee Historical Society, James Needham undertook an exploratory journey in April 1673 into the Tennessee Valley.[53] Needham apparently kept a journal in which he recorded:

---

[52]Naylor, *Sang Spell*, 46.
[53]Kennedy, *The Melungeons*, 10-11.

> [A]fter a small time of rest one of my men returns with his
> horse, ye Appomatock Indian and twelve Tomahittans, eight men
> and foure women. One of these eight is hee which hath been a
> prisoner of ye white people. . . . ye prisoner relates that ye white
> people have a bell which is six foot over which they ring
> morning and evening and att that time a great number of people
> congregate togather. . . . [54]

The tie-in to Latin culture can be traced to allegations by Jean Patterson
Bible and Bonnie Ball, two Melungeon historians. We see this tradition
in Naylor's Canara. "There were no clocks in Canara. No calendar, even.
There was only the rising of the sun and the clang of the dinner bell to
mark the day."[55] Mavis also uses the bell for another purpose; she rings
it to sound an alarm the fateful night of the autumn equinox. "*Clang!
Clang!* Mavis was ringing the bell by the cookhouse, and she rang it again
and again, two by two, the sound of alarm. *Clang! Clang! . . . Clang!
Clang!* it pealed out over Canara."[56]

The other things that Naylor bills as traditions are probably a blend
of tradition and fiction. The wedding celebration is the first of these.

> The next rest day Sylvania and Tom were married. . . . Two
> of the pigs were slaughtered and their carcasses then roasted
> slowly over an open pit. The aroma seemed to bring life to the
> village. Children gathered around to watch the basting, and the
> older girls went to the cabin where Sylvania lived, bringing with
> them ribbon and squares of handmade lace. . . .
> While Sylvania was being bedecked in lace, Tom—a slim,
> handsome young man—was engaged in a wrestling match with
> his old friends down by the river. Stripped to their waists, the
> men rolled and jostled and laughed, as though Tom were
> signaling to every rival he'd ever had that Sylvania was now his,
> and her lips belonged to him alone. Then they washed, dressed,
> and gathered in the clearing. Sylvania came dressed in bright
> colors, specially dyed cloth that had been subject to no washings
> yet. Her red and yellow dress, lace, and scarves completely
> covered her body, and her hair was festooned with ribbons.

---

[54]Kennedy, *The Melungeons*, 11.
[55]Naylor, *Sang Spell*, 65–66.
[56]Naylor, *Sang Spell*, 165.

Josh recognized everything and nothing in the ceremony. There was a canopy under which the bride and groom were to stand, symbolic, he thought of a Jewish ceremony; a cross held by Pardo was such as might appear in a Christian wedding; drums provided the music afterward for the dancing, in which mostly the men took part, reminiscent of a Mideastern custom; and the roasted pigs for the feast, Josh decided, was the ususal banquet food of none of the above. Though Pardo officiated during the nuptials, the public declaration by the couple that each was the other's intended seemed sufficient, and here in Canara, at least, Tom and Sylvania were officially wed.

When the women joined the dancing, Sylvania danced with every man in turn, Tom with all the women, and finally, when they went off to the woods for their wedding night in a small cabin a family had lent them, the whole village followed after and stood around the outside singing and calling, some rattling the door handle as if to go in, until finally Tom came to the door and offered sweets to all. Thus satisfied, the crowd dispersed.[57]

The pig barbecue and the shivaree are recognizable Appalachian customs. Some of the other details seem fabricated for this story.

After the wedding another Canara tradition is celebrated.

Mavis, smiling, clutched Josh's arm as they left the woods [Tom and Sylvania's cabin] and purposefully guided him toward the river.

"Where are we going now?" he asked.

"To swim," she said.

[The older people] smiled at the silent parade of single folk who were slipping down to the river's edge. Josh was startled to see them quickly disrobe, male and female alike, and slip into the water. He turned to ask Mavis what it was all about, and was astonished to see her pulling her dress over her head, emerging naked in the moonlight, half of her breasts in shadow. Feeling curious, excited, and somewhat awkward, Josh took off his clothes also and ducked into the water behind her.

The coldness of the water took care of any thoughts he might have had of sex. He wasn't sure what he expected would happen next, but in truth, nothing much did. The line of naked figures

---

[57]Naylor, *Sang Spell*, 122-24.

slowly moved deeper and deeper into the water until most were
in up to their waists, some to their shoulders, There were giggles
and whispers as the water reached their chins, and the river at
last became a shadowy sea of bobbing heads.

Josh had felt embarrassed at first facing Mavis in his
nakedness. . . . But finally, when the river covered them both, he
managed to say, through chattering teeth, "What is this? This
ceremony?"

"I don't know," she said. It doesn't have a name. We just
always do it—the single people—after a summer wedding,
anyway. And some nights just for fun. Eulaylia says more people
get engaged in the water after a wedding than at any other
time." She laughed. "Daniel says it's a way to see the merchandise before you buy it."

"Then the parents don't mind?"

"They did it themselves. It's tradition."[58]

Another created legend that Naylor puts into the novel is the concept
of immortality for certain Melungeon people in the village. Mavis insists
that the Melungeons of Canara are truly different from all people, even
those with Melungeon blood, who live Beyond.

"We *are* different. Because of the way we live here. And
because of . . . of the Changeover."

"The what?" he murmured.

"They say . . . Pardo has told us . . . that those with pure
Melungeon blood—direct descendants of the Santa Elena
settlers—have the ability to live forever if they reach a certain
age. Then they become young again, and all the events of their
present existence are added to those of the past. They are the
'Old Who Remember.' "

"Mavis, that's nonsense."

"Is it? Is there any place in Beyond that is like Canara, where
to go forward you must first go back?"

"No, but if some of you live forever, it means you are a kind
of ghost, and you certainly feel like flesh and blood to me."
When she didn't reply, he asked, "So who are the purebreds in
Canara? Who will live forever?"

---

[58]Naylor, *Sang Spell*, 124-25.

"I didn't say they *would*, Josh. I said if they didn't die before the Changeover, they begin again, just as they have been doing for a long, long time. I'm not sure who they are. Perhaps they don't even know themselves until it happens."

"Isobel?"

"I think so. She certainly seems to be getting to that age, and if she does—if she doesn't meet up with an accident or illness before then—well, it's this that keeps Canara going. Pardo says we need people who know the past in order to preserve our future."

"What about the rest of you?"

I've heard that there can be an immortal in every generation, and sometimes we joke about it—we who are young. We kid about which of us it might be. But it's not a joke, Josh. It's real. At least, I've been told that it's so."

He could not believe she swallowed all this. "And if for some reason, something happened to the 'Old Who Remember'—before they got to the Changeover—then Canara would mix with the rest of the world and you could go anywhere you wanted?"

"Should that happen, Eulaylia says, there is a good chance Canara would cease to exist at all, and we along with it."[59]

One other element that Naylor uses convincingly to create the mood of mystery is names. "Canara" has already been discussed. The names of the characters are just as carefully chosen and just as interesting. The first, of course, is Joshua Vardy. The matriarch Isobel tells him that Joshua means "whom God has saved."[60] Even without this reminder of the meaning, the name "Joshua" carries rich connotations—the wise Old Testament warrior who led the Israelites into the Promised Land of milk and honey comes immediately to mind. And then the name Jesus is the New Testament version of the Hebrew name.

"Vardy," Josh's surname, is also rich with layered meaning. Not willing to leave its significance entirely to chance or her readers' possible research, Naylor has Mavis explain one origin of the name. "Vardy" does, in fact, come from Navarro or Navarrah, a region in northern Spain. Kennedy suggests in his book that Vardaman, the first name of one of Hancock County, Tennessee's first-recorded Melungeon settlers called Vardaman Collins, "is pronounced identically to the Turkish *var duman,*

---

[59]Naylor, *Sang Spell*, 147-48.
[60]Naylor, *Sang Spell*, 97.

meaning literally 'everything I own has gone up in smoke.' "[61] This meaning certainly applies to Josh who, when he arrives in Canara, has lost everything familiar to him. His displacement is both literal and figurative. Old Vardy Collins settled in a valley on the north side of Newman's Ridge in Hancock County. That community still bears his name today— Vardy. It was in Vardy that Presbyterian missionaries came to establish a church and a school in the early twentieth century. Many Melungeon children walked to the school at Vardy and attended there until eighth grade. R. C. Mullins, a man I met at the Sneedville Fall Festival, was one of those. So Josh's schooling in Canara to learn about his heritage is all tied up with the essence of who he is that is embodied not only in his story spun out in the pages of the novel but also in his name.

"Mavis" is also a name that has a meaning that fits with who she is in the story. Mavis (from Middle French *mauvis*) is another name for a song thrush. This European songbird migrates to Scotland where it is hailed as the harbinger of spring. As already noted, every day, when the ginseng diggers return within sight of the village, Mavis bursts into spontaneous song. That Mavis should have a French name instead of a Portuguese name is also significant. Mavis is not a pure Melungeon; she stays in Canara by choice; therefore, she has an outsider's name.

"Pardo" is also explained in the story. This character is named for Juan Pardo, who incidentally was really *Joao Pardo*, a Portuguese commissioned by King Philip II of Spain to forge a path from Santa Elena to connect with the inroad that de Soto's party had made from their landfall at Pensacola twenty-five years earlier. Thus, soldier of fortune Juan Pardo would mark a land route that would go from the Atlantic coast to the Gulf of Mexico without sailing around the Florida peninsula. This captain, Juan Pardo, had both soldiers and clergy in his group. His mandate was to explore, find a route, build forts, Christianize the indigenous inhabitants, and claim the land for the king of Spain. As he carried out his orders, he left communities of men at four, or possibly five, forts. We know exactly how he did this from his extant journals and from another journal kept by one of his subordinates. Many believe Pardo's men were at least some of the European progenitors of Melungeons. For the person who knows this Spanish/Portuguese part of the history of North America, the name "Pardo" speaks volumes.

---

[61]Kennedy, *The Melungeons*, 139.

"Eulaylia" is used by Naylor for the woman in the village who is not only the teacher, but also the woman who adopts Mavis when her own mother, Leone, is rendered mute by grief and shame. Kennedy notes that

> The name "Eulaylia" (*Yūlyū* or "Yo-le-yah") is Arabic for the month of July and also the name of an ancient, well-known church in Spain, as well as two villages (Santa Eulalia) in eastern and western Portugal.[62]

Names of other characters have obviously also been chosen deliberately for their meanings or associations. Helena, Alonso, Elvas, and Sylvester are mentioned by Kennedy. The first three are merely mentioned by Mavis when she is talking to Josh about his name, but Sylvester, Mavis's grandfather, gets more treatment in the story. Sylvester means "of the forest" in Latin. Its short form is, of course, Sly. "Old Sly" in this novel is a gruff and suspicious man. He drives the wagon that carries the diggers to the forest to dig "sang," and he seems as threatening as Pardo is soothing. Josh's first encounter with Old Sly is intimidating.

> Josh felt a rough hand on his shoulder and turned to see a large man whose face seemed older than his body. His complexion was ruddy, the skin lined as old leather. He had flowing gray hair and beard, and bushy brows, beneath which black eyes stared intently as though from the mouths of caves.
> "Who are you?" he thundered. "And how did you get here?"
> . . .
> "Eulaylia sent me," he said. . . .
> "When did you get here" Leone brought you in?"
> "Yes. I was mugged out on the road and she found me. I've got a broken rib."
> "You will work," said the man.[63]

Josh's relationship with Old Sly never gets any easier, but we don't learn why until nearly the end of the novel. It is Old Sly, along with Pardo, who apprehends Josh when he has taken the rowboat in an escape attempt and is dangerously close to finding the fenced secret cache of growing ginseng on the island in the river.

> [Josh] discovered himself in the light of a lantern and, shielding his eyes, found he was looking into the face of Old Sly.

---

[62]Kennedy, *The Melungeons*, 140.
[63]Naylor, *Sang Spell*, 27.

A large hand reached out and roughly seized his clothes, jerking him forward so swiftly that Josh could smell the man's breath in his nostrils.

He could have fought, could have jerked himself free, but the growls of the approaching dogs told him how futile the effort would be. And something more—the fury on Old Sly's face, fury mixed with such sadness that Josh remained immobile till Pardo, holding the dogs on a leash, came crashing through the woods and caught up with them. . . .

Old Sly released Josh's shirt, but continued to hold the lantern so they could see each other's faces. His voice was strangely gentle.

"A boat without a passenger goes Beyond," he said. "A man from Canara stays in Canara. I have tried it many times."

"You mean if I had rowed downstream, I wouldn't have moved, really? I would still be in Canara? . . . Then where are we now?" Josh asked, confused.

"An island, only an island, and Canara still. You have been going in a circle."

Josh refused to believe it. He *wouldn't*. "Then why the dogs and the fence?"

"Look." Old Sly bent down then lowering the lantern to the ground, and Josh saw that the forest floor was covered with ginseng. He stared at the profusion of plants—thousands and thousands, he guessed. Acres of ginseng. A spell of 'sang.[64]

If Josh is surprised by this discovery, he is even more surprised by Old Sly's subsequent revelation, which indicates that the nickname "Sly" is more than just the shortened form of Sylvester. "You and Kaspar are two of a kind, and I know you well, for I was once as you are. Troublemakers. I knew it from the beginning."[65]

Sylvania is the feminine form of Sylvester ("of the forest"). Isobel is the Spanish form of Elizabeth, a Hebrew name that means "oath of God." Leone means lion in Greek and also is the name of a region in Spain. Leonard is the patron saint of horses, and Leone in the story drives the horse-drawn wagon. Daniel, young Gil's father in the story, is an Old Testament name that means "God is (my) judge." In the Book of Daniel, the young Israelite is among the exiles in Babylon; he is valued at the

---

[64]Naylor, *Sang Spell*, 134-36.
[65]Naylor, *Sang Spell*, 137.

court as a reliable interpreter of the king's dreams. His refusal to bow to the emperor causes him to be thrown into the lion's den, the occasion of God's miracle of deliverance. Naylor's Daniel is one of the teachers of the children, perhaps as such a nurturer of dreams.

Kaspar is a northern European (Dutch, German, or Scandinavian) form of Jasper; jasper is a green gemstone. I think this name is used ironically in the novel; it means "treasurer" in Persian. Kaspar cheats his way to extra money that he hoards against his escape by stealing ginseng from the other diggers. The name is also traditionally thought to designate one of the wise men who came to pay homage to the infant Christ. Kaspar *thinks* he is wise, but the reader knows better.

There is also a young man in Canara called Chad Tolliver, who clearly has designs on Mavis. Tolliver is a common Appalachian name, a variation of Taliaferro. This name has an interesting and distinguished history.[66] One legend dates back to 58 BC when a barbarian saved the life of Julius Caesar. Caesar invited the man into his camp and made him an arms bearer. This bearer was called *Tallefer*, from the Latin *Tatum*, meaning dart or spear, and *ferre*, to bear. Another story has it that *Taillefer* was the name of a warrior-bard who was at the Battle of Hastings with William the Conqueror in 1066. In this version the etmology is traced through French to Latin: *Talia*, to cut, and *ferro*, iron. The Taliaferro family was well established in England and can document emigration to North America around 1640. How the Tollivers got to Appalachia is not clear.

The last important name to discuss is the novel's title *Sang Spell*. Both words have multiple denotations and connotations. "Sang" is, of course, Appalachian vernacular for ginseng, the plant that is valuable as a trade item both in the story and in present-day reality. Many stories with Melungeon characters connect the Melungeons with gathering ginseng as well as other native plants. "Sang" is also the past tense of "sing."

"Spell" means to say the letters of a word one by one and by extension to explain something, as in "spell out." A "spell" is a magical state that a person or place can be put under, as in "The wizard cast a spell on me." A "spell" is a measure of time, as in "Come set a spell with me on the porch." And to "spell" someone is to stand in for that person or to take over his/her duties.

---

[66]These notes on "Taliaferro" are from <http://assentweb.com/taliaferro/page3.html> and < . . . /page5.html>, accessed 7 June 2000.

Weaving all these senses for the words together is surely what Naylor has intended in her title. The ginseng holds the people and perhaps even Josh and Kaspar in Canara. Canara works its magic on Mavis, the "song thrush," who sings when she approaches it each evening. Josh spends time, a *spell*, in the village gathering ginseng and learning about his roots (the valuable part of the ginseng plant is its roots). The secret ginseng patch on the island is to quote Old Sly, "a *spell* of 'sang.' "[67] Canara works its magic, its *spell*, on Josh to bring his healing and his enablement. Learning about his Melungeon heritage shows Josh, *spells* out to him, important things he needs to understand. There may be even more permutations and combinations of the meanings of these two small words.

We cannot leave *Sang Spell* without touching on its themes. These ideas are the vital spots where this novel connects the Melungeon story with the broader life that all human beings share. While not uniquely related to Melungeon history or culture, they are still important to the work. The first is the importance of discovering the secrets of the past, the roots of one's heritage and being. Also one of the strong messages in *The Devil's Dream, Big Stone Gap, Kinflicks,* and *M.C. Higgins, the Great,* this message is strong in the novel. Isobel tells Josh, "[T]o go forward, you must go back, for you have lost your way."[68] Initially he thinks this almost proverbial saying does not apply to him because he deems she has not really answered his question ("Do you know—is there anyone here who knows what I must do to leave Canara?"[69]). The example of the tame crow is a brutal interlude—a powerful metaphor—and warns the reader if not Josh that the stakes in life are high, that preparation for life is serious business.

> When he saw Mavis that afternoon, she was feeding a crow that had become a pet, and he sauntered over, bemused. The crow was standing on the railing at the far end of the fence while Mavis held a piece of bread in her outstretched hand. The crow studied the hand and the bread sideways and moved about from one foot to the other, then tipped back its head and cawed. Other crows answered, flying in from tree to tree, until dark bundles of birds hovered in the branches overhead.

---

[67]Naylor, *Sang Spell*, 136.
[68]Naylor, *Sang Spell*, 98.
[69]Naylor, *Sang Spell*, 98.

Cockily, hesitantly, the crow did his strut-walk down the fence rail, stopping now and then with one foot raised to survey the situation, till at last it reached the outstretched hand. The head darted forward, the beak snatched up the bread, and the crow flew skyward.

"If he's smart, he'll circle back and share that with the others," Mavis mused. "It wouldn't pay to just fly off."

"How long did it take you to teach him that?" Josh asked, watching the crows watch them.

"Several seasons," she said. "Midnight, we call him. Crows are wary, but he's the tamest of them all." . . . She turned away . . . and stared up at the sky, where all the crows were flying now, Midnight still in the lead, a dim speck against the clouds. . . .

There was a commotion in the sky and Josh and Mavis looked up to see a whirlwind of crows against the clouds.

Mavis sucked in her breath. "He wasn't ready," she said. "He shouldn't have gone."

Josh wasn't sure whether she was talking about her father[70] or her crow, but the huge flock of birds was circling rapidly now, faster and faster, a vortex of black that suddenly spiraled downward like a dagger, and a moment later a crow lay dead at their feet.

It was Midnight.[71]

Josh, often as he tells himself he wants to leave, does not. The longer he stays in the mountain hollow and the more he learns about what it means to be Melungeon, the surer he becomes that knowing his heritage is what frees him to leave Canara when the time comes and to face the dragon that awaits in Dallas at his new school.

This segues into a second theme already alluded to above, in the introductory paragraphs of this discussion about Naylor's own childhood. That theme is the terror and anguish that goes with being "the new kid."

---

[70]Mavis's father Jack was an outsider who came to Canara, but never felt comfortable there. In his zeal to leave, he started a fire in hopes that someone would see the smoke and come to help. Instead the entire village was destroyed and four people lost their lives. Jack was sentenced to death by stoning. Mavis's mother, Leone, was pregnant with Mavis at the time. Leone became mute from that day forward.

[71]Naylor, *Sang Spell*, 65-67.

This is especially difficult for a "star" like Josh. In Massachusetts he was a valuable member of the basketball team and a more-than-competent swimmer; he had good friends; and the girls were beginning to come around; he had the security of a mother who loved him and the promise of college (Boston University) and a career (sports medicine). In Texas he will have to start over. There are no guarantees he will stand out, make the team, or find the friends he wants and needs. Throughout *Sang Spell* he keeps up a running dialog with himself concerning the fantastic events he is living through in Canara. He judges he can mesmerize an unknown Texas audience by narrating his adventures in a disparaging mode with a lot of bravado. He mentally adds to his list of tales to tell every time he has a new experience. This enables him to distance himself from what is going on around him, to refuse assimilation into the web of life in the Melungeon community. However, when enmeshed in Kaspar's plans and forced to choose which side he is really on, Josh grows up in an amazing way. He sees with a new kind of insight both appreciating what the sojourn in the spell of the Melungeon world has meant and finding the strength he needs to move on. His decision to save Isobel and Leone and bring the elders in to mete out justice to Kaspar changes him forever.

> Everything he was going to tell his new friends in Texas, he knew he would never tell now. His "ace in the hole" was a card he would never play, for fear that ginseng diggers would descend on the hills en masse, searching for the prize. He would go on to Dallas as the person he was meant to be, that he had found himself to be, without needing the story of Canara to pave his way.[72]

Another interesting theme in the novel is the existentialist idea that choices an individual makes shape that individual in profound ways. Mavis sees Josh's choices in a limited way: "You can either be angry and turn out like Kaspar or you can settle in and make the best of it."[73] Josh sees his choices differently. Mavis accuses him of always looking on the dark side, but Josh struggles with the temptation to stay or to leave.

> If he stayed in Canara, he would never have to face a new, uncertain life in Dallas. He would never have to risk being lowest man on the totem pole—possibly not making a team at all,

---

[72]Naylor, *Sang Spell*, 173.
[73]Naylor, *Sang Spell*, 118.

any of them. He fought against this fear, banishing it from his mind, ever watchful it would creep back in again.[74]

He decides to leave. When the schoolhouse vanishes the night of the autumn equinox, Josh determines he will be inside. This choice makes him think twice when Kaspar's plan intervenes. However, Josh in that final analysis chooses honor and integrity by saving Isobel and Leone from certain death and saving himself from a life of guilt.

This whole idea of the importance of choices is ironically annihilated by the fact that Josh's Melungeon heritage is the biggest and most important shaper of his life. His time in Canara and what he learns there are not things he can prevail against. He is who he is, and that means most of all.

Phyllis Reynolds Naylor is not an Appalachian writer, not even a Southern writer. However, in this novel I see the Melungeon story coming full circle. Naylor, an outsider to both the region and the legend, came upon Brent Kennedy's narrative about his family and the ethnic minority they belong to and was compelled to take notice. Like Ted Anthony and like me, she could not forget what she had read. Naylor was fascinated by the Melungeon predicament, and the compelling history of the Melungeon people piqued her curiosity and stimulated her imagination. She gathered facts. Being who she is and doing what she does, she put articles and artifacts into one of her big black three-ring binders. The information came together with what she knows from inside herself about feeling like an outsider and being thrust into a new situation. From this rich mixture, *Sang Spell* emerged.

People inside the Melungeon legend, who have bona fide Melungeon blood in their veins, may not feel comfortable with Naylor's interpretation. They may be saying—as Mark Twain reputedly said about a woman using profanity—"The words are right, but the tune is wrong." However, melodious or cacophonous, this fine piece of writing deserves both notice and praise, for it shows how a talented outsider can adeptly employ the Melungeon metaphor.

---

[74]Naylor, *Sang Spell*, 150.

14

Conclusion:
The Powerful Metaphor

When I think about this project and its outcome, an entire book, my mind goes two different places. There are people I immediately want to contact to say that I am finished at last and that I have something important to tell. One cluster of people is my immediate support group. This group is small. It consists of two—first, a colleague specializing in Appalachian Studies, who has read every chapter as soon as I finished it, who has offered criticism and encouragement, who has taken the time to write editorial notes and comments, and second, a friend, also a writer, who has mentored me by e-mail through the research and the writing processes, who encouraged me when the task seemed overwhelming, who gave me permission to find my own writer's rhythm, and who told me from the outset that even scholarly writing must come from the heart.

Another group is bigger and growing. I can see the Spanish face of Mr. R. C. Mullins of Morristown, Tennessee, the man I met at the Sneedville Fall Festival who grew up in Vardy across Newman's Ridge from Sneedville and went to the Presbyterian mission school. I can visualize the e-mail addresses (alas! not the faces) of many regulars on the Melungeon e-mail list whose postings that revealed insights into their own Melungeon experience kept me working through to a real conclusion because they so often take umbrage at one or another of these stories I love so much.

I also at last can imagine an audience that is farther abroad: first, other interested researchers and scholars I have encountered through their work and met face to face in the process of doing my own; second, those people Darlene Wilson refers to as lay readers with Appalachian connections; and, finally, those people whose interest is the books and the authors I have considered.

To all those and others, I am ready now to share what I believe about Melungeon connections that exist in the stories of some significant writers. I'm eager to say what I think is going on not in the newspapers, magazines, and scholarly journals, but in the arts—the novels and the short stories.

Authors do choose with purpose and with passion to create Melungeon characters, incorporate Melungeon lore, and replicate the

Melungeon experience. They do these things because *Melungeon* is convenient shorthand and a powerful metaphor. *Melungeon* says mystery, unpredictability, isolation, prejudice, passion, volatility, superstition, adventure, and pride. *Melungeon* suggests a predisposition toward making and drinking "shine," a knowledge of herb medicine, fetching dark-skinned blue-eyed women, handsome reckless men. It conjures a vision of living free on misty ridges, knowing one's own way apart from the monotony of urban America, challenging death in church by eyeballing a rattlesnake or a copperhead, and painting colorful figures with bold strokes against a background of poverty and prejudice. All these things emanate from just one word.

> One lousy word. An obscure word. A powerful word, uttered over the centuries in confusion, derision, and most recently, pride.[1]

Melungeon.

Having read this far, my conclusions will not surprise you. Yet I am compelled to summarize a bit. All the literary works I have considered talk about and illustrate the prejudice against people with Melungeon heritage that has existed for many years in Appalachia. This prejudice is the one thing the Melungeon characters in these fictions all endure. We can remember Haun's despicable character Linus who hates Melungeons with startling intensity. We can hear Claud Hulett telling his daughters "A Melungeon is all alone in the world."[2] We remember John Fox, Jr.'s "Malungian" with his head cracked open. We're back to Ted Anthony's depiction:

> For 300 years, racial, social, and cultural stigmas made second-class citizens of anyone in [Appalachia] who was branded with that one word. Scattered in pockets through the mountains, they sat on the bottom of the white-trash pile—discriminated against, denounced, denied voting rights, branded "colored" by the government in the days when that was a fighting word.[3]

---

[1]Ted Anthony, "Forging a Common Present from Mysteries of Long-Hidden Past Lineage: A Quest for Ancestral Secrets in the Appalachians Leads a Researcher to the Melungen People—and to Controversy," *Los Angeles Times*, Bulldog Edition, 28 June 1998, A:1.

[2]Lee Smith, *The Devil's Dream* (repr.: New York: Ballantine Books, 1993) 57.

[3]Anthony, "Forging a Common Present."

Melungeon.

We're back to Darlene Wilson's opened closet door that reveals "Appalachia's ugly history of racism, caste- and class-differentiation."[4] We're back to Brent Kennedy's own summary of his findings:

> [L]ike a lost and wandering biblical tribe condemned to perpetual homelessness, these dark-skinned pioneers, most likely— and ironically—of at least partial Jewish origin themselves, finally gave in or gave up. They surrendered their dreams of decent land and peaceful coexistence, yielded in their vain effort to preserve their heritage, and simply took what few securities a life of abject poverty would begrudge them. As a people they fell asleep, drifting off to a netherworld of forgetfulness, losing their most precious cultural, historical, and spiritual memories to an enforced collective amnesia. . . .
>
> . . . I know that we are bits and pieces of many peoples and all races, and that we arrived not only when the first Europeans or Moors set foot on our coast, but also when the earliest Native Americans crossed the Bering Strait.[5]

Why is it that a writer would choose to depict a character so unattached, so down-and-out? Well, think about it yourself. What characters do you remember best from the stories you love? Is it the predictable person whose life holds no excitement? No, of course not. You remember the hero or the heroine who triumphs against overwhelming odds—young David risking his life against the giant Goliath, Oedipus caught inextricably in a web of circumstance, beautiful and maligned Desdemona, tortured Heathcliff, orphaned Jane Eyre, disadvantaged David Copperfield, destitute yet plucky Scarlett O'Hara. Choosing to make a character first, last, and indelibly Melungeon can speak volumes in the whispering of the single magic word.

Melungeon.

Most writers who use Melungeon characters feel compelled to talk about what these people look like, but phenotype is not their most distinguishing feature in stories. The thing I believe makes Melungeon charac-

---

[4]Darlene Wilson, "A Response to Henige," *Appalachian Journal* 25/3 (Spring 1999): 288.

[5]N. Brent Kennedy, *The Melungeons: The Resurrection of a Proud People. An Untold Story of Ethnic Cleansing in America*, 2nd ed. (Macon GA: Mercer University Press, 1997) 139-40.Kennedy, *The Melungeons*, 166, 168.

ters so attractive is the elusive mysterious puzzle of their natures. It's the quality that inspires old man Harkryder to say, "Ain't no telling what them folk will do."[6] It's what makes Catfish think about banning Melungeons from his smokehouse poker games. It's the myth that Melungeons hoard indescribable treasure in buried strongboxes on mountain ridges. It's their romantic names like Vashti, Eulaylia, Mavis, Sabrina, Deutsia, and Destry; Joshua, Zephaniah, Pardo, and Ephriam. It's the magic of mountain-gathered ginseng purported to lengthen life and enhance sexual prowess. It's what Deputy Goins knows when Beulah Mullins steps into the jail in Rocksalt, "[He] didn't know her, but he knew her. It was as if the mountain itself had entered the tiny room, filling it with earth and rain, the steady wind along the ridge."[7] It is Clem Cloyd's propensity for flirting with his own demise—what he terms "the ultimate orgasm." It is R. C. Bailey putting the gun in his mouth because he has never—through all the years and through all the music—found his way in the world.

These are reasons an author would choose a Melungeon character—it makes that author's task so much less arduous. The author has said already a great deal with this one eytmologically disputed word.

Melungeon.

Outside Appalachia most people are clueless. They have never heard of a Melungeon. "A who?" they ask. "A what?" Even inside Appalachia many are uninformed. The writers considered here do a creditable job of explaining things. Thirteen of the fourteen give some information about the theories of Melungeon origin. Nine of the fourteen tell incidents of actual historical significance related to people with Melungeon heritage. However, in spite of some explanatory information, the general reader still may be clueless. Remember: the winners write the history. It will take more than one aside in a work of fiction to bludgeon down our firmly entrenched presuppositions. Americans have no historical pegs to hang this "new" information on. The ideas about possible Melungeon origins and the events that legally suppressed this group are new and foreign notions to even well-educated citizens. People who have gone through the public school system know about Columbus. They know about Jamestown and the Pilgrims. They think that in the years between—from 1492 to 1607—what is now the United States of America was empty. Sure, there were Indians here, but the *real people,* the progenitors of white Americans, had not yet arrived. Annoying and pain-

[6]Sharyn McCrumb, *She Walks These Hills* (New York: Signet, 1994) 119.
[7]Chris Offutt, "Melungeons," in *Out of the Woods* (New York: Simon & Schuster, 1999) 49.

ful as these facts are to Americans with racial heritage other than white, they are for the most part true facts. It will take more than one or another paragraph buried in a novel or short story to change the prevailing notions and the history textbooks.

I firmly believe that until assumptions change—perhaps even afterwards—writers both inside and outside the Melungeon legend will continue to do what they do so well, to make one thing stand for many other things, to stretch their readers' caches of experience, to look for ways to express what they know in their hearts to be *truth*, by using from time to time this powerful metaphor, the *Melungeon* shortcut.

Appendix.
Chart of Melungeon Traits

As I worked carefully through the fiction, I found that similar descriptions, ideas, and attitudes surface again and again. The visual representation of these factors in chart form shows how authors incorporate the characteristics that are commonly associated with being Melungeon. Even though I was very familiar with the texts I was analyzing, the way the display turned out surprised even me. I expected descriptions of physical traits might be the most prevalent characteristic. However, the only idea mentioned in *every* narrative is *prejudice*.

My original chart is large and records each mention of a particular characteristic. I have reduced the chart to a list of texts and a key that lists the traits to give readers the benefit of the chart's visual impact.

One category, "Beliefs and Attitudes" (column D), deserves further explanation. Often a story turns on a particular piece of lore about Melungeons. Melungeon baby boys will have dark skin, girls light. Melungeons are known for honesty and integrity. Melungeons often disregard the law (understandable since it was so often used against them). For example, they make and sell moonshine; they drive fast; they participate in blood feuds. Shooting the chimney off someone's house should serve to warn the occupant that he is in danger. Perhaps the most interesting ideas are superstitions: parsley in a garden plot invites death; planting must be done according to the signs; when the cat washes herself, company is coming, bad storms bode evil; a dry cow signals bad luck; seeing a snake skin is a malevolent sign, a coyote's howl means something bad will happen.

AUTHOR'S NAME	A	B	C	D	E	F	G	H	I	J	K	L	M
Haun	✓	✓	✓	✓	✓	✓							
Dykeman	✓	✓	✓	✓	✓	✓		✓	✓		✓	✓	
McCrumb/Hills	✓	✓	✓	✓		✓		✓	✓				
McCrumb/Bones	✓	✓	✓	✓	✓	✓	✓	✓	✓		✓	✓	✓
Smith	✓	✓	✓	✓	✓	✓		✓	✓				
Alther	✓	✓	✓	✓	✓	✓	✓		✓		✓		✓
Stuart	✓	✓	✓	✓	✓		✓	✓	✓	✓	✓		
Hunter	✓		✓	✓	✓		✓		✓	✓	✓	✓	
Offutt	✓	✓	✓	✓	✓	✓	✓	✓	✓	✓			✓
Aswell/Miller	✓	✓	✓	✓		✓	✓			✓	✓	✓	
Hamilton	✓	✓	✓		✓		✓	✓				✓	
Fox	✓	✓		✓		✓			✓	✓			
Trigiani	✓	✓	✓		✓		✓	✓	✓	✓			
Naylor	✓	✓	✓	✓	✓	✓	✓	✓	✓	✓		✓	

Key to the Chart

- A Prejudice
- B Unpredictable, mysterious nature
- C Discussion of possible origins
- D Beliefs and attitudes
- E Phenotype
- F Violence
- G History (documentable)
- H Isolation
- I Poverty
- J Names
- K Moonshine
- L Herb lore
- M Denial of being Melungeon to pass for white

Bibliography

"About the Folklore Project and the Life Histories." Web page: <http://memory. loc.gov/ammem/wpaintro/wpalife.html>.

Alther, Lisa. *Kinflicks: A Novel*. Reprint with a new introduction by the author: New York: Plume/Penguin-Putnam, 1996. Original: New York: Knopf/Random House, 1975.

_____. "The Melungeon Melting Pot." A talk at the Kingsport Public Library, 19 October 1999.

Anthony, Ted. "Forging a Common Present from Mysteries of Long-Hidden Past Lineage: A Quest for Ancestral Secrets in the Appalachians Leads a Researcher to the Melungeon People—and to Controversy," *Los Angeles Times*, 28 June 1998, Bulldog Edition, A:1. The *Los Angeles Times* version of this important article is available (for a fee) at <http://www.latimes.com/cgi-bin/archsearch-cgi?DBQUERY=Forging+a+common+present&DATE=1998&SECT=part +a&TYPE=&WORT=d%3Ah&NITEMS=25&x=38&y=r>. Earlier versions of this article appeared in the *Cincinnati Enquirer* (7 June 1998) and in the *Knoxville News-Sentinel* (18 June 1998).

Apseloff, Marilyn. "A Conversation with Virginia Hamilton." *Children's Literature in Education* 14/4 (Winter 1983): 204-13; in *Children's Literature Review* 40:58.

Aswell, James, et al. *God Bless the Devil! Liars' Bench Tales*. Tennessee Writers' Project. Facsimile edition with a new introduction by Charles K. Wolfe. Tennesseana Editions. Knoxville: University of Tennessee Press, 1985. Original: Chapel Hill: University of North Carolina Press, 1940.

_____. "Lost Tribes of Tennessee's Mountains." *Nashville Banner Magazine*. 22 August 1937: 5.

Ball, Bonnie Sage. *The Melungeons*. Eighth edition. Big Stone Gap VA: privately printed, 1991. Other versions of this work include: (1) *The Melungeons, or a Vanishing Race*. A 5-page pamphlet reprinted from the Summer 1960 issue of *Mountain Life and Work*. Chillicothe OH: Ohio Valley Folk Research Project, Ross County Historical Society, 1960. (2) *The Melungeons: Their Origin and Kin*. Haysi VA: privately printed, 1969. 71 pages. (3) *The Melungeons: Notes on the Origin of a Race*. Illustrations by Randy Hodge. Revised edition. Johnson City TN: Overmountain Press, 1992. x+114 pages, illustrations.

Barr, Phyllis C. "The Melungeons of Newman's Ridge." M.A. thesis, East Tennessee State University, 1965.

Burks, Jacqueline Daniel. "The Treatment of the Melungeon in General Literature and Belletristic Works." M.A. thesis, Tennessee Tech University, 1972.

Bible, Jean Patterson. *Melungeons Yesterday and Today*. Rogersville TN: East Tennessee Printing Co., 1975.

Coady, J. "State's Poet Lauerate, Jesse Stuart, Dies." *The Courier Journal*, 19 February 1984, as found in "Jesse Stuart" by Jamie Ballard, accessed 15 February 2000, at <http://www.english.eku.edu/services/kylit/stuart1.htm>.

Cryer, Dan. "Kentucky Bluegrass Runs in Their Veins." *Newsday*. Accessed 14 June 1999 at <http://www.elibrary.com/s/edumark/836498@library_I&dtype +0~0&dinst+0>.

Davis, Louise Littleton. *Frontier Tales of Tennessee*. Gretna LA: Pelican Publishing Co., 1976.

_____. "Pushing for a Happy Ending." *Nashville Tennessean Magazine* (30 August 1970): 13.

de Marce, Virginia Easley. "The Melungeons." A review essay. *National Genealogical Society Quarterly* 84 (1996): 134-40.

Donelson, Kenneth L., and Alleen Pace Nilsen. *Literature for Today's Young Adults*. Fifth edition. New York: Longman, 1997. Original: Glenview IL: Scott, Foresman, 1980.

Dorson, Richard. "Fakelore." In *American Folklore and the Historian*. Chicago: University of Chicago Press, 1971.

Dykeman, Wilma. Introduction to *Daughter of the Legend*, by Jesse Stuart. Ashland KY: Jesse Stuart Foundation, 1994.

_____. *The Tall Woman*. Newport TN: Wakestone Books, 1962.

Elder, Patricia Spurlock. *Melungeons: Examining an Appalachian Legend*. Blountville TN: Continuity Press, 1999.

Eller, Ron. "Lecture Notes for History 580." Accessed 16 February 2000, at <http://www.uky.edu/RGS/AppalaCenter/lec12.htm>.

Everett, Chris. "Melungeon History and Myth." *Appalachian Journal* 26 (1999): 358-409.

Fox, John, Jr. *Christmas Eve on Lonesome, "Hell-fer Sartin," and Other Stories*. New York: Charles Scribner's Sons, 1909. Especially the following stories: "Down the Kentucky on a Raft"; "Man-Hunting in the Pound"; "Through the Gap"; and "To the Breaks of Sandy."

Gallegos, Eloy J. *The Melungeons: The Pioneers of the Interior Southeastern United States 1526-1997*. Volume 2 of *The Spanish Pioneers in United States History*. Knoxville: Villagra Press, 1997.

Hamilton, Virginia. *M. C. Higgins, the Great*. Reissue edition. New York: Aladdin Paperbacks, 1988. Original: New York: Macmillan, 1974.

Haun, Mildred. *The Hawk's Done Gone and Other Stories*. Edited by Herschel Gower. Nashville: Vanderbilt University Press, 1968.

Henige, David. "The Melungeons Become a Race." *Appalachian Journal* 25/3 (Spring 1998): 270-86.

Hunter, Kermit. "Walk toward the Sunset." Unpublished script for the Melungeon Outdoor Drama in Sneedville, Tennesses, 1976 season.

Ivey, Saundra Keyes. "Oral, Printed, and Popular Culture Traditions Related to the Melungeons of Hancock County, Tennessee." Ph.D. dissertation, Indiana University, 1976.

"Jesse Stuart Biographical Sketch." Accessed 11 February 2000, at <http://www.morehead-st.edu/projects/village/bio.html>.

Johnson, Mattie Ruth. *My Melungeon Heritage: A Story of Life on Newman's Ridge.* Johnson City TN: Overmountain Press, 1997.

Judge, Joseph. "Exploring Our Forgotten Century." *National Geographic Magazine* (March 1988): 330-63.

Kennedy, Brent. Afterword to *Daughter of the Legend,* by Jesse Stuart. Ashland KY: Jesse Stuart Foundation, 1994.

Kennedy, N. Brent, with Robyn Vaughan Kennedy. *The Melungeons: The Resurrection of a Proud People. An Untold Story of Ethnic Cleansing in America.* Macon GA: Mercer University Press, 1994. Second, revised, and corrected edition, 1997.

McCrumb, Sharyn. *Lovely in Her Bones.* Reprint: New York: Ballantine Books, 1990. Original: New York: Avon Books, 1985.

_____. *She Walks These Hills.* Reprint: New York: Signet/Penguin Books, 1995. Original: New York: Scribner's, 1994.

"Naylor, Phyllis Reynolds." *Contemporary Authors.* New Revision Series. Volume 24. Farmington Hills MI: Gale Group, n.d.

Naylor, Phyllis Reynolds. "Phyllis Reynolds Naylor." Internet Public Library Youth Division: Ask the Author. Accessed 25 August 1999, at <http://www.ipl.org/youth/AskAuthor/Naylor.html>.

_____. *Sang Spell.* New York: Atheneum Books for Young Readers, Simon & Schuster, 1998. Reprint: New York: Aladdin Paperbacks, 2000.

Offutt, Chris. "Melungeons" (a short story). In *Out of the Woods: Stories.* New York: Simon & Schuster, 1999.

_____. "Smokehouse." In *Kentucky Straight.* Vintage Contemporaries. New York: Vintage, 1992.

Ralph, Brett. "Chris Offutt." Feature essay in *Rain Taxi Review of Books* 3/3 (Fall 1998). Accessed 6 October 1999, online at <http://www.raintaxi.com/offutt.htm>.

Reeves, Rhonda. "Back to the Woods." Cover story in *Ace Magazine* (now *ACEWeekly*) (25 November 1998). Accessed 9 October 1999, online at <http://www.acemagazine.com/backissues/981125/coverstory_981125.html>, but now online at <http://www.aceweekly.com/acemag/backissues/981125/coverstory_981125.html>.

Russell, David L. "Cultural Identity an Individual Triumph in Virginia Hamilton's *M. C. Higgins, the Great.*" In *Children's Literature in Education* 21/4 (December 1990): 253-59; in *Children's Literature Review* 40:63.

Short, Martha. "Signs and Superstitions." Melungeon Resource Page: Folklore. Accessed at <http://homepages.rootsweb.com/~mtnties/signs.html>.

Smith, Lee. *The Devil's Dream.* Reprint: New York: Ballantine Books, 1993. Original: New York: G. P. Putnam's Sons, 1992.

Sovine, Melanie L. "The Mysterious Melungeons: A Critique of the Mythical Image" Ph.D. dissertation, University of Kentucky, 1982.

Spurlock, John H. Preface to *Daughter of the Legend,* by Jesse Stuart. Ashland KY: Jesse Stuart Foundation, 1994.

Stuart, Jesse. *Daughter of the Legend.* Edited and with a preface by John H. Spurlock; introduction by Wilma Dykeman; afterword by N. Brent Kennedy; illustrated by Jim Marsh. Ashland KY: Jesse Stuart Foundation, 1994. Original: New York: McGraw-Hill, 1965.

"Taliaferro Homepages." Accessed 7 June 2000, at <http://assentweb.com/taliaferro/page3.html> and at <http://assentweb.com/taliaferro/page5.html>.

Trigiani, Adriana. *Big Stone Gap: A Novel.* New York: Random House, 2000.

Tucker, Edward L. "John Fox, Jr." *The Dictionary of Literary Biography.* Volume 9: *American Novelists 1910–1945.* Edited by James J. Martine. Detroit: Gale Research Co., 1981. As accessed 17 May 2000, at <http://www.galenet.com/servlet/lit . . . [parameters missing] Fox+JR&PX=0000033326DT=Biography>.

Wagner, Rick. "Writer Sets Sights on Region Again." *Bristol Herald Courier,* 20 September 1999, A:1 and A:12.

Waugh, Hilary. *Hilary Waugh's Guide to Mysteries and Mystery Writing* (aka *Guide to Mysteries & Mystery Writing*). First edition. Cincinnati: Writer's Digest Books, 1991.

Williams, Monica. " 'Gap' a Portrayal of Peculiarities." Book review. *Boston Globe,* 16 May 2000. Accessed 18 July 2000, online at <http://www.omaha.com/Omaha/OWH/Storyviewer/1,3153,338776,00.html>.

Wilson, Darlene. "A Melungeon Homepage." Accessed 20 September 1999, at <http://www.melungeons.org/mel_fox.htm>. (This "Melungeon homepage" internet site, however, is now defunct.)

_____. "A Response to Henige." *Appalachian Journal* 25/3 (Spring 1999): 286-96.

_____. "Some Reflections on Appalachian and Melungeon History." Accessed 21 June 2000, at <http://www.melungeons.org/dgw-hist.htm>. (This internet site is now defunct.)

Wiltse, Henry Martin. *The Moonshiners.* Chattanooga: Times Printing Co., 1895.

Wolfe, Charles K. "Introduction to the New Edition," in James Aswell et al., *God Bless the Devil! Liars' Bench Tales.* Tennessee Writers' Project. Facsimile edition with a new introduction by Charles K. Wolfe. Tennesseana Editions. Knoxville: University of Tennessee Press, 1985. Original: Chapel Hill: University of North Carolina Press, 1940.

Index

(Characters and settings from the fiction are indicated by quotation marks. Traits from the novels that are noted in the chart in the appendix are in boldface type).

medical care denied, 47, 118, 146
Melungeon(s) (Melungeon people), vii,
    viii, ix, x, 1, 2, 5, 6, 7, 8, 9, 10, 11 12,
    13, 14, 15, 16, 17, 20, 21, 22, 23, 24,
    25, 28, 35, 37, 39, 40, 41, 44, 48, 52,
    54, 55, 56, 57, 61, 68, 71, 72, 78, 90,
    96, 97, 98, 99, 100, 102, 105, 106, 107,
    108, 112, 114, 120, 124, 125, 128, 133,
    138, 139, 141, 142, 143, 144, 145, 146,
    149, 150, 155, 156, 157, 158, 160, 161,
    165, 166, 170, 171, 172, 173, 174, 175,
    176, 177, 178, 183, 184, 185, 188, 189,
    190, 192, 194, 195, 199, 201, 203, 206,
    219, 223, 225, 226, 233, 235, 236, 237,
    243, 244, 245, 247, 248, 251, 256, 257,
    260, 261, 262, 263, 264, 265, 268, 270,
    275, 277, 280, 281, 282
  blood, 111, 115, 257, 277
  character(s), vii, viii, ix, x, xii, 1, 17,
    20, 30, 34, 39, 40, 97, 156, 159,
    179, 183, 188, 190, 198, 233, 236,
    242, 259, 279
  history, 173, 177, 178, 259, 261
  heritage, 7, 11, 14, 41, 48, 55, 61, 248,
    260, 277
"Melungeons" (short story), 181, 183,
    190-98
"Melungeon Colored" (short story), 23-
    25, 111
Melungeon e-mail list, ix, 5, 12, 13, 179,
    279
Melungeon Research Committee, 2, 13
Melungeonness, 190
Methodist, 15, 157
midwife, midwives, 7, 15, 20, 216
Miller, Elva E., 137, 141, 148-55, 161-66,
    167
"Milo," 43
Mira, Manuel, 15, 139
missionary movement in Appalachia,
    99, 104, 110, 116
moonshine, 30, 32, 44, 74, 112, 128-29,
    148-55
The Moonshiners, 149
Moors (Moorish people), 263

"Mos," 24
"Mr. Zed." *See* "Hull, Mr. Zed."
Mulatto, 7
Mulberry Gap TN, 97
"Mulligan, Ave Maria," 235-42
Mullins, "Brandy Jack," 14, 145
Mullins, "Counterfeitin' Sol," 14
"Mullins, Beulah," 192-96, 197, 282
"Mullins, Big Betsy," 150-55
"Mullins, Fleeta," 236
Mullins, Mahala ("Big Haley") Collins,
    13, 97, 128, 148, 149, 151, 154, 245
Mullins, R. C., 270, 279
Murfree, Mary, 140
Muslims, 261, 263
mysterious nature. *See* **unpredictable
    nature.**
myth, 12, 13, 140, 142

names, 14, 30, 98-99, 156, 178, 197, 265,
    269-74
"the nameless mountaineer," 230-35
"the nameless mountaineer's woman,"
    230-35
Native Americans, 47, 90, 178
Naylor, Phyllis Reynolds, vi, ix, 243-77
Needham, James, 265
Negro, 6, 21, 23, 125, 143
"The New Jerusalem" (short story), 20-
    23, 25
Newman's Ridge TN, 1, 14, 48, 68, 96,
    97, 117, 138, 139, 147, 148, 176, 177,
    270
nigger, 144
North Carolina, 6, 14, 29, 39, 44, 117,
    159, 161, 169, 172
Northeast Tennessee, xii, 8, 12, 39

"Oak Hill" (setting in *Daughter of the
    Legend*), 96, 112, 113, 115, 120, 124,
    131
Offutt, Chris, 167, 181-98
Ohio, 199, 200, 212
"Old Horny" (the devil), 142-48